Tim Clar.   KT-493-483   1
went on to spe.   f
the world's leading   ...nor Partner. Since
retiring as a lawyer, Tim ... .ake.. on board positions in a number of
corporate, arts and charitable organisations, and senior advisory roles
at a number of international think tanks. He lives in London with his
wife, close to their two sons.

Nick Cook is an author, journalist, broadcaster and entrepreneur.
In 1986, he joined the world-renowned *Jane's Defence Weekly* as a
reporter, rising quickly to become Aviation Editor, a position he held
until 2005. His first novel, *Angel, Archangel*, was published in 1989
to critical acclaim. Nick's first non-fiction title, *The Hunt for Zero
Point*, followed in 2001, reaching number one in Amazon's non-fiction charts. He has also written, hosted and produced two documen-
taries about the world of aerospace and defence – *Billion Dollar Secret*
and *An Alien History of Planet Earth*. He lives in London with his wife
and two children.

Super Patrons

Celia Sheils
Paul Sheils
Richard Slater
Tom Storey
Ian Thomas
John Tucker

TIM CLARK & NICK COOK

MONOPOLI BLUES

unbound

First published in 2018
This paperback edition first published in 2019

Unbound

6th Floor Mutual House, 70 Conduit Street, London W1S 2GF

www.unbound.com

LONDON BOROUGH OF WANDSWORTH		
9030 00006 8143 6		
Askews & Holts	20-Jun-2019	
920 CLAR	£9.99	
	WW19001655	

A CIP record for this book is available from the British Library

ISBN 978-1-912618-50-7 (eBook)
ISBN 978-1-78352-818-9 (trade paperback)
ISBN 978-1-912618-51-4 (paperback)

Printed and bound in Great Britain by Clays Ltd, Elcograf S.p.A.

1 3 5 7 9 10 8 6 4 2

This book is dedicated to Bob Clark (1924–2013) and the story which he never told.

I've got Monopoli blues, Monopoli blues
I'm blue – I'm through; this isn't the life I'd choose
I've got Monopoli blues, Monopoli blues
Oh Lord, I'm bored and I don't like Monopoli booze

I sit drearily in the mess
Life doesn't strike me as good
I'd like to see the FANYs
But they couldn't care less
And I don't see why they should

I've got Monopoli blues – I've had Monopoli properly
I've got Monopoli blues…

Contents

List of Photographs & Maps

Alberton, Aintree/Avonmouth and Ampthill – January–March 1944) *(© private collection)*
- Tim on the beach at the mouth of the River Tenna (Operation Anon – Popksi beach reconnaissance – May 1944) *(© private collection)*

Plate 5

- Termoli *(© private collection)*
- Pop with Robin Richards on Robin's 90th birthday *(© private collection)*
- Halifax B.II Series I *(© Sons of Damien)*

Plate 6

- Sergio Curetti with 2 other partisans in Mondovi *(© Curetti family)*
- Sergio Curetti (aged 16) *(© Curetti Family)*
- Le Nuove Prison, Turin *(© private collection)*
- Floor of Le Nuove Prison on which the Clarion team were held *(© private collection)*

Plate 7

- Mop in Siena (March 1945) with Christine Drury (FANY coder), American serviceman and unknown FANY *(© private collection)*
- The marshalling yards at Bolzano *(© private collection)*
- Moosburg PoW Camp, Munich *(© private collection)*

Plate 8

- Celle Airfield today *(© Celle Archive)*
- Mop and Pop wedding party 1949 *(© private collection)*
- Mop and Pop after the war *(© private collection)*
- The reunion – Pop and Sergio Curetti meet in Mondovi

almost 50 years after the Clarion Mission *(© private collection)*

Other photographs in the book

- Page 39: Nancy in FANY uniform (February 1944)
- Page 46: Commander Gerry Holdsworth, Commander of No.1 Special Force in Monopoli *(© National Archive)*
- Page 47: Commander Hilary Scott, Commander of Sea Operations of No.1 Special Force *(© Slaughter and May)*
- Page 49: Dick Laming , member of No.1 Special Force *(© National Archive)*
- Page 109: Roy Taylor, member of No.1 Special Force *(© National Archive)*
- Page 156: Major Duncan 'Huffy' Campbell, Commander of the Clarion Mission *(© National Archive)*
- Page 159: Commander Enrico Martini (Mauri), Founder and Commander of the partisan I Group Alpine Divisions (which operated in the Cuneo region)
- Page 160: Carluccio Dalmasso with Daniela Curetti (Sergio's daughter) and Tim *(© private collection)*

Maps

- *Map 1:* Italy, 1943–1945 *(page 61)*

- *Map 2:* Clarion Area of Operations, November – December 1944 *(page 162)*

- *Map 3:* Central Europe, January 1945 *(page 224)*

Foreword

Paddy Ashdown

There is a very good – and very human – reason that explains the recent sharp increase of interest in the personal stories of the Second World War. For the most part, the stories of the great events have been written and have now passed into history. But the stories of what our fathers and grandfathers did remain untold, fresh, personal and within reach. Many of us are drawn to these tales of the individual cogs in the great machinery of global war out of amazement and bewilderment. We are amazed at how perfectly ordinary people, like ourselves, were able to do such extraordinary things when called upon to do so. And bewildered because understanding this forces us to an act of self-examination: 'how would we have done in their place?'

Monopoli Blues is as much about Tim Clark's search for his father (and mother) in World War II, as it is an account of an ordinary man who proved exceptional at a time of great trial and turbulence. It is charmingly and compellingly written and radiates with the fundamental decency of both the writer and the subject. Its quiet matter-of-fact tone perfectly reflects the age and attitudes of those like Robert Clark and his contemporaries who had such adventures and did such remarkable things as they made their contribution to the struggle against the tyranny that so nearly overwhelmed their age. It is completely devoid of the pomposity and self-aggrandisement that so frequently infects this kind of book. There is room here for humanity and humour and eccentricity (Falla the bear for instance) and all those absurd and bizarre little events that always seem to inhabit the corners and cracks of great historical events. There is much courage and fortitude here too – but it does not leap out and grab you by the throat. It lies unspoken but unmissable below so much of what Robert Clark, and those who worked with him, did.

There is high romance here too. The happenstance meeting between Robert Clark and his future wife, Marjorie, an SOE radio operator who would be assigned to receive his secret radio messages behind the lines, their odyssey of parting, capture and reunion, is the stuff of films and thrillers.

This is, however, not just an interior story of their war. The Special Operations Executive's role in creating and leading the French Resistance is well known and well documented. SOE's role in Italy is far less well known. *Monopoli Blues* throws important light on this, so far only skimpily told, part of the secret war in Europe.

In this book, Tim Clark and Nick Cook have given us a moving and elevating picture of Tim's parents' war and of his quest to bring this to light. This is a charming, moving and compelling book, which will enlighten and enliven all who read it.

Introduction

The origins of this book and why my brother, sister and I were so determined for it to be written are at the same time both clear and unclear. The clear part is that we always believed there was an extraordinary story to be told and that we would have the opportunity eventually during my father's life to find out from him the details which were necessary to write it.

The first element is undoubtedly true – the story of how my mother and father met and fell in love in Italy and their time in special forces, in a theatre of the Second World War which has, at least until recently, received little attention, is a truly extraordinary one. All this at a time when they were, apart from the last few months, under the age of majority – the story in this book ends at the time when they are back in England having to start their working civilian lives upon the conclusion of hostilities.

The second element we never achieved, mainly because of my father's insistence upon not telling us more of his story beyond the occasional fleeting reference or amusing anecdote of things going wrong. The only obvious legacy of the war was his insistence on the extraordinary courage of the partisans and – in contrast to his usual even temper – his fury when people would make derogatory remarks about the bravery of Italians.

Perhaps as a defensive mechanism, my father would tend to default to the strategy of the war and the contribution (or otherwise) of generals. I remember when he agreed to give a talk to the John Locke Society at Westminster School, which formed much of the information which we had when we embarked on this project; being suspicious of his approach, I asked him to show me a draft of what he was planning to say. It was a brilliant analysis of the war in Italy in 1943–5 but mentioned nothing of his or my mother's personal experiences. I said to him that, while that would work well in a lecture on strategy, the pupils at the school would really be interested in what it felt like – at the age of 18 – to be there on a boat or submarine or parachuting into mountains in the dark. He re-wrote the talk and we did get something more of his personal experiences. But, as the book makes clear, precious little in the big scheme of things.

My father's steadfast refusal to talk about the war was not unusual – indeed it was, and largely still is, characteristic of his generation who, with protests about the fact that there was nothing unusual about their experiences, would insist that the important focus was on the future. Also, interestingly, although one might say that he had great cause to feel otherwise as a result of his experiences, he had no feelings of antipathy towards his former enemies; quite the opposite, he was a firm believer in the need to be close to Germany, initially in the Common Market and then the EU.

This refusal has intrigued me over the last few years as Nick Cook and I have worked on the book and I have sought on numerous occasions to explore it with people ranging from psychiatrists (including an American psychiatrist who had treated the New York firemen who had responded to 9/11 – whom I happened to be sitting next to on a flight to Mozambique) to current and recently serving military officers. To all of them there was a general theme: that people with experience of war will generally only talk to people who have had that experience – just as Siegfried Sassoon returning from the trenches in 1917 was keen to engage people in London while on leave, but decided it would be a futile exercise. It is illustrated, perhaps, in my father's case by the fact that he only revealed his traumatic experiences in Turin jail to another former member of special forces and not to any of his family.

So, perhaps the unclear aspect of the project is why, given my father's reluctance to talk about his experiences and our belief that, had we asked for his consent to write the book, he would have absolutely refused it, did we proceed with the project and effectively ignore his wishes – something which I never wanted to do and rarely did.

I think that there are three reasons which have guided us. First, this is not just my father's story. It is also the story of two others – principally, of course, my mother, whose contribution to the story is scarcely less incredible than my father's – turning down Oxford at the age of 17 and a half and joining special forces after a childhood in rural Wales. She was, from the start, very happy to support and participate in the project notwithstanding the great sadness of my father's recent death. The other 'person' in this story is Falla (pronounced 'Fire') – the unique bear who was with my father from the first year of his life and whose ashes were scattered with my father's. Falla was with Pop throughout the whole of his war including the time in Monopoli and Mondovi – we believe that he was the only bear to have been captured by the enemy and held in prison. If there were medals for bears, Falla would have been given them.

My father's love for, and devotion to, Falla was second only to that for his family. Falla met my mother not long after she first met my father. He was part of all of our lives – buying us Christmas and birthday presents in generous fashion – and my father never went anywhere without him. He came, for example, as the story makes clear, to the Special Forces Club 70th anniversary dinner in 2010 and featured in the subsequent article in *The Times*. He also appeared on Radio 4 – *A Point of View* – with David Cannadine reflecting on the relationship between men and bears. If this is a book about my father, it is also very much a book about Falla, even though we have decided not to refer to him throughout the text as he too remained silent until the end about his war.

The second reason is that we felt that it was important that the story was known to the family and that we should all understand what it was to have parents who went to war at the age of 18 showing great courage and being rewarded by falling in love. We also thought that, if the story was interesting to our family, it might be interesting to others and – in our less modest moments – that it might in some way convince people to write about their own families. In the UK (in contrast to the US), we have been too slow to recognise the importance of recording the stories of 'the ordinary soldier' as opposed to the generals. Many families have parents or other relatives with stories to tell – and I have met a large number of them while discussing this book – and it is so important that the stories are preserved; in particular, in the context of the Second World War where so few veterans are still alive.

The third reason – which may appear to be self-serving, although I don't believe that it is – is that, while my father would not have supported us starting the project, I rather think that, now it is completed, he would be quite pleased (even if perhaps a little embarrassed). My belief in this is enhanced by a feeling that, wherever he is now, if he had not wanted us to complete the book, we would not have had the various pieces of huge good fortune along the way – without which the story could not have been told.

I think of two instances in particular: the discovery of the account by Duncan Campbell of the chaotic end to the Clarion mission and subsequent imprisonment and transfer to Germany, and the meeting with Clara Muzzarelli. Clara is the niece of Max Salvadori – a distinguished Anglo-Italian member of SOE whose story intertwines with that of my father (both during the war and, in fact, on occasions afterwards). We met Clara quite by chance at her home in Fermo while we were looking – without much science – for the Salvadori villa, which itself plays a part in my father's story. In fact, we must have looked rather suspicious staring at the house when she happened to return and asked us – very charmingly – what we were doing. It led to an enormously helpful meeting as she filled in many of the details of SOE and its participation in the exfiltration of escaped POWs and gave us subsequently much advice and arranged introductions. We are very grateful to her for all of her help. It was only after that meeting that I found out that Oliver Pawle – whom I had known for many years through the City – was a nephew of Max. This led to other introductions to Oliver's sister, Audrey, and her husband, Paul, and to Max's son, Clement, who has recently edited a new version of his father's book – *The Labour and the Wounds*. By extraordinary chance, too, Nick's mother, Hilary, was great friends with Max's daughter, Cynthia, whom she knew in Kenya. And so it goes…

I have to confess that when, not long after my father's death in early 2013, I started to feel that something had to be done to tell the story, I thought that the obvious medium would be film/TV rather than a book. This was not due to any informed insight on my part but rather the result of talking to others with knowledge of storytelling. So armed with this misplaced belief, I went – along with my television producer brother-in-law, John – to see Nick with a view to asking him to write a storyboard which we could use to see if there might be any interest on the part of producers. Nick has been a friend of the family for many years and, importantly, knew my father as well as my mother (who were at his and Ali's wedding). We were so fortunate that Nick (with his background in defence journalism, research and book writing) shared our enthusiasm for the project. Nick rapidly persuaded me (and John) that we should produce a book (and any film or television could work off that). This is the first of many pieces of wisdom that Nick has contributed to the book.

Perhaps the second piece was the structure of the book. When we started, we thought that we should simply write a history of my parents' experiences in the context of the war. It would tell the story – and this is what we did. However, when it was finished, we felt that there was no real access for readers into the story and that, while the facts were important (and, indeed, key), it didn't really capture all of the essence of the story. By that time, Nick and I had spent three years working on the book and had had, ourselves, a number of experiences in uncovering the story (and the pieces of great good fortune I have referred to) which we felt were interesting in their own right. It was Nick then who suggested that the book should, in effect, combine *two* stories – the story of my parents' war and our tale of discovering that story with the latter building off the central story and (we hope) providing insights into the experiences which my parents had.

We hope that the structure we have chosen is one which tells the story in the way it should be told. Nick and I have benefitted greatly from the contributions, support and encouragement which have been given by a wide range of people – without which the book could not have been written and the story told. We are enormously grateful for all of this help – and for the luck which it has represented and, on occasion, created. We have included at the end of this book a list of acknowledgements and, if there are any people whom we have inadvertently omitted, we hope that they will forgive us. It does not represent an absence of gratitude.

Having said that, there are two acknowledgements which I would like to make here – each key to the completion of this project. The first is to my family – to my mother who has always supported us and has (relatively!) patiently put up with Nick's and my incessant questions and refusal to believe that more than 75 years after the extraordinary events of her youth, she can't remember every day's happenings. Her contribution has been remarkable. There has also been wonderful support from my brother, Will, my sister, Catherine, and brother-in-law, John, and above all from my wife, Caroline, and sons, Nick and Richard, whose advice and willingness to make suggestions has been invaluable. Caroline has also brought her great talents as a photographer (and devoted a great deal of time) to guide us on the pictures in the book and to ensure that they are shown to their greatest effect. Ali, Nick Cook's wife, has likewise been enormously supportive in getting the book off the ground and helping to make it fly.

But the final word should be for Nick. I have referred to his wisdom in the structuring of this project but that is only a small part of his enormous contribution to this book. When we started out to research and write the book – almost five years ago now – we had no idea where it would take us or what it would involve. More fundamentally, we didn't know if we would ever find out enough of the story to write the book – especially when starting out with information that covered only five sides of A4 paper. The project has taken us across Europe from Arisaig and the Helford River to Monopoli, Bari, Ortona, Termoli and Ancona and, as we followed the trail of my father's captivity from Mondovi, Turin and Bolzano to Munich, Bremen, Hamburg and, finally, Celle in North Germany.

Nick brought to the project his professionalism and rigour combined with great insights and capacity to tell a story. It is this which is reflected in the writing of this book. His writing skills are extraordinary and most of the time I think my role was to be the (no doubt rather irritating!) grit in the oyster. This book is very much the work of both of us – built, as I have said, on the contribution of many others. I never thought that when I retired, 10 years ago, from my career as a lawyer, that I would ever have the title 'co-author' next to my name – a coincidental piece of luck.

In addition, we could not have spent this considerable period working and travelling together unless it was also fun. I have learned an enormous amount during the project thanks to Nick, but it has been hugely enjoyable.

Finally, Nick and I are happy to lay this story before you. We hope that you find it interesting and moving – and that, if there are stories which you have to tell, you will tell them too.

Tim Clark

London – July 2018

Timeline of Events

1 September 1939	Germany invades Poland; two days later, Britain and France declare war on Germany.
	Pop, in Canada when war is declared, returns by ship to start Sixth Form at Highgate School.
10 June 1940	Italy enters the war.
22 June 1940	France surrenders. Within weeks, Winston Churchill issues a directive for the foundation of the Special Operations Executive (SOE).
September 1941	Pop goes up to Cambridge to read modern languages; Mop starts Sixth Form at Cheltenham Ladies College.
27 May 1942	Reinhard Heydrich, head of the Reich Main Security Office, the RSHA, and acting *Reichsprotektor* of the Protectorate of Bohemia and Moravia, is attacked in Prague by Czech agents, trained by SOE. He dies a week later.
Summer 1942	Pop undergoes initial Navy training at HMS Collingwood (Fareham).
Autumn 1942	Pop joins HMS *Fleetwood* in Londonderry. Within weeks *Fleetwood* is assigned to convoy escort duties in the western Mediterranean (Malta).
8 November 1942	Allied invasion of Morocco, Algeria and Tunisia begins under Operation Torch. Later that month, Gerry Holdsworth, who will lead SOE's No.1 Special Force in 1943, sails for Algeria in the *Mutin*.
Beginning 1943	Pop arrives for officer training for the Royal Naval Volunteer Reserve (RNVR) at HMS *King Alfred*, near Brighton. He is posted to administrative duties at Chatham Dockyard, Kent. Within a few weeks he is recruited by SOE.
April 1943	Mop leaves school and joins the First Aid Nursing Yeomanry (FANY). She is sent to Overthorpe Hall, Oxfordshire, for basic training.

May 1943	Pop arrives for SOE training at Arisaig on the west coast of Scotland.
June 1943	Pop is dispatched to the Helford River in Cornwall for para-naval training and operations.
9 July 1943	Allied forces invade Sicily. Six weeks later, they capture the island. On 25 July, Benito Mussolini is arrested on the orders of King Victor Emmanuel III.
3 September 1943	British and Canadian troops land on the Italian mainland in Calabria. Main Allied invasion takes place six days later at Salerno and Taranto. Italy surrenders on 8 September.
28 September 1943	No.1 Special Force formed at Monopoli, near Bari, in Puglia; Holdsworth is appointed to lead it.
September 1943	Pop arrives in Algeria from the Helford River.
1 October 1943	Allied troops enter Naples.
3 October 1943	British Commandos capture the key east coast port of Termoli, a harbour central to SOE naval operations in the months to come.
5/6 October 1943	SIMCOL operation to rescue Allied POWs in Italy begins.
Early November 1943	Pop departs Algeria for Malta; he sails later that month in the *Gilfredo* to Monopoli.
	Mop sails from Liverpool in the *Monarch of Bermuda* for SOE's Mediterranean HQ, Algiers.
End November 1943	No.1 Special Force begins dedicated para-naval operations along the Italian east coast.
Early December 1943	Pop arrives in Monopoli.
26 December 1943	Pop sails in the Italian submarine *Marea* on his first mission, codenamed 'Rodney/Renown', an agent insertion operation near Venice.
27 December 1943	Ortona, another key east coast Italian port, 75km north of Termoli, is captured by the Allies.

January 1944	Mop sails to Taranto from Algiers; she is transported by truck to Monopoli.
	Mop and Pop meet.
17 January 1944	US Army begins assault on the Gustav Line, German defensive fortifications stretching from north of Naples on the west coast to Ortona in the east.
20/21 January 1944	Pop takes part in Operation Aberton, dropping four agents at the mouth of the Chienti River, near Civitanove Marche; he returns with 17 Allied POWs.
22 January 1944	Allied landings, designed to leapfrog German defences, take place successfully at Anzio; troops fail to break out and dig in for the rest of the winter.
Late January	Pop sails to Vis on a resupply mission to British Commandos supporting Yugoslav partisans in the eastern Adriatic.
19–22 March 1944	Pop takes part in Aintree/Avonmouth and Ampthill sabotage missions behind German lines inland from the mouth of the Chienti River and Porto San Giorgio.
April 1944	The para-naval members of No.1 Special Force, including Pop, are 're-reroled' for land-based special forces missions.
15 May 1944	Pop and Robin Richards undertake Operation Anon, a beach reconnaissance for a landing operation by Popski's Private Army on 14 June.
18 May 1944	Polish troops capture the key German stronghold of Monte Cassino after months of heavy fighting.
End May 1944	Pop and his boss Hilary Scott head 'up country' towards Ancona in their first mission as land-based SOE liaison officers.
5 June 1944	Allied troops enter Rome.
	Mop in Rome within days of its liberation.
18 July 1944	Polish II Corps, part of the British Eighth Army, takes Ancona; Hilary Scott enters the city hours later.

15 August 1944	US and French troops launch Operation Dragoon, an airborne/amphibious invasion of southern France. Allied troops in Italy regroup prior to assaulting German forces' formidable Gothic Line, which stretches from Pisa to Rimini.
25 August 1944	Allied assault on Gothic Line begins.
August 1944	Pop and Robin Richards are briefed on behind-the-lines Rankin missions at Monopoli.
	Field Marshal Albert Kesselring, C-in-C German Army Group C, floods the Liguria/Piedmont region with battle-hardened troops in response to increasing partisan attacks in Northern Italy; SOE by now has 33 separate 'missions' in the region.
Early September 1944	Pop begins parachute training at Brindisi-San Vito dei Normanni; from 15 September he is on standby to jump into Northern Italy.
2 September 1944	Allied forces capture Pisa.
21 September 1944	Allies take Rimini; the August offensive against the Gothic Line halts at the Po Valley. Rankin missions are put on hold four days later.
October 1944	Planning for Operation Clarion, Pop's mission to the Mondovi region in Piedmont, begins.
Early November 1944	Atrocious weather hampers Allied air-drop operations to Northern Italy. The bad weather continues throughout the winter into 1945.
13 November 1944	Gen. Alexander, C-in-C Allied Armies, Italy, issues his infamous 'Winter Directive' to the partisans – the cessation of large-scale hostile operations due to the inability of the Allies to supply them with enough food and weapons. The same day, a German *rastrellamento* begins around Mondovi.
16 November 1944	Pop and Eddie Cauvain parachute into the Mondovi region as one third of Clarion.

9 December 1944	The remaining members of Clarion jump into the Mondovi area of operations.
	Two nights later, Pop and three other Clarion members are captured near the village of Fontane. They are imprisoned briefly in Mondovi before being taken to jail in Cuneo.
20 December 1944	Distinguished Service Crosses (DSCs) awarded to Pop and Robin Richards for Operation Anon are announced in *The Times*.
29 December 1944	Cauvain is captured and imprisoned. The next day, the captured members of Clarion are transferred to Le Nuove prison in Turin.
Early January 1945	No.1 Special Force transfers its HQ from Monopoli to Siena in Tuscany.
6 January 1945	Pop celebrates his 21st birthday in Le Nuove.
14 January 1945	Pop, Campbell, Stevens and Williamson are transported to the Dulag 339 transit camp near Mantua; Cauvain and Banks follow later.
Late January 1945	Mop arrives in Siena.
Early February 1945	Clarion POWs, including Pop, arrive at Stalag VIIIA, Moorsburg, Bavaria.
Late February 1945	Pop arrives at Marlag und Milag Nord, near Bremen.
23 March 1945	Allied armies cross the Rhine into Germany.
	Mop leaves Siena for Naples.
1 April 1945	Mop sails from Naples to England; she arrives in Liverpool one week later.
10 April 1945	British VIII Corps prepares to attack Hamburg; the battle for the city will rage for two weeks.
	Marlag O POWs, including Pop, begin forced march to Lübeck.
23 April 1945	Marlag O POWs arrive at Oflag XC, Lübeck.

24 April 1945	Soviet Red Army completes encirclement of Berlin.
28 April 1945	Mussolini killed by Italian partisans.
30 April 1945	Hitler commits suicide in Berlin.
2 May 1945	Berlin surrenders to the Soviet Red Army. German forces announce their surrender in Italy.
	Oflag XC liberated by the British Second Army.
4 May 1945	Field Marshal Bernard Montgomery takes the unconditional surrender of all German forces in the Netherlands, Denmark and northwest Germany at Lüneburg Heath.
6 May 1945	Pop flies from Germany to Biggin Hill, Kent; he makes his way home to East Finchley, North London.
8 May 1945	VE Day – Victory in Europe.

Dramatis Personae – Principal Characters

Lieutenant Ezio Aceto	Commander 15th Val Casotto Brigade, a partisan unit of Mauri's 1st Group Alpine Division, operating south of Mondovi with Pop.
Able Seaman Fred Albin	One of the Helford 'originals'; frequent crewmate of Pop on boat missions into enemy waters.
Petty Officer William 'Faithful' Banks	Radio operator (Telegraphist), No.1 Special Force.
Flight Lieutenant Christopher Brock	Head of 'Rankin' planning at No.1 Special Force.
Major Duncan 'Huffy' Campbell	Argyll and Sutherland Highlander British Army veteran of campaigns in Sudan, Egypt, Abyssinia, Libya and Greece. Flew to Italy to become SOE officer commanding Pop's Clarion mission.
Petty Officer Eddie Cauvain	Radio operator who parachuted into Northern Italy with Pop on Operation Clarion; one of the Helford 'originals'.
Major Alan Clark	No.1 Special Force 'original' (who sailed with Holdsworth on the *Mutin* into Brindisi harbour in September 1943); composer of 'Monopoli Blues'.
Captain Piero Cosa	Leader of the 3rd Alpine Division, another partisan unit under Mauri operating south of Mondovi.
Sergio Curetti	Sixteen-year-old partisan from Mondovi who resumed contact with Pop in 1991, 47 years after they had last seen each other.
Carluccio Dalmasso	Partisan, Mauri bodyguard.
Hugh Dalton	British Minister of Economic Warfare, the government department in charge of SOE.

Ettore Damini	Sixteen-year-old translator for A-Force (MI9 ops in support of POW escape missions); documented SOE's missions behind the lines in the Chienti and Tenna river valleys.
Major Neville Darewski (a.k.a. Major 'Temple')	SOE's head of the Flap mission in the Langhe, Clarion's designated reception unit.
Captain Teddy de Haan	Former trainee manager at the Savoy, one of the first SOE officers in Italy post-invasion – his task: make contact with the Italian government; later Hewitt's deputy.
Lieutenant Colonel Douglas Dodds-Parker	Head of operations at 'Massingham', SOE's Mediterranean HQ in Algeria.
Marian Gamwell	Head of the First Aid Nursing Yeomanry, the FANYs; the woman who recruited Mop to SOE.
Major General Sir Colin Gubbins	Seconded from the Army by Hugh Dalton to SOE, Gubbins, initially responsible for training, became head of SOE by the time Pop was recruited. Sir Colin was father of Captain Michael Gubbins, an officer attached to No.1 Special Force.
Major John Henderson	SOE liaison officer dropped behind enemy lines to coordinate partisan/Allied assault on Ancona.
Major Dick Hewitt	Holdsworth's second in command at No.1 Special Force, later his successor (from August 1944).
Commander Gerry Holdsworth	Head of No.1 Special Force, Monopoli. Holdsworth, who ran an advertising agency before the war, was an expert on sailing in small boats, which caught the attention of Section D, Secret Intelligence Service, one of the original pillars of SOE. He went on to co-found the Helford Flotilla and was the mastermind of SOE operations in Italy.
Captain Colin Irving-Bell	Campbell's deputy on the Clarion mission.
Lieutenant Dick Laming	Dutch-born Royal Naval officer with para-naval unit under Scott; Pop's frequent captain for boat-based missions behind the lines.

Lieutenant Tom Long	Officer with para-naval unit under Scott; one of the 'originals' who sailed into Southern Italy on Holdsworth's sailing ship *Mutin*.
Captain Charles Macintosh	Holdsworth's deputy for land and air operations, No.1 Special Force.
Sergeant Dick Mallaby	The first SOE agent to be dropped into enemy-held Italy. Captured in summer 1943, he helped establish a channel of communications that led to the Italian armistice.
Major Enrico Martini (a.k.a. 'Mauri')	Commander 1st Group Alpine Division, the main partisan body operating in the Mondovi region, Northern Italy.
Major Malcolm Munthe	Son of a Swedish doctor and writer, recruited into the British Army and the Gordon Highlanders; one of SOE's most decorated operatives in the Mediterranean.
'Nancy'	FANY colleague of Mop from the early days of SOE training.
Gerry Pattinson (pseudonym)	Ex-MI6 friend of Pop's and mine.
Susan Pattinson (pseudonym)	Gerry's wife, also ex-MI6.
'Peggy'	Secretary in the Naval Office, No.1 Special Force, Monopoli.
Colonel Vladimir Peniakoff	Head of British Army's No.1 Demolition Squadron, better known as 'Popski's Private Army'.
Corporal Bill Pickering	Radio operator, No.1 Special Force and author of *The Bandits of Cisterna*.
Captain Edward Renton	Peacetime conductor at the newly opened Glyndebourne Opera; another No.1 Special Force 'original'.
Brooks Richards	Brother of Robin, co-creator of the Helford Flotilla; director of SOE naval operations in the Mediterranean.

Lieutenant Robin Richards	Naval officer, para-naval unit, No.1 Special Force, who, together with Pop, was awarded the DSC for a successful recce of the beach where Popski's Private Army landed in June 1944. Robin was co-creator of the Helford Flotilla with his brother Brooks and a lifelong friend of Pop. He was also my godfather.
Max Salvadori	Anglo-Italian liaison officer with the British Army, who became a central player in SOE operations following the Allied landings at Salerno and Anzio. A staunch pre-war anti-fascist, he was invited by the British to help create a new Italian government after the fall of Rome while continuing to assist SOE in supplying and organising the partisans.
Lieutenant Commander Hilary Scott	Head of the para-naval unit, No.1 Special Force, Monopoli; Holdsworth's deputy for sea operations; later gave Pop a job at his pre-war law firm, Slaughter and May.
Captain Derrick Scott-Job	Head of the Signals Office, No.1 Special Force, Monopoli.
Lieutenant Colonel Selby Cope	SOE liaison officer in Cuneo (returned to Monopoli in November 1944 following death of Darewski).
Corporal Stephens	Clarion team member.
Colonel John Stevens	SOE liaison officer who flew into the Langhe after Darewski's death in an attempt to bolster the command structure of partisans operating in the region.
Lieutenant Roy Taylor	Bermuda-born, former Lincolnshire Regiment para-naval colleague of Pop, No.1 Special Force.
Corporal Williamson	Cope's radio operator; stayed behind in the Val Ellero to operate the 'Coelum South' radio set, Pop's only telecommunications link with No.1 Special Force, Monopoli.

Prologue

Liberation Day

Le Nuove prison, Turin, 25 April 2015

The talking stopped abruptly – as if we'd suddenly stumbled into a funeral or a place of worship. Long rows of cells stared down at us from two levels of a tall, narrow atrium. A thin shaft of light shone on to the floor from a window just below the high vaulted ceiling.

In one of the very few references my father ever made to the prison that had held him in Turin, he had said that it resembled one of those state penitentiaries that had been popularised by American post-war gangster movies – something that had always managed to lend it a touch of glamour, as if he'd had Humphrey Bogart or Jimmy Cagney for company. But there was nothing remotely glamorous about Le Nuove. It filled me, as it must have filled Pop, with hopelessness.

My mother and I had managed to attach ourselves to a party of school children that had come here to commemorate Italy's Festa della liberazione, Liberation Day, on 25 April, when Italians celebrate the fall of fascism and the end of Nazi occupation.

According to our guide, a retired professor of history, the atrium had been one of the few places in Le Nuove where its better-behaved inmates had been allowed to meet and mingle – a clunky, dust-covered projector, indeed, was still in evidence at the back of the room. They'd shown films in here. But this, the professor said, had been a privilege introduced long after the war. In 1944, the rooms off the atrium had housed the administrative staff as well as the surgery where the prison's doctor and dentist had worked. In one of them you could still see a bed fitted with straps and beside it a table with old saws, syringes and scalpels laid out across it.

Le Nuove, remarkably, had remained a prison until 2003.

In its 145-year history, it had incarcerated intellectuals, political prisoners, partisans who'd fought against fascism, Red Brigade terrorists and a handful of wartime 'enemy combatants', including Pop.

My father, the professor said, would have been housed in the wing run by the SS, a part of the complex given over to the incarceration of partisans and Jews and the odd hardened criminal.

We were heading there next.

There were no privileges to be had back then, not in 1944; unless you allowed for the fact that POWs had not had to endure the solitary confinement that was the norm on all the other wings – that Pop and other members of Clarion, the codename for Pop's six-man mission into northwest Italy towards the end of the war, had at least been allowed to remain together in the same louse-ridden cell.

Pop had once told me that he'd been unable to picture himself as a prisoner of war. Dead perhaps. Alive certainly. But never a POW. As a member of Britain's special forces, he'd been conditioned to believe that captivity wasn't an option. In the binary world of special ops, you lived and worked behind the lines or you were put up against a wall and shot. This was very much in accordance with Hitler's 'Führer order', the directive that enemy 'commandos' – any Allied operative, military or not, caught behind the lines – would be executed if caught. I'd wanted to ask him how he *had* survived, but he'd clammed up – as he had about so much of his wartime activity.

'Mop', my mother, extrovert to his more studied introvert, hadn't been able to tell me much more, which, on the face of it, was surprising as both my parents had served from 1943 to 1945 with No.1 Special Force, a unit set up by Special Operations Executive to do what SOE had been doing since the beginning of the German occupation of Europe: fighting the Nazis behind their own lines.

For years, I had wanted to learn about their war – what Pop in particular, such a huge presence in my life, had done, but it had been one of those things he'd only ever discussed at odd moments, and then only reluctantly and with no detail.

All I'd ever known were the rudiments of his story – that he'd been recruited to SOE from the Royal Navy Volunteer Reserve (RNVR); that he'd met my mother while they'd been stationed near Bari, in Puglia in the heel of Italy; that for a while he had been part of a team that had in- and exfiltrated agents behind the lines by boat and by submarine; that he had been parachuted into the north of Italy; that he'd planted the odd bomb and blown up the odd train; and that he'd ended up captured there.

During his illness, in the last 10 years of his life, I kept thinking we'd sit down and talk about it – that I'd finally get to find out those elusive details. But we never did. And beyond the nine months they had spent together at No.1 Special Force, Mop, it turned out, had known precious little about the operational side of his war, too.

His attitude in life, she reminded me, had always been to look forward, not back, a trait that also seemed to sum up the attitudes of his generation, especially those who had fought in the war.

So, for the past year and a half, I'd been on a mission. I'd started with five pages of handwritten notes culled from the snippets of all the conversations I'd ever had with Pop about his time in SOE. I'd journeyed to all the places he'd been during the war: Scotland, Cornwall, Italy, Austria and Germany. I had learned things about his war I couldn't have guessed at when I set out to chart his story: from the time he'd joined up, through his recruitment to SOE, his training as an agent and the operations that had taken him behind the lines – and what had emerged was a quiet tale of unrecognised heroism; something, I felt, the family needed to know about.

Le Nuove, though, was different. It had sucked in the light in a way that none of the other waypoints had. Something had happened here; something that put everything else into perspective; something, perhaps, that explained Pop's reluctance to speak.

On the level above, in the wing where he had been held, I wandered into one of the cells and reflected on the only three things I'd known about his time here before I'd set out to get the facts – that he'd spent his 21st birthday in Le Nuove, that he'd shared his cell with a murderer and that an egg given to him by a nun that day had been the best present he'd ever received. The cell was bare but for a stove and what looked like a pallet that had served as a bed. On the wall was some graffiti: '*Abasso* Mussolini' crossed out and replaced with '*Abasso il re*'. This, too, had been replaced with '*Abasso tutto*' – '*down with everything*'.

I turned to find the professor standing in the doorway. '*Signor*

Clark,' he said softly, 'perhaps you would like to join our small ceremony. It is about to begin.'

He explained that the children would be lighting some candles in the gallery outside; that he would say a few words about the prison, the people who lived and died here, as well as about the war, and offer a few short prayers. He then asked if I would say some words to the children about what had brought me all the way from England and something, too, about Pop. I told him I'd be honoured, but added that I wasn't altogether sure what to say.

The professor smiled kindly. 'Just say whatever comes naturally and do not worry about the language.' He glanced at my friend Egidio Gavazzi, who had helped to arrange the trip, and asked if he would act as interpreter.

Egidio said he would be happy to. Two of his uncles had been prominent partisans during the war.

I followed them outside. The children, around 30 of them, were gathered in a semi-circle at the end of the gallery. Each held a candle. They were, I guessed, aged around 14 or 15.

Silently they parted to admit us to the middle of the group.

I stood in front of the rusted steel door of a cell and the professor handed me a candle. He looked at me. I looked at Egidio. We began to tell the story of how my father had come to be at Le Nuove.

Chapter 1

'Ero qui durante la guerra'

Guildford, England, 1960

In 1960, when I was nine, my parents moved to a largish house close to Guildford. Just outside the spare room at the top of the stairs was a big old cupboard. One day, I was rummaging through it when I came across Pop's naval uniform. The thing that grabbed my attention was the parachute badge sewn on to the sleeve. In all my reading on the war – and, being of the generation that had grown up in its immediate aftermath, I'd read a lot – I'd never come across a naval parachutist before. Why did Pop have a parachute on his uniform? Could it be possible that there had been more to his wartime service in the Royal Navy, as I thought of it then (he had actually been in the Royal Navy Volunteer Reserve, the RNVR), than he had been letting on?

When I asked him about it, he said he'd done some parachuting, but had dismissed it with a wave of the hand – telling me that parachuting itself had been no more frightening than jumping off a 12-foot wall. This, however, coupled with a training manual tucked amongst a pile of vintage Second World War *National Geographic* magazines I'd found under a bed in my grandparents' house round about the same time – it had contained a set of instructions on how to make bombs as well as stripping and reassembly notes for a Bren gun – hinted that my father's wartime career had been more interesting than he'd been letting on.

A year or two after this, we went on holiday to France. One day, to give us a break from the beach, Mop and Pop took us to visit the port at St Nazaire – the place where, in 1942, HMS *Campbeltown*, her bow packed full of explosives, had rammed and destroyed a dock used for repairing German battleships. The St Nazaire raid had been legendary, one of the most daring of the entire war, and it had struck me as curious that Pop had known quite so much about it. My naïve view of the way the Navy waged war had been supplanted by a more mature appreciation of combined land–sea operations, the St Nazaire raid being a prime example of the way in which the roles of sailors, commandos and soldiers had blurred when the need arose – usually when there was a requirement to hit the enemy via unconventional warfare.

But I still wasn't able to equate 'being in the Navy' with doing anything subversive. So, the plot thickened when, that same holiday, Pop took us to see a memorial to French Resistance fighters in the Loire Valley. He had clearly been moved by it, but had said nothing.

It was only the following year, on our next holiday, driving around Puglia in Southern Italy, that the penny finally dropped. We arrived at a fishing port called Monopoli, where, out of the blue, my parents announced they'd met each other. '*Ero qui durante la guerra*,' Mop would tell any local she came across in her broken Italian. *I was here during the war.* I learned, from other asides, she'd been a wireless operator/coder. But neither she nor Pop ever divulged the essential point: that the reason they'd been in Monopoli was because it had been the operational HQ of the Special Operations Executive in Italy from 1943 to 1945.

In the mid-1960s, SOE was barely on anyone's radar, because 20 years after the war most of its operations remained highly secret. Bits and bobs had come out in books like *The White Rabbit* by Tommy Yeo-Thomas, which I'd read avidly, but it was only when I was at university, and I got hold of Professor M.R.D. Foot's seminal history of the SOE in France, which had recently been published, that I appreciated how big Special Operations Executive had been and what it had done.

In Pop's case, it had clearly involved guns, because shortly after our Italian holiday my brother, Will, and I had found his weapon: a Beretta automatic, complete with its magazine and ammunition. Even though it couldn't fire, we'd played with it, mouldy green bullets and all, until one day, during one of those amnesties that used to get held every so often, a policeman turned up to ask if Pop had any old weapons he wanted to hand in.

My father's best friend had been a man called Tommy Walmsley.

Tommy, big, kind and always on hand with an amusing story, had been Pop's drinking buddy for many years in a touching weekly tradition they never, ever broke. Tommy had been in the Lancashire Fusiliers and described his greatest military achievement as saving the regimental wine at Dunkirk. He and Pop had met while they'd worked together at Slaughter and May, the legal firm, where, years later, I also ended up.

Every Sunday evening, Pop and Tommy would meet for a couple of hours at the Seahorse, a pub near Guildford where they would set the world to rights. Tommy died in 1982 at the age of only 60. Pop had many friends, but nobody quite filled the vacuum left by Tommy or the enjoyment of those Sunday evenings down at their local. When I became a lawyer and Pop had moved on from law to forge a career as a banker, for 15 years our offices were less than 500 yards apart. In all that time, however, we met for lunch or for an after-work drink maybe half a dozen times, until he retired in 1989 – though 'retirement', in actual fact, simply meant work at a less frenetic pace and several days in London as opposed to the whole week. He and I then started to implement our own tradition of the weekly drink. Every Tuesday, after work, for an hour and a half, in the convivial atmosphere of an old-fashioned 'local', Pop began to open up a little more, in part because of my continual prompting, but perhaps also because, being away from home, he was less 'on guard'.

The stories were, at best, episodic – snatches, more than anything else – and it never took too much for the conversation to move on.

Until, that was, the day in April 1991 he announced he'd received a letter from Curetti.

Who, I asked Pop, *was Curetti?*

Sergio Curetti, he told me, was the man – he was not much more than a boy then – who had rescued him and taken him in the night that he parachuted behind the lines.

He reached into his jacket, produced a letter, unfolded it and handed it to me. I started to read:

> *Dear Sir, I'm writing to you hoping that you are the person I
> have tried to trace these following years. This person is someone*

who I have met in Italy in 1944. If you are not the person I am
seeking, please excuse me.

It was on November 16, 1944, at San Giacomo di Roburent
(a small town in the mountains), where I was a 'partigiano'. Two
English soldiers were parachuted.

Sergio Curetti explained he had written to Pop because he'd recently read a book in which Pop and a man named Cauvain had been mentioned as the parachutists who'd dropped into San Giacomo. The Italian declared that he had been trying to track Pop down ever since the end of the war, but, knowing Pop had been captured, had feared he had been killed.

The book mentioned that Sub-Lieutenant Robert Clark RNVR had gone on to carve out a distinguished career for himself in the City and it was via this snippet of information that Curetti was able to track him down.

I asked Pop about Cauvain and to my surprise he replied without hesitation. Later, I took this as evidence of just how much Curetti and the letter had meant to him.

Eddie Cauvain, Pop said, had been his radio operator. They were part of a small team that was supposed to work with the partisans against the Germans, but it started to go wrong from the beginning. Instead of dropping into the place they were meant to, Pop (and his 'unholy' baggage) had ended up in a tree in the garden of a priest and had broken his ribs. He and Cauvain had landed more than 15 miles from the drop-zone. But they had ended up captured before they could do much good. Three-quarters of the party didn't drop that night – they came in a month later.

When I asked Pop if he was going to reply to Curetti, he told me he already had, and that he and Mop were going to go to Italy to meet him and his family.

The visit (including a return to the locations of their wartime activities), took place the following year and turned out to be a great success; a few years later, during a second visit to the Curettis, I joined them. The Curettis lived where they'd always lived, in the lee of the Alps, in a town called Mondovi, close to where Pop had made his jump. They were delightful and made me feel – as they have done ever since – as if I were part of their family.

Slowly, between our weekly sessions in the pub and the visit to the Curettis, a few more pieces of the puzzle had come together. Even though we'd never actually sat down and spoken about the arc of his wartime career, many of the episodes of which Pop had spoken over the years had now knitted into a narrative of sorts.

I knew that he had been recruited to SOE from the Navy after telling someone he'd 'mucked about in small boats'; that he'd trained in Scotland where the weather was atrocious and where he'd apparently ended up meeting the assassins of Reinhard Heydrich, Hitler's Reich-Protector of Bohemia-Moravia and one of the main architects of the Holocaust; that shortly afterwards, he'd been dispatched to the Helford River in Cornwall, where SOE had taught him how to infiltrate and exfiltrate by boat; that after this, and a short stint in Algeria, he'd sailed an old fishing smack from Malta to Southern Italy, where his operational career with SOE began.

It was in Monopoli that he met my mother and from Monopoli that he'd made a number of missions up the coast, delivering and collecting agents, and carrying out sabotage missions. He'd also divulged, with some reluctance, how he and my godfather, Robin Richards, whom he'd met while training on the Helford, had been awarded DSCs: for carrying out a recce for a beach landing by a small force of commandos, known as 'Popski's Private Army', led by a man called Colonel Vladimir Peniakoff, a Belgian of Russian-Jewish descent who'd fought with the British Army; and that despite the success of the mission the landing itself had gone spectacularly wrong.

From my Italian trip, and a return visit by the Curettis to us, I also learned how Pop had been selected for the parachute drop into Northern Italy, that it had gone awry and after his capture he'd been incarcerated in a number of prisons – including a civilian jail in the middle of Turin. Thanks to the rescinding of Hitler's order, late in the war, that all commandos caught behind the lines be shot, Pop had avoided execution to be sent instead as a POW into Germany, where he'd ended up first of all in a camp near Bremen, and then in another near Lübeck, where he was finally liberated. On that day, he'd enjoyed a whisky in the company of the legendary Battle of Britain flying ace Johnnie Johnson and, pitifully thin, had promptly fainted.

In addition to a short interview he'd given to researchers at London's Imperial War Museum – part of the IWM's campaign to record oral histories of as many people as possible who had fought in the world wars – a short talk that he'd given at Westminster School, where his grandchildren, my two sons, had been at school, was probably the fullest account he'd ever made of his war. But, while all this gave me knowledge, it wasn't any more than the version I had, by now, assembled piecemeal – one that was woefully incomplete.

Pop's code in life had always been to look after those he felt responsible for, both at home and in the workplace, and it was a duty he could not have discharged any better if he'd tried. He loved and looked after my mother with a passion and dedication that even my brother, sister and I could see was a rare and precious thing – and he did the same by us, too. But there comes a moment in most of our lives when our relationship with our parents changes and mine changed on the day that Pop, by now well into his seventies, got food poisoning at an SOE gathering in Oxford. The bacteria, they told us later, had been in the gelatin of some pâté he'd eaten and the resulting sickness so severe that it had disrupted the rhythm of his heart – and Pop went from being a man who had never had a day's illness in his life to someone who started to rely on others to help him cope. He bore this shift in his circumstances with great dignity and when, in 2003, he was diagnosed with cancer as well, with considerable courage, too.

After a number of operations, he was confined to a wheelchair, but the prognosis from his doctors was generally encouraging: Pop, they said, was of an age where the spread of the disease would be slow and, therefore, we shouldn't worry unduly – he was, even after the food poisoning, they told us, a robust individual, who wouldn't be leaving us any time soon.

Nevertheless, we all knew that the time we had left with him was finite and that we had to make the most of it.

And I knew that if the full story of his time with SOE was to come out at all, it needed to do so in its own time – in *his* own time – and that there should be no pressure on him to divulge it.

In 2010, I spoke to an old friend I'll refer to as Gerry Pattinson who'd previously chatted with Pop about his time in SOE – and Pop had opened up to him, because Gerry had a background in the security services and knew a great deal about operations behind the lines. Gerry had asked me if Pop was coming to the SOE 70th anniversary dinner.

The event commemorated the 70 years since SOE's foundation in 1940. There were by now only 300 surviving former field officers, some 30 of whom were due to attend the dinner at the Imperial War Museum, and Pop announced he was keen to go. I accompanied him, and Pop sat next to Gerry and his wife, Susan (who also has a security services background). During the evening, Pop was introduced to a journalist from *The Times* who was fascinated by Falla (pronounced 'Fire') – the threadbare teddy bear Pop had had from the earliest days of his childhood, who had also made it to the dinner. Falla, who had been in the car for the early part of the proceedings and had, by popular demand, joined us for the speeches and toasts, had been with Pop through thick and thin during the war. The journalist asked Pop whether he would be happy for Falla's story (and his own) to be the subject of an article and, knowing of Pop's dislike of the limelight, I waited for his reply with apprehension. 'I'd be delighted,' he said.

The article, which emerged a couple of weeks later, featured a colour photo of Pop, Mop and Falla – Falla looking jaunty in a blue knitted suit; Mop and Pop both smiling and happy, and both proudly wearing their medals.

Falla was the hook for the story that appeared with the picture, which, while not revelatory, marked a shift, because it signalled, I felt, that Pop was ready for a lengthier account of his war to come out – that it was only the manner in which he told it that needed to be decided, and picking the right moment in which to sit down to get the details.

The shift had come because of the time he'd spent at that dinner with his former colleagues and with it, perhaps, the sense that what he had done – what *SOE* had done – amounted to something that was still important.

In the discussions I went on to have with Pop after the dinner, he was particularly keen to tell me about the Italians he had fought alongside. And while the details I'd craved from the beginning continued to remain elusive, the one thing I did come to appreciate was the esteem in which he held his *partigiani* co-combatants: 'Forget all those stupid jokes about the tanks with four reverse gears. [The Italians] were amongst the bravest people I ever met,' he said. Shortly afterwards, during a 90th birthday lunch for my godfather, Robin Richards, with whom Pop had served in No.1 Special Force, I listened as the two of them started to talk unselfconsciously about some of the experiences they had shared in Italy. Robin, I knew, had not dropped with Pop into Northern Italy, but had been with him on many other missions, and thus would be an invaluable source of information in building the picture.

I resolved to contact Robin as soon as possible to see if he would be amenable to contributing to the story. But, a week before Christmas, Pop suffered a stroke. He had fought so many battles and won that I found it hard to believe that this one would be any different, a view that was given impetus, when, over Christmas, with the family around him, he regained some of his strength and we allowed ourselves to believe that he'd pull through. But, on 3 January, Mop rang me to say that he wasn't eating and wasn't talking and appeared to be going suddenly and rapidly downhill. I left work, picked up the family and drove as fast as I could down the A3 to my parents' home. It was there, surrounded by his family, and with Falla by his side, that my father finally gave up the fight for life, three days short of his 89th birthday.

I gave little thought in the weeks and months afterwards to the idea of continuing to research Pop's war. But, bit by bit, as the rawest part of our grief began to heal, the desire in me to *know* only grew stronger.

By the summer, my brother, Will, and I had resolved to go on a journey to find out. But with Will living in Australia, it was accepted that I would do most of the on-the-ground sleuthing. The problem, of course, was how to go about assembling the facts now that the principal of the story was no longer with us.

I had never talked to Mop much about Pop's war, because I'd always imagined that one day I'd sit down and talk with *him* about it. But Mop was very obviously the place to start.

Chapter 2

'Booted and spurred'

Ystalyfera, South Wales, 1924

My mother, Marjorie, had had a remarkably happy childhood, one marred by the tragic loss of her mother, who had died giving birth to her. To enable my grandfather to continue running the small mine he owned, in a little village called Ystalyfera about 12 miles from Swansea in South Wales, my great-grandmother moved into the family home to bring up her and her sister, Gwenda. They were a close-knit, loving family. My grandfather had distinguished himself on the Western Front, and had been wounded three times between 1916 and 1918.

Prior to the war, he had played rugby and earned five caps for Wales. Afterwards, despite his wartime injuries, he continued to captain Swansea, but the war had taken its toll and soon he stopped playing to concentrate on the business. In later years, my grandfather admitted that he had been plagued by horrific nightmares of his time in the trenches. He never elaborated, but my mother once told me she used to hear his screams at night.

The family spoke Welsh and English at home and the girls were taught in both languages at their primary school in the village, which was halfway up a mountain. 'I walked up and back four times a day, there being no school lunches,' she would tell people in later life, 'and sometimes I had to be bribed to return in the afternoon by being given a halfpenny, which bought a lot of sweets in those days.'

When she was 10, Mop went to a convent school in Swansea, which was an hour's journey by bus, with a 20-minute walk the other end. She used to play hockey on Swansea beach, with the team having to wait until the tide was out to mark the pitch.

Back in the village, the milk came by horse and cart and the postman was the source of most of the local gossip. On Sundays, the family went to chapel three times and, to observe the Sabbath, the girls weren't allowed to sew, knit or play ball games. 'Once a year we were taken on the chapel outing to the seaside for the day and to me it meant new white socks and a pretty dress,' Mop remembers. This image of butter-wouldn't-melt-in-the-mouth innocence is belied by another story she likes to tell, which is how she once got into trouble by throwing her rice pudding out of the school bus at a group of pedestrians.

Because she had been what she'd always described as a 'bit of a handful', as soon as she was 13 my grandfather did something extraordinary – at least by the standards of the day and the relatively modest circumstances in which they'd lived – he packed her off to one of the finest girls' public schools in the country: Cheltenham Ladies College.

Cheltenham was a bittersweet experience for my mother.

On the one hand, she'd loved the opportunities that it had offered, especially in sport. She opened the bowling for the cricket team and ended up captaining the First XI. On the other, she detested the snobbery and was teased mercilessly about her Welsh accent.

During the holidays, while most of the other girls were up in London attending debutantes' balls, Mop and her friend Christine spent all their spare money at the cinema, so that they had something other than tittle-tattle from London society to discuss at the beginning of each term. They talked about film stars in the same way that the others talked about the Earl of This and the Marquis of That.

When war came, the playing fields were dug up to make way for potatoes. The war gave school an edge it had lacked in peacetime – bombs used to fall perilously close by as the Germans attempted to destroy aircraft factories in Gloucester and Cheltenham – and Mop and Christine developed a morbid fascination with the death columns, which they used to pore over in the school library. One day, in May 1941, this came sharply and poignantly into focus when the headmistress, Miss Popham, announced in school assembly that the battleship HMS *Hood*, pride of the Royal Navy, had been sunk by the *Bismarck*, with the loss of almost all hands. The daughter of the captain, one of the 1,415 casualties, was at the school. Mop and Christine stopped reading the death columns after that.

Mop was bright and particularly good at maths, which may explain what happened next. In January 1943, soon after the start of the spring term, a man showed up at Cheltenham from an anonymous ministry in London and interviewed two specially selected girls for a job that he couldn't tell them anything about. One of the girls was my mother. The 'man from the ministry' opened her interview with an odd question: 'Can you keep a secret?'

Clearly she could – or at least convinced him she could – because she passed the test.

Miss Popham, who seemed to be oddly complicit in steering her in the direction offered by the man from the ministry, then urged her to attend a second interview in London; this despite the fact that she had just been offered a place at Oxford.

In London, Mop was interviewed by Marian Gamwell, the commandant of the FANY, the First Aid Nursing Yeomanry. To this day, she still refers to Gamwell as 'the Queen Bee'.

The FANY had been founded in 1907 by one Captain Edward Baker. Baker's idea was that women recruited to the FANY wouldn't just be first-aid specialists but skilled in areas that would allow them to make their own way to the battlefront – an astonishing concept in a country in which women didn't yet have the vote. The original members were trained in cavalry work, signalling and camp-work. By the outbreak of the Second World War, these duties had morphed into four distinct areas: motor transport, wireless telegraphy (W/T), code work and general duties. What was not divulged, because it was 'top secret', was the fact that the FANY had become the parent unit for many women who would become SOE agents. By 1943, it had become intimately associated with SOE, supplying it with all its female personnel in the administration and technical support roles at its Special Training Schools and at its three main operating hubs – in North Africa, India and the Far East. Mop, in line with the secrecy, had not been told why she had been recruited, but her personnel file at The National Archives, which I had managed to obtain, stated, for the record, that my 17-and-a-half-year-old mother had turned up at FANY headquarters – a former vicarage in Wilton Place, near Hyde Park Corner – 'for possible employment as [a] W/T operator' on 6 February 1943.

The file said that she appeared at Wilton Place for a second interview five days later.

I asked her if she could remember what happened next.

'Marian Gamwell told me, as I was Welsh, that I was going to be a wireless operator. I think there was some suggestion that as the Welsh are known for their love of music and singing that I'd be able to master the wireless set and the coding process – perhaps via some tenuous relationship to the piano.'

There is precious little in the archives on what SOE was looking for when it recruited women like my mother. According to Hugh Popham, author of *The FANY in Peace and War*, SOE tended to recruit from the British public-school system because this reflected the composition of the people running it. It was clearly also keen for its women recruits to have mathematical backgrounds, as it wanted 'the right kinds of brain' for dealing with codes and ciphers. It has always mystified my mother that this wasn't made more explicit – that her 'Welshness' was the thing Gamwell picked up on. But this seems very much to have been in line with the secrecy ethos. Very little during the SOE recruitment process, as Pop would discover later on, was as it seemed.

Returning to Cheltenham, and further encouraged by Miss Popham, my mother then had to call my grandfather to tell him that she wouldn't be taking up her place at Oxford, but would be joining the FANY instead.

This was *all* she was able to tell him. My grandfather, Mop told me, had to take it on trust that she was doing the right thing. And it was to his credit, she added, that he did.

Mop left Cheltenham just before Easter 1943 and was sent for basic training to Overthorpe Hall, a requisitioned stately home, near Banbury in Oxfordshire. Here, corps history, drill, first aid and chores were the focus – but, 70 years on, somewhat frustratingly for my purposes, all my mother could really remember of her time at Overthorpe Hall was that she'd 'cleaned taps'.

This was an early manifestation of the challenge I found myself up against. While Mop was wholly supportive of my effort to dig into

Pop's wartime story, she couldn't quite understand what any of it had to do with her. I read this later as avoidance – so typical of her generation – of any suggestion that she'd done anything that might be characterised as 'brave'.

'I wasn't brave; I was just doing my bit. How could I have possibly gone to Oxford, when London was being bombed?' she told me on one of my numerous attempts to 'debrief' her. Increasingly, therefore, I found myself relying ever more heavily on what little information existed on my mother in documentation at The National Archives and the Imperial War Museum.

With basic training under her belt, she was dispatched (according to her demobilisation papers, which she had managed to hang on to) on 29 May to Fawley Court, near Henley, also known as SOE station STS 54. Here she was introduced to all SOE's systems of codes and ciphers then in use, both for communicating with agents in the field and mainline stations such as Cairo.

By the time of Mop's recruitment, an elaborate system of coding and decoding called 'Playfair' had recently been replaced by a 'one-time pad', which tended to be used exclusively for field traffic and was considered virtually unbreakable.

Due to the pressures of operating in the field, agents often left out their checks – codes hidden within the message – when transmitting their reports and it was down to the FANY base coder to determine whether this was a genuine oversight or the set had fallen into enemy hands.

This, as I was to discover later, placed an intolerable burden on the coder/decoder – young girls, more often than not, barely out of their teens (and often, like my mother, still in them) – to know whether the agent was genuine.

The system checks were supposed to be strenuously enforced, but this, tragically, wasn't always the case.

Between 1941 and August 1943 – a month before my mother completed her training – a basic failure to implement the check system, compounded by a litany of other errors, resulted in the compromise of SOE's entire Dutch Section and consequently in the deaths of dozens of agents and possibly hundreds of Dutch Resistance fighters.

At one point, one of the base coders even signalled to an *Abwehr* intelligence officer, presuming him still to be the Dutch agent he purported to be, that 'you ought to use your security checks' when his key-stroke behaviour appeared out of character. This lapse then alerted the *Abwehr* to the existence of such checks and the compromise deepened.

The fallout rate for male and female wireless telegraphy operators, WTOs, training at Fawley Court was high. Some of those who did not last the course became coders; others became registry clerks or were entrusted with the copying and distribution of signals. Still others became teleprinter or switchboard operators. The pressure derived from WTOs having to achieve a high speed in words per minute – at least 20. This was essential so as to keep radio transmissions to 15 minutes or less, the time it was estimated the *Abwehr*'s direction-finding vans needed to locate a set.

On 27 September, according to Mop's demob papers, she was sent to Belhaven Hill, near Dunbar in Scotland, a specialist training school, designated STS 54B, that had been opened a few months earlier.

Using all the skills she had acquired at Fawley Court, now re-designated STS 54A, she spent the next month transmitting and receiving signals to and from Henley, almost 400 miles away, under conditions mirroring those she would experience in the field – in particular, how to understand signals distorted by the kind of climatic and atmospheric conditions that plagued wireless transmissions across Europe.

At the end of October, she had to break the news to the family in a difficult phone call from Belhaven Hill that she was about to be sent abroad.

A note that she wrote to my grandfather shortly afterwards survives. *I want you to be very cheerful about this decision of mine*, she told him, *because I feel I am doing the right thing. Just you be happy too – that's all I want in the world and I too will be all right.*

When I talked to her about it, Mop remembered – or affected to remember – just seven things about the voyage that took her to North Africa: that she was being put to work in an organisation that nobody had yet told her anything about; that the ship was called the *Monarch of Bermuda*; that Peter Ustinov, the actor and raconteur, had been on board; that she and her friend Nancy *(pictured)*, with whom she had trained, were one of just a handful of women on the ship; that Nancy and Ustinov had gone on a 'date' during the voyage; that the convoy had been attacked; and that tomato ketchup had been on the tables.

There is, however, an online account of the early stages of the journey of the *Monarch* recorded by Tom Nevin, an able seaman on board the British light cruiser HMS *Birmingham*, which acted as one of several escorts for the convoy in which the *Monarch of Bermuda* found herself. It was from Nevin's diary that I'd learned that the weather had been fine the day that she slipped out of Liverpool docks in early November 1943. Nevin also described how at midday on Tuesday 16 November, in a calm, slight swell,

the captain announced over the ship's tannoy that the convoy was ferrying 43,000 troops and supplies to Algiers, Alexandria and Bombay via the Suez Canal.

This was the first they knew of their destination.

Pursuing a westerly course almost 1,000km into the Atlantic to avoid enemy aircraft, *Birmingham* joined the convoy off the coast of Ireland, the crew on their toes for up to 40 U-Boats they had been told were active in the North Atlantic at that time. Before long *Birmingham* rendezvoused with the rest of the convoy, including the *Monarch of Bermuda*. Requisitioned as a troopship when war broke out, her elegant pale-grey pre-war livery, complete with red and black funnels, had been swapped for a hastily applied iron-grey paint scheme, mottled with oil stains and chipped and rusted from the constant battering of the high seas.

Two days later, still heading westwards, they were overflown by an unidentified aircraft and two days after that, on 20 November, the convoy to the northeast of them was attacked by U-Boats.

For all her veneer of forgetfulness, Mop's memory had been spot on. The record stated that there were 12 FANYs on board the *Monarch* and that they were under the command of Lt Jean MacLachlan, formerly a don at Girton College, Cambridge. According to Margaret Pawley, a former FANY, who recorded details of this particular voyage in her book *In Obedience to Instructions*, MacLachlan was very regimental, took her duties seriously and insisted that her charges should carry their own luggage. Her favourite expression, Pawley said, was 'being booted and spurred'.

After safely negotiating the Strait of Gibraltar, the convoy came under attack before entering the port of Algiers in early December. Mop then casually told me something she'd never divulged before: that the ship next to the *Monarch* had been struck by a torpedo, which had exploded spectacularly, lighting up the night sky. I was stunned that I'd never heard this before, but Mop just shrugged, disappeared for a few moments, then returned with an old newspaper cutting.

> *An attack by thirty German heavy bombers on an Allied convoy off the North African coast on Friday evening was broken up by fighters of the North West African Coastal Air Force. Eight enemy planes were shot down into the sea and a ninth was destroyed by the guns of a naval landing craft…*

Upon disembarking at Algiers, the 12 FANYs divided, according to Margaret Pawley, with five heading to a hotel called the Oasis, where their first duty was to clean up vomit left on the stairs by some troops who'd stopped by for the night. Both groups, Mop's included, ended up after a couple of days' acclimatisation at a secret location called 'ISSU6', as the SOE base codenamed 'Massingham' was also known – a place called the Club des Pins, 25km outside the Algerian capital.

Massingham, according to the man who became its operations officer, Lt Colonel Douglas Dodds-Parker, had been set up soon after the Allied landings in North Africa, 'with wide but undefined duties', but in essence 'to establish a base for later operations northwards'.

The objective of the landings in Morocco, Tunisia and Algeria in November 1942 – codenamed Operation Torch – had been to bring about the surrender of Vichy French forces in North Africa and to provide a forward command, communications, supply and training base for subversive operations against southern France, Corsica, Sardinia, Sicily and Italy – the 'soft underbelly of Europe' that Churchill had identified as a viable strategic objective in advance of Allied landings in northern France. By the time Mop arrived, in early December 1943, Massingham was already overseeing SOE operations in Italy – this in the wake of the Allied invasion three months earlier.

The camp, whose personnel came from Britain, the US, France and Spain (the latter comprised 50 Spanish Communists imprisoned by the Vichy French and set free by General de Gaulle), was a hive of activity, with paramilitary and demolition training taking place on a variety of nearby ranges. There were lecture rooms, weapon and demolition stores and even a 'museum' in one of the Nissen huts showcasing different types of foreign weapons, booby traps and enemy uniforms. The rooms in the villas occupied by the FANYs had stone floors, no furniture and no heating. The girls slept on camp beds issued with grey Army blankets. This might have been all right in summer, but was miserable in winter, which was probably why my mother had retained so little memory of it. Apart from a short school trip to Germany, Algeria was Mop's first real experience of foreign travel and would have come as a shock. Margaret Pawley records that letters home from girls in Mop's intake requested pillows and dressing gowns. FANYs improvised by stuffing their underclothes into their khaki pillow cases; and kitbags, according to Pawley, remained the only receptacle for clothes and possessions. Bedside tables were created from orange boxes and decked with parachute silk.

On 9 July 1943, Allied forces had invaded Sicily and, after six weeks, captured the island. On 24 July, Italy's Grand Council of Fascism voted against the dictator, Benito Mussolini, and the following day he was arrested on the orders of the king, Victor Emmanuel III.

With Mussolini locked up, the Italian government started to make overtures to the Allies for an armistice that would take Italy out of the war.

On 3 September, just hours before an advance guard of British and Canadian troops came ashore on the Italian mainland in Calabria after crossing the Strait of Messina, Italy surrendered.

On 9 September, the main Allied invasion of Italy took place at Salerno and Taranto. While this was not the second front that Churchill and US President Franklin D. Roosevelt had promised Marshal of the Soviet Union Joseph Stalin – that would come nine months later, in June 1944, with the D-Day landings in Normandy – it was the beginning of the assault on the European underbelly that Churchill believed would help speed Hitler's defeat.

Operation Axis, Hitler's response to Italy's collapse, resulted in German troops taking the surrender of a million Italian soldiers in Italy, France, Greece, Yugoslavia and the Aegean. In the ensuing confusion, some Italians sided with the Allies, others with the Germans. Others went home or disappeared into the hills. The result was, in effect, a quasi-civil war, in which Italian fascists and those against the armistice sided against the anti-fascists, many of them Communists.

Soon after Christmas, my mother and Nancy were told they would be heading for Italy.

In January 1944, Mop, Nancy and four other FANY WTOs arrived in the port of Taranto, in the Gulf of Taranto between the toe and the heel of Italy, in some of the worst weather to hit Italy for several decades – winter storms that had stalled the Allies' offensive north following the September invasion and which would persist well into the spring.

Mop's memory of this part of her journey was remarkably good. As the FANYs disembarked, they were greeted by the sight of German POWs, holed up on the lower decks of the ship on which they'd just sailed, sticking their tongues out at them. Not put off by the fact they were the first enemy she'd seen – or maybe because of it – my mother, and Nancy, responded in kind.

Two hours later, after a cold and bumpy journey on a Bedford truck, they hopped down from the tailgate and surveyed their new home: Monopoli, a fishing port of around 30,000 inhabitants built around a walled medieval harbour halfway between Bari and Brindisi.

They were led a short way through the town to the FANY mess. Mop recalled that they passed black-clad peasant women, some of them without shoes. Their escort, one of the seven FANYs who had arrived the previous autumn, trotted out what would soon become a familiar refrain: 'Italy begins at Florence and Africa begins at Rome.' Massingham seemed luxurious by comparison.

Once in the mess, the six newcomers were introduced to their sleeping quarters: a more austere version of the dormitory Mop had slept in at school, with camp beds lined up against the walls. To make room for them, beds had to be placed on an adjoining terrace covered by a tarpaulin. There was no heating and next to no hot water, because the locals had scavenged all the wood. Their welcoming meal consisted of porridge and bacon – the cooks, recruited locally, hadn't quite got the hang of the idea that these were best served separately.

It was here, for the first time, they were told that they were part of a secret unit known as No.1 Special Force.

The captain in charge of the Signals Office was a man called Derrick Scott-Job. Bill Pickering, a sergeant with SOE who recorded his experiences at Monopoli in *The Bandits of Cisterna*, worked in the Signals Office alongside the FANYs and described the bespectacled Scott-Job as 'studious looking'. Mop remembered him more vividly as a 'miserable thing', a quality she also ascribed to the working conditions: 12-hour shifts, they were told, would be the norm, until more coders and WTOs arrived from Massingham. Mop and the other coders were trained in a village called La Selva around 15km south of the town. Inevitably, perhaps, Scott-Job acquired the nickname 'Oddjob'.

Fred Tillson, formerly a warrant officer in the Royal Corps of Signals, who worked at No.1 Special Force, recalled introducing the FANYs there to the Italian operators with whom they would be working in the field. It was important, Tillson told them, as he went through the routine, that they learned to recognise the characteristic 'keying' of each agent before the agents went behind the lines. If any of them were captured and their sets taken over by the enemy, the way in which they communicated, the keying characteristic, known as a 'fist' – how individual agents tapped their Morse keys – needed to be as familiar as their own handwriting. Mop detested W/T work – a momentary lapse on her part meant the capture or death of an agent. As part of her training, she had spent months learning to recognise different fists. There had been no adequate method for teaching this – it came with experience and through listening – and for this, she reflected, perhaps it did help that she'd had a musical ear. A fist was almost impossible to fake or replicate by an enemy. But would she recognise it if any of the young Italians she'd trained with were to be captured and replaced?

Mop came away struck by the youth of these men – these 'Italian boys', as she described them to me 70 years later. It was her first brush with the agents that she would soon come to be working with around the clock – many of whom would subsequently be killed.

In the darkness of the signal room, with one hand pressed to her headphones, the other by her keypad, coding and decoding, she told me, would become a curiously intimate ritual – the thinnest of bridges to someone under threat of capture at any moment in an intensely hostile environment.

To escape from the stress of it, she would go down to the harbour whenever she could. It had changed little in centuries. Old stone houses overlooked a sheltered port bobbing with small fishing boats. On a promontory to the south, a medieval castle looked out over the Adriatic.

It was in the middle of January that she and Nancy found themselves introduced to the four officers of the para-naval unit of No.1 Special Force: Lt Cdr Hilary Scott, Lt Dick Laming, Lt Robin Richards and the new boy, Sub Lt 'Bob' Clark.

Chapter 3

'Massingham'

Algeria, September 1943

Pop, I knew, had arrived in Algiers in late September 1943, almost three months before Mop, at a time when SOE would have been abuzz with events that had led to the Italian surrender – events that were now focused on the Allies' advance north.

At the time of his arrival, news was coming through that large swaths of Naples were in the throes of a popular uprising against the Germans, a rebellion that would culminate in Naples's surrender to the Allies on 2 October. SOE personnel were embedded with forward Allied units in the front line at Salerno, 40km south of Naples, in the formative stages of trying to corral Italian Resistance against the Germans and Italian fascists.

That Pop was in Algiers at all was down to a man named Commander Gerry Holdsworth, RNVR, the head of No.1 Special Force – and the man who would later help to found the Special Forces Club, of which Pop had been an early member.

Pop, in fact, on one of the rare occasions he'd opened up about his time in SOE, had told me he'd had a great deal of respect for Holdsworth, a man with a swashbuckling pedigree. An expert on sailing small boats, he had spent time on a rubber plantation in Borneo during the 1920s, but returned to England in the early 1930s to make films for an advertising agency. His connection to Britain's clandestine special services began just before the war by virtue of his being a part-owner in a pilot-cutter, *Mischief*, based in the Bristol Channel.

In 1938, SIS, the Secret Intelligence Service, also known as MI6, established its Section D as a sabotage and subversion unit. Part of Section D's remit was to survey and reconnoitre parts of the continental coastline that might assume strategic significance during wartime. Through *Mischief*, Holdsworth became part of a distinguished group of amateur sailors, known as the Royal Cruising Club, who would gather such data for Section D.

In 1940, Section D became one of the founding pillars of SOE. David Stafford, whose book *Mission Accomplished* is one of the definitive works on SOE's Italian campaign, described Holdsworth *(pictured)* as a 'quiet character with an occasionally explosive temper', who would later be summed up by one of the partisan leaders who worked with him as 'more southern than north-

ern, generous and warm, half-hero and half-pirate, the ideal companion for a big game hunt or an adventure in Shanghai'.

A few weeks after the war broke out, Holdsworth was summoned to St Ermin's Hotel, in St James's, London, where Section D had established its headquarters. After receiving a short course of instruction in demolition, he was sent to Norway under commercial cover to plot the flow of Swedish iron ore to Germany – and to see how it might be disrupted. For at least part of the time, he was accompanied by his wife, Mary. After the German invasion of Norway, Holdsworth's mission was compromised and he was arrested by the Swedish authorities. He eventually made it back to the UK where he was put in charge of covert resistance plans in East Anglia in the event of a Nazi invasion, before being dispatched to Cornwall to establish SOE's 'Helford Flotilla' – a 'sea-transport service' to and from Brittany on the French coast. He eventually left for Algeria soon after the Allied invasion of North Africa.

By September 1943, SOE's centre of gravity for operations in Italy had started to shift from North Africa to Italy itself.

It had been clear to Douglas Dodds-Parker, SOE's head of operations at Massingham, that SOE would need a dedicated base in Italy once British forces were established there – somewhere that would not just oversee the burgeoning need to coordinate behind-the-lines missions in Italy, but in the Balkans as well. The man who immediately sprang to mind was Holdsworth, but Holdsworth had initially declined on the basis that, 'as a simple sailor', he would not be up to the job. Dodds-Parker reminded him that he had just been awarded his second Distinguished Service Order (DSO) and was more than up to it.

It was only, finally, when he told Holdsworth that he had agreed to his request that the new base could be codenamed after his wife – the quiet, redoubtable Mary – that Holdsworth relented.

On 28 September, a little over two weeks after SOE's four-man scouting team first arrived in Monopoli – now codenamed 'Maryland', the coordinating centre for all SOE operations in Italy and Yugoslavia (Massingham retained its role as a coordinating HQ for SOE in the wider Mediterranean) – Holdsworth and his ship the *Mutin* sailed into Brindisi harbour, the second British ship to do so since the Allied invasion.

The *Mutin* was skippered by Dick Laming, a tall, blond Englishman born and brought up in the Netherlands (Laming, along with Pop, was one of the first people Mop met from SOE in Monopoli), with another SOE veteran, Tom Long, serving as coxswain. Two other  team members of note were Lt Cdr Hilary Scott *(pictured)*, RNVR, and Captain Charles Macintosh. Born in Uruguay to New Zealand parents, Macintosh was dark-haired, brown-eyed and a keen sportsman. He was quickly drafted from the Intelligence Corps into SOE and was something of an all-action contrast to the more bookish Scott, who had been a distinguished partner at Slaughter and May, my old law firm, and my brother Will's godfather. He had found himself drafted into SOE in the early part of 1940, joined the Naval Section in 1942 and in January 1943, a few months after the Allied invasion of North Africa, wound up in Tangier. From there it was a short hop to Algiers and thence to Malta. He remained in Malta until scooped up by Holdsworth and the *Mutin*.

Like other early recruits to SOE, Scott seems to have been recruited on the strength of his knowledge of countries that were central to SOE's directive to 'set Europe ablaze'. Before the war, he had visited – on holiday and business – France, Italy, Switzerland, Sweden and Norway. His personnel file describes him as having personality, intelligence and a strong work ethic. He was quite some way older than all the others and after the war, I knew, had offered Pop a job at Slaughter and May. At Monopoli, Scott would deputise for Holdsworth in all matters relating to sea work; Macintosh would do the same for air and land.

After establishing a direct signals link to London and to agents in the field, carrying out an assessment of operations to be planned and the selection of agents to be trained and infiltrated behind German lines in Italy, the immediate aims of the mission in Brindisi were to establish contact with SIM, Italian Military Intelligence, as well as the Italian Navy and Air Force contingents that were attached to the Badoglio government and the king.

But, as pointed out in a retrospective account of SOE's activities in Italy held in The National Archives at Kew, 'as Scott had little experience of naval matters and Macintosh had no air experience, they had to rely on their intelligence and natural charm to produce results'. If this all sounded a little amateurish and Boy's Own, it was by no means a true reflection of the picture.

Macintosh had landed in Sicily soon after the Allied invasion and had been put in charge of rounding up and refurbishing captured enemy weapons and recycling them – via a number of boat trips in and out of Brindisi – to partisans in Italy and the Balkans. It was while in Sicily that he crossed paths with *my* future godfather, Robin Richards, who went on to become one of Pop's best friends. Robin had left England at the end of July on a troopship heading to Algiers. Upon arrival there, he found himself – in the aftermath of the Italian landings – allocated to an air–sea rescue launch. I knew this because I had managed to access an interview given by him to the Imperial War Museum.

From Algeria – most likely, it seems, just before Pop's arrival there – Robin was directed to take the air–sea rescue launch to Malta. One of his passengers was none other than Marian Gamwell, the FANY 'Queen Bee' who had interviewed Mop just over three months earlier. From Malta, Robin managed to get to Catania, Sicily, where he picked up a 'rat-ridden Italian cargo-schooner' called the *Gilfredo* for gun-running operations between North Africa and Sicily. 'It was rough living,' he recalled in his IWM interview. 'There were rats at the foot of my bunk. We slept on deck. And our drinking water came out of abandoned 50-gallon oil drums,' he noted sanguinely to his IWM interviewer. It was in Sicily that he met Macintosh, who deputised Robin to ship his requisitioned German and Italian weapons to North Africa, where they were cleaned and overhauled prior to being handed over to Italian and Yugoslav partisans. They made two runs, their final port of call being Brindisi.

At the end of September, the *Gilfredo* again set sail for Brindisi, this time without any recycled weapons. On board, in addition to several ratings, were Richard Hewitt, Peter Lee, Francis Donaldson – the only Italian-speaker in the party – and Captain Michael Gubbins, the son of Major General Colin Gubbins, the head of SOE. Gubbins Senior had risen to become head of SOE in the wake of his initial appointment as the director of all SOE training. All on board the *Gilfredo* had amassed experience of running operations at Massingham.

On 29 September, one day after Holdsworth's *Mutin* sailed into Brindisi, the *Gilfredo* joined her in harbour. Dick Laming,

Holdsworth's skipper on the *Mutin*, had already set about contacting Admiral De Foscari, part of the Badoglio/King Victor Emmanuel government-in-exile contingent that had been in Brindisi since announcing the armistice at the beginning of the month.

De Foscari was the Italian Navy's Chief of Staff-Intelligence. What Laming *(pictured)* wanted to know was whether he could get the Italian Navy's cooperation in running clandestine missions up the coast. Laming, who described De Foscari as 'an absolutely splendid fellow', gained the admiral's full cooperation. This would have critical ramifications for No.1 Special Force as it found its feet in Italy – SOE having a need for an 'Italian fleet' with which to mount its covert operations.

Before they could begin, however, the advance party had to find somewhere to set up its operations.

As all the appropriate accommodation in Brindisi had already been grabbed, two of the party – Donaldson and Major Maurice Bruce, a training officer who had also flown in from Massingham – journeyed around 70km up the coast until they reached Monopoli. David Stafford, quoting Holdsworth, described it as 'a small place, not already committed to one of the armed forces, and, therefore, requisitionable. A harbour for a couple of boats from Africa, it also provided the opportunity of keeping ourselves to ourselves without being too hopelessly remote.'

Donaldson and Bruce found some suitable houses for accommodation and, by mid-October, a large facility just outside the town for their training headquarters. Holdsworth joined them in November. Thus it was that 'Maryland HQ' – Monopoli – was now operational.

The immediate priority confronting SOE's band of operators in Monopoli was what to do about the thousands of Allied POWs who had absconded from fascist-run prisoner-of-war camps at the time of the Italian armistice.

The fog of war in the wake of the Allied landings in Italy had resulted in some misguided attempts at avoiding confrontations between General Montgomery's advancing Eighth Army and Allied POWs heading in the opposite direction. Brigadier Crockett, head of MI9 – the British Directorate of Military Intelligence Section 9 charged with assisting the escape and return of British POWs to Allied lines – had instructed POWs in Italian camps to remain where they were, but this, not unnaturally, was widely disregarded. In the end, while some POWs did stay, between 10,000 and 20,000 did escape. As of the beginning of October 1943, many were still at large in the Apennines.

On 23 September, an experienced escape and evasion specialist at MI9's 'A-Force' attached to the Central Mediterranean theatre, Lt Col Anthony Simonds, had been tasked with putting together a rapid operation to rescue as many of these POWs as possible. At that time, the front line on the Adriatic coast was established between Pescara and Ancona, which was a long way north of the furthermost point of Allied advance on the other side of the country. The plan, code-named 'SIMCOL' (after Simonds), was to parachute-drop uniformed parties into four sectors and make contact with the groups of POWs within them. They would then be directed to four pre-selected rendezvous points on the coast, where, along with other uniformed parties, they would be given protection prior to being embarked by boat safely down the coast to the Allied lines. The troops to form these uniformed parties were hastily assembled from the US 1st Airborne Division, two British Special Air Service (SAS) groups and an OSS (Office of Strategic Services) Italian operational group, which was made up of Italian Americans who had just made it across from North Africa.

The next problem was transport. There were precious few air or maritime assets available to the operation, forcing Simonds to rely principally on landing craft that had been sequestered from the landings that had taken place at the beginning of the month. At around the time that the SOE advance party settled in Monopoli, Douglas Dodds-Parker relayed a request to Gerry Holdsworth for SOE to assist in the operation. Charles Macintosh – J Section's 'land officer' counterpart to Hilary Scott's 'sea officer' – had had some success in requisitioning some ancient Italian bombers – splendid-looking, but outmoded, double-decker machines called Savoia-Marchetti SM.82s – but these were only good for parachute training and night operations. Dick Laming, on the other hand, via his meeting of minds with Admiral De Foscari, had managed to avail himself of an asset that would become not just useful for the SIMCOL operation, but on a much wider basis to No.1 Special Force as it planned its clandestine operations in Italy during late 1943 and early 1944. Under an agreement formalised between the British and Italian Navies, Laming could now access six MS and seven MAS boats – Italian vessels similar to

Germany's E-Boats and Britain's motor torpedo boats – as well as six submarines that were based at Brindisi and Taranto.

The boats adopted by SOE were mainly of the MS type. These were Italian-built copies of German E-Boats sold to Yugoslavia before the war that had been captured by Italy in the Yugoslav port of Catarro in April 1941. The MS boats were better able to weather rough seas than the MAS boats, but both were sleek and impressive vessels. The MAS boats displaced between 23 and 30 tons, their 2,300 horsepower Isotta Fraschini Ace 1000 engines giving them a top speed of 42 knots. They were armed with two 450mm torpedo tubes and bristled with 20 and 13.2mm calibre anti-aircraft guns. The MS boats, though bigger, slower and sturdier – they had a top speed of 34 knots – were still impressive, displacing around 65 tons, and had better range and heavier armament. The MS boats were engineered with an underwater exhaust system, making them perfectly adapted for close, silent inshore work.

Laming, who clearly had a knack for charming just about anybody, described the commander of the MAS/MS flotilla at Brindisi and Taranto, Captain Giorgio Manuti, as a 'lovable rogue' and struck up an even closer bond with two of his vessel captains. It tickled Laming that MS63, which had sunk the British cruiser HMS *Manchester* the previous year, had the silhouette of the *Manchester* stencilled on the side of her bridge. Her captain was a Lieutenant Tedesci.

Although the SIMCOL mission was outside SOE's formal charter, London agreed to the request, as long as it didn't detract from No.1 SF's core duties, on the grounds that SOE would soon need all the help it could get in the form of quid pro quo support from other Allied entities in-country. Laming had already decided that the *Mutin*, antiquated sailing vessel that she was (and also because technically she belonged to the French Navy), should be kept well away from the 'shooting war' and that they should avail themselves, if at all possible, of the MAS/MS fleet for SIMCOL operations. As preparation, on 1 October, Laming, Scott and Michael Gubbins took the Italian trawler *San Vito* and another former fishing boat up the coast to the Gargano peninsula, around 170km north of Monopoli, and anchored off its northern shore.

The front situation on the east coast in October 1943 was extremely fluid, but in essence comprised a line of German resistance from the coast just north of Naples in the west to the north coast of the Gargano peninsula in the east. A notable German stronghold was the port of Termoli, just to the north of the peninsula, 50km or so from where the party was at anchor.

In the early hours of 3 October, a fleet of landing craft and commandeered Italian fishing boats steamed past the *San Vito*, heading directly for Termoli. On board were British Commandos tasked with taking the town and its port – a port that wasn't just integral to the plans of the Eighth Army, but also to the SOE party. Laming, Scott and Gubbins knew that if Termoli could be captured it would act as a vital staging point for the MAS/MS fleet to steam north on its SIM-COL mission. They learned afterwards that 40 Commandos managed to penetrate deep into the town before the Germans even woke up to the fact they were under attack. There was some fierce close-quarter fighting in the streets with paratroopers of the 1st *Fallschii-mjäger* (Parachute) Division, but by 0800 hours the Commandos had captured the town and were in control of its main approaches. German infantry, later supported by tanks from the 16th Panzer Division, counter-attacked repeatedly until 6 October, but, by noon that day, the Commandos managed to link up with the Eighth Army and put the enemy into full retreat.

Early the same afternoon, Laming manoeuvred the *San Vito* into harbour and moored off the end of one of its breakwaters. Moments later, the Luftwaffe appeared and straddled the vessel with bombs. Laming stood at the end of the gangway, and was apparently completely unperturbed by the proximity of the blasts, but the *San Vito* was mortally struck. Her seams opened by the explosions, she settled slowly on to the harbour floor. One SAS member was killed and four SAS and OSS were injured in the attack.

With the harbour secure – and efforts by the Luftwaffe notwithstanding – the SIMCOL missions could begin. The *Mutin* – SOE's de facto mobile HQ and something of a talisman by now – was moved north from Monopoli, but only as far north as Manfredonia, a port on the southern side of the Gargano peninsula. In the end, Laming and co. were unable to use the MAS/MS craft, having to rely on slow and vulnerable LCIs (Landing Craft Infantry vessels) instead. Laming carried out a first pick-up on the night of the 5/6 October and a second on the 9/10. But by then, the 'bright of the Moon period', as it was known, during which clandestine missions had to cease due to the ambient light conditions, had begun and operations had to be stalled for a further fortnight.

All in all, according to Brooks Richards – brother of my godfather, Robin – writing in his book *Secret Flotillas*, the definitive work on SOE naval operations, 'SIMCOL was not a great success', but it set the scene for operations to come. As part of the initial effort to gather information on the size and location of the POW groups, scattered as they were throughout central and Northern Italy, SOE decided to send in so-called 'Italian Liaison Missions' consisting of a military observer, a W/T set and a set-operator to areas where the larger and more reliable groups were located.

These 'missions', according to the SOE official archive history at Kew, were told to transmit the size and potential value of the POW groups, as well as the make-up of enemy strength in the area and any supplies, weapons and demolitions that might be needed for dealing with enemy units likely to pose a threat to recovery operations. The seeds of SOE's behind-the-lines activities in Italy were now sown – activities that would be integral to decisions that led to Pop being parachuted into enemy territory a little over 12 months later.

The rationalisation process at Monopoli gathered pace with the arrival from Massingham of the first mobile signals unit. This was composed of four-axle wireless trucks built by the Morris Commercial Company, known as 'PUs'. In charge of the unit, which had been established initially at Brindisi, was 'Captain Oddjob' – soon to become Mop's boss in the Signals Office. He described the new equipment, which was often unserviceable, as a nightmare.

Getting communications right between Brindisi and the Italian W/T operators and 'organisers' who had already been infiltrated behind the lines – their task to corral the partisan bands that were forming all over the country – was a top priority. These behind-the-lines missions were codenamed 'Pearl' in Bologna, 'Marcasite' and 'Ruby' in an area south of Ancona and 'Sapphire' in Sardinia.

In early November, the decision was taken to move the signals unit up the coast to Monopoli. On 14 November, in a reflection of Maryland's newfound permanence, as well as its graduation from the training base initially established under Major Bruce, the first seven FANYs arrived from Massingham.

Almost immediately, a request went out for more to be sent over, a directive that would result in Mop's arrival two months later.

The MS boats under the effective command of Dick Laming were soon joined by a second 'flotilla' – a fleet of MS/MAS boats that had been running infiltration missions along Italy's west coast. These operations had been coordinated by a soon-to-be-legendary SOE figure, Major Malcolm Munthe.

Munthe had acquired as a base ship a 130-ton vessel built in 1941 for Italy's Atlantic fishing fleet called the *Eduardo*. She had been converted by the Italians into a minesweeper – and would soon become intimately linked to Pop's own story – serving, I knew from my discussions with Mop, both as his floating quarters and, on several occasions, as 'parent ship' for the MS boats.

The *Eduardo*, indeed, was the boat on which Pop and Robin had been living when my parents first met.

The loan of the flotilla by the Royal Navy to SOE had been contingent on it being available for jobs the Navy needed performing in the area – principally, air sea rescue and beach reconnaissance. These missions, in addition to running agents up and down the coast, were placing intolerable manpower demands on No.1 Special Force. Consequently, in a memo to HQ in Monopoli, dated 2 November 1943, I found a request specifically asking for Pop to be sent there from North Africa, where he was still waiting to join operations in Italy.

Chapter 4

'The new boy'

Malta to Italy, November 1943

I had been able to find frustratingly little about Pop's time in Algeria beyond a reference to a stay he had made in the port of Sidi Ferruch, a few miles to the west of Algiers. This, at least, made sense, as Holdsworth had established a small naval training base there. In any case, he wasn't in Algeria long, no more than eight or nine weeks, because, from my notes, I saw he'd departed in early November for Malta, where he was given an 80-ton Italian schooner, used for inter-island trading before the war, and told to sail to Monopoli.

'With this ship I was given eight ratings, all of whom, with the exception of the Cockney cook, had been fishermen on the east coast of England. They were all very good seamen,' Pop had relayed, 'but not good at accepting orders.

'So, with a totally inexperienced skipper in me, we set forth from Malta around Sicily to southeast Italy. We had a maximum speed of seven knots.' With contrary winds, he continued, it took six days to reach Monopoli. The trip was marked by heavy storms and an encounter with a landing craft off the coast of Sicily, whose crew had become lost. By the time he sailed into Monopoli harbour, it was the middle of December.

In Maryland, he found an organisation full of wrinkles, bumps and teething issues – but one, even so, that was beginning to hit its stride. Six W/T operators were now in place with resistance groups and starting to send back information. Twelve others were in training. Over 100 Italian organisers and sabotage experts were being instructed to work with the nascent partisan movement. The Italian Supreme Command, including Italian Military Intelligence, SIM, was cooperating fully in setting up training schools for Italian agents and initial recruits. At the same time, recruiting and training had begun

– unknown to SIM – of covert agents under the sole control of the British at Maryland.

Aware perhaps of the procedural lapses that by this stage had led to serious questions being asked about the integrity of its Dutch Section – the entire network having been compromised since 1941 – SOE put fire breaks in place between Maryland's organisational infrastructure and its agent network. Thus, operatives responsible for ferrying agents – para-naval personnel like Dick Laming, Tom Long and my godfather, Robin – would be unable to divulge anything about the agent network itself were they to fall into the hands of the enemy.

Gerry Holdsworth wanted Maryland to replicate, wherever possible, the facilities in place at Massingham.

A parachute training school was therefore set up in place near the airfield at Brindisi; a paramilitary battle school was established at Castello di Santo Stefano – a large and imposing medieval house on a promontory, surrounded by high walls known as 'Maryland Castle' by Monopoli personnel and later simply as 'the Castle' – on the coast a few kilometres south of Monopoli; and a wireless training school 'up the hill' at La Selva.

'Holding houses' for different types of agents were located at various points in the town, and a FANY mess established (where Mop had been greeted by porridge and bacon on her arrival) in a large building in the town centre.

Close by, all within the confines of a central complex in the middle of the town, was the officers' mess, the operations and country section offices, the orderly room, the sergeants' mess, the other ranks' mess, motor transport, stores and a workshop.

While No.1 Special Force at that time was composed of around 100 people from all three services, the naval section had just four officers: Hilary Scott, Dick Laming, Robin Richards and Tom Long.

Long, Laming and Richards had just carried out No.1 Special Force's first true para-naval operation on behalf of SOE itself (the SIMCOL series of POW pick-ups the previous month having been on behalf of Military Intelligence's MI9 escape and evasion arm) – an operation codenamed 'Gearbox'. For this, at the end of November, they had journeyed north from Brindisi in the *Mutin* to Manfredonia – around 100km up the coast – and there switched vessels to the faster, sleeker and stealthier MS61 with its Italian crew. From Manfredonia and the Gargano peninsula, they ventured a further 250km north to the mouth of the River Chienti near the port of Civitanova Marche, where they landed three groups of six agents in total. The first team was codenamed 'Opal' and tasked with working in the Marche, the mountainous region bordering the Adriatic halfway up Italy. The second, codenamed 'Zircon', was dispatched to the Romagna region further to the north and a little way inland. The third was an A-Force/MI9 agent on a POW round-up mission. Laming and Richards had attempted to land the six agents near Ancona, the Marche's regional capital, but were successful only when they moved south to a quieter spot on the coast by the mouth of the Chienti. This innocuous fact would take on a deeper significance – one that would affect Pop later on.

Having been driven out of Termoli the previous month, the Germans had now dug in on the coast at Ortona, another heavily fortified medieval deep-water port and therefore of special value to whoever held it. Allied forces had crossed the Sangro River around 16km to the south of Ortona at the end of November and shelling of the town had commenced on 5 December. Allied planners had expected little or no resistance from the German defenders, anticipating that they would not want to be outflanked and would thus retreat north behind their defensive bulwark, whose southernmost line, a little to the north, formed part of a series of defensive lines, constructed by the Germans and Italian fascists, known collectively at that stage as the 'Winter Line'. What Allied planners had not picked up, certainly at this point, was a directive from Hitler to the troops holding Ortona – troops of the crack 1st Parachute Division or *Fallschirmjäger* – that they were to hold it at all costs. When Canadian troops attacked under a fearsome artillery barrage on 20 December, the *Fallschirmjäger* were already well dug in. The subsequent fighting was some of the fiercest of the entire Italian campaign and saw eight days of close-quarter battle as the Canadians cleared the town house by house. This they did largely by 'mouse-holing', a process by which platoons moved through a defended street using anti-tank weapons to blow holes through the wall of one house into the next. They would then flush out the defending paratroopers with grenades and, when those ran out, via hand-to-hand combat. Not for nothing was the battle nicknamed 'Little Stalingrad'. Eventually, on 27 December, Ortona fell.

In the meantime, Laming had been invited up to Termoli, the next nearest port in Allied hands, for Christmas. The invitation had come from the head of Termoli's naval contingent, a 'Captain Black', who was described by Laming as 'a hard thing if ever you met one'.

The following morning, with a storm howling around them and waves pounding the harbour, Laming was roused from a bleary-eyed state by the local commander, invited into the ops room and shown the last known position of a raft filled with American aircrew that had ditched into the sea and was now reported to be drifting 12km off the coast near Pescara.

Pescara was 25km north of Ortona and, stirred up like a hornet's nest by the fighting there, the last place anyone in the Allied camp would have wanted to carry out an air–sea rescue, especially on Christmas Day. Even so, Laming took the only available transport he could find – an LCI that leaked like a sieve in the storm-tossed seas – and proceeded to head for the search area. He found the raft a mile and a half off the breakwater at Ortona and within sight of the German front line. For whatever reason – but, perhaps, I like to think, via the providence of a Christmas miracle – the Germans had allowed the operation to go ahead; or, more prosaically, they had simply been unaware of it. The aircrew, in any case, was saved.

Pop, who arrived in Monopoli just before Laming's Termoli trip, but, for reasons that were about to become clear, wasn't on it, made up the fifth member of this battle-blooded team and, after a week's acclimatisation, undertook his first operation – codenamed 'Rodney' and 'Renown' – a double mission to deliver three Italian agents deep behind the enemy's front lines. Alone, perhaps as a test of his mettle as the new boy, he was given orders to join an Italian submarine on Boxing Day in harbour at Taranto and to set sail the next day. The objective was to land two agents behind the lines near Venice and the

ITALY, 1943-1945

Detail, see Map 2

— Winter line 1943-44
········· Winter line 1944-45

0   50   100 miles
0   50   100   150 kilometres

Map 1

third near Trieste to the northeast. The agents were tasked with join-ing partisan groups already operational there.

There are scant records of this mission in official sources, so it is dif-ficult to assess its impact on SOE's para-naval operations at this time. What I did learn from several references that I'd discovered online was that the submarine was called the *Marea*, a *Tritone*-class boat that resembled a German U-Boat, and that her commander was called Lt Attilio Mario Russo.

The *Marea* had only entered service the previous May, but was clearly not in a grand state of repair. A report by Russo around the time of Pop's mission to Chioggia, near Venice (it may even be *from* his mission – the report is unclear on this), praises his crew for having wrestled with a number of difficulties: the concurrent failures of the depth-meter, the fact that the submarine's dive planes had to be oper-ated manually and, 'more seriously', as Russo put it, the inability to replenish the air tanks due to a failure of the compressors. The *Marea*, in any case, sounded little more than a death-trap.

Pop, for his part, did provide a short and pithy description of the week-long voyage years after the war – one that is noteworthy for the way in which it downplayed the technical issues, the squalor, the claustrophobia and the terror of operating with people, who, not four months earlier, had been his enemy.

The submarine was reasonably primitive, he wrote in this account, *and commands were given from mouth-to-mouth. My knowledge of the Italian language was nil and, as we sailed to the north, every command sounded like 'abandon ship'.* He described how they were spotted off Venice, in perilously shallow waters, and depth-charged by surface vessels. The Italian crew behaved in an exemplary manner, he added, while he was 'all for moving off and coming back another day'. But the crew, he said, made it quite clear they would sit on the bottom of the Adriatic and surface at night, which they did.

He went on to express his admiration for the bravery of his crew-mates, fully aware that his own Royal Navy uniform would have provided him with some guarantees were they to be captured. The Italians, he said, 'would be in a most unhappy position' were this to happen to them.

All, however, went reasonably well. Brooks Richards's log of the operations in *Secret Flotillas* states that Rodney failed on 30 December, but that Renown, later that same night, was a success, the agents being delivered by rubber dinghies and Pop getting his feet wet, as it were, as their ferryman.

In his own very succinct account of this mission long after the war, Pop said that the only thing he had managed to accomplish on the voyage was reading Plato's *Republic* in the Everyman edition. His only other preoccupation, he said, was a 'few hours rowing agents ashore'.

Instead of being seduced by this bravura performance of the stiff upper lip, which was typically Pop, I found myself imagining what it must have been like in this stinking, leaking tin can, surrounded by unfamiliar people speaking an unfamiliar language, as the *Kriegsmarine* (the Navy of Nazi Germany) pummelled them with depth charges. I tried, too, to imagine whether it might have been remotely possible, with or without all this going on, to have read Plato's *Republic*, or anything else for that matter, as, hour after hour, the submarine had lain on the bottom, in the shallow waters off Venice, with the metallic sound of E-Boat engines transmitted through the hull and the stench of oil, fetid water, sweat, human waste and fear – of men in close proximity and, worse, my own – assaulting my nostrils. Did this explain why, in later life, Pop dismissed those who denigrated the bravery of Italians? I could think of few things more terrifying. More to the point, this insouciant account made me want to know things that I had not even thought about when I set out on this journey.

Pop was 19 when he arrived in Monopoli. My research had given me certain facts, but there was one about which I was clueless: what it was that had caused him to be recruited by SOE in the first place. He wasn't a Charles Macintosh or a Dick Laming when he arrived in Italy. Far from it.

I thought back to the conversation I had had with him when, as a child, I'd discovered his naval uniform with the parachute badge on the sleeve. He'd hardly left school and was colour-blind. SOE must have seen something in my father, some innate quality, that had led them to recruit him in the first place. In 1943, they could have picked anybody to join one of Britain's most elite fighting units, but they picked him.

Why?

Chapter 5

'Set Europe ablaze'

London, England, July 1940

On 1 July 1940, nine days after France surrendered, a meeting was held of senior British diplomats, ministers and administrative officials at the Foreign Office in London to discuss what could be done to help those people in France and the other occupied countries of Europe who wanted to continue fighting – *resisting* is what it now boiled down to – the occupiers.

The following day, Hugh Dalton, Britain's Minister of Economic Warfare, wrote to Lord Halifax, the Foreign Secretary, outlining the foundation of a new organisation to 'coordinate, inspire, control and assist the nationals of the suppressed countries, who must themselves be the direct participants'.

The letter passed to Winston Churchill, the new prime minister – Neville Chamberlain having resigned six weeks earlier over his failure to prevent defeats that had seen Poland, Norway, the Low Countries and France all capitulate to Hitler within nine months of the outbreak of war. Dalton, whose energy and enthusiasm earned him the nick-name 'Doctor Dynamo', campaigned strenuously to be given the task of running the new organisation.

SOE, as it became, grew out of capabilities extant within three of Britain's clandestine intelligence organisations: Section D of the SIS, the Special Intelligence Service, which, even before the war, had been developing plans to undermine Germany's military and economic capacities via sabotage, propaganda and subversion; MI(R), a think tank of the Military Intelligence Directorate of the War Office, which had led efforts to develop guerrilla warfare in areas of German occupation; and Electra House, the secret propaganda arm of the Foreign Office. In the end, it was the Ministry of Economic Warfare, not the Foreign Office or the armed services, that would be given the job of setting up and running SOE. Upon getting the role he'd campaigned for, Dalton was tasked with galvanising SOE under Churchill's 'set Europe ablaze' directive. While Axis-occupied Europe attracted much of the fledgling organisation's initial attention – SOE agents being sent to destinations as far afield as occupied France, Belgium, the Netherlands, Poland, Denmark and Yugoslavia – its operations quickly extended much further: to the Middle and Far East, with theatre HQs established in Cairo, India, and Kandy in Ceylon (now Sri Lanka).

Dalton, according to an official history of SOE that I'd picked through at the Special Forces Club, was both disliked and admired by Churchill at the same time. While the 'set Europe ablaze' order has come informally to be thought of as SOE's founding mantra, its more prosaic – and accurate – tasking was 'to coordinate all action, by way of subversion and sabotage, against the enemy overseas'.

The organisation's early recruits, according to the SF Club official history, came from 'industrial, commercial and city firms with experience of doing business in foreign countries'. A good example of the kind of individual drawn from this unusual recruiting pool was Sir Charles Hambro, of the banking family, who had strong connections to Norway, an early focus of SOE's attention. Other prominent recruits came from Courtaulds, the 150-year-old textile company, and the legal firm Slaughter and May. Indeed, the Slaughter and May connection had even prompted a question in 1943 in the House of Commons: why, MPs had been asked, were so many partners of Slaughter and May recruited by the intelligence services? The answer is a relatively simple one. Because these men had been adept at doing international business at a high level before the war, they were viewed as exactly the kind of people needed to woo the support of the exile community of Allied governments that had established themselves in London in 1940. They were also discreet.

Colin Gubbins had written a number of Army manuals on guerrilla warfare in the 1930s. He was also responsible for the training and running of several military units that had emerged from early British attempts to form behind-the-lines assault units – units that would later coalesce as the Royal Marines Commandos. In November 1940, on the request of Dalton, he was seconded to SOE and took over as its executive leader from Hambro in September 1943. He would stay as its head till the end of the war.

SOE became known after the war for a small number of spectacular one-off successes, most notably the destruction of the German heavy-water plant in Norway that was central to Nazi efforts to develop an atomic bomb. It also became known for the capture of Antwerp by Belgian Resistance before it could be destroyed by retreating German troops in 1945. But it was the steady, relentless effort put in place to undermine Germany's occupation of Europe – especially in France – for which its reputation has rightly endured.

During the course of the war, SOE sent 470 agents into France, many of them women. While sabotage and subversion by these agents were key components of the SOE mission – blowing up trains, bridges and factories – working with the 'nationals of the suppressed countries', as per the wording of Dalton's original letter to Lord Halifax, formed the greater part of its tasking.

To prosecute this objective, it was the unglamorous radio set – as opposed to explosives and advanced weaponry – that turned out to be the most crucial piece of equipment in the SOE inventory. This was a 30-pound short-wave transceiver that fitted into a 2-foot-long suitcase. Although portable and easy to disguise, its deficiency by modern standards was the fact that it relied on a 70-foot aerial. The deployment and repacking of the aerial complicated the set-up and shutdown procedures and exposed the operator to discovery at any moment.

On top of this, complicated coding and decoding practice meant that WTOs had little choice but to remain on air for long periods.

The work was amongst the most hazardous of any mission of the Second World War and, before the war's end, hundreds of SOE agents would die, often after long periods of interrogation by the Gestapo.

Two years after Pop died, I flew up to the tiny airport at Oban, the nearest airfield to Arisaig, a village on the west coast of the Scottish Highlands. For four weeks in late May and most of June 1943, Pop had been based here at what was officially known as 'Basic Training

School No.26'. Arisaig House, on which the school was centred, was actually a group of houses, cabins and hunting lodges spread over several Highland estates where groups of agents – separated according to the countries in which they would be operating – were housed. The area was both remote and tough, the perfect place to train for covert missions.

Upon arrival at Arisaig, I met up with Henrik Chart, an expert on SOE at the local Land, Sea and Islands (visitor) Centre, who immediately drove me over to Arisaig House, now a rather grand hotel, where it was still possible to see traces of SOE's activity from the war. Standing in a meadow in front of the former training HQ, with views towards the sea, Henrik pointed to two small buildings tucked into some trees that had been used by SOE during the war.

One of them was a place where they would subject students to mock interrogation techniques, the other was used as a store room for explosives, he told me cheerfully. Apart from the vegetation, in fact, Arisaig had hardly changed at all in the 70-plus years since Pop had been there, allowing me to glimpse what it must have been like when he arrived in May 1943.

Security throughout the war had been all-important. From 1940, all land running northwest of a line that extended along Loch Ness, from Fort William in the west to Inverness in the east, was designated a military zone – Scotland's so-called 'No.1 Protected Area'. Anyone entering or leaving No.1 Protected Area, and all communication to and from it, was watched.

The job of implementing course security at the Arisaig complex was carried out by an Intelligence Corps detail from the Army's Scottish Command and this was based in Arisaig House. The detail was also responsible for monitoring the arrival and departure of all SOE students as well as their movements during the four or five weeks they spent on the course. I kept all this in mind when I thought of Pop arriving on the train that pulled into Beasdale, a request stop at a point where the railway line intersected the road close to Arisaig House. It remains a request stop to this day. As one security officer – quoted in a book by Stuart Allan called *Commando Country* – said: 'This was the ideal spot where a request halt would allow troops to be set down, with no one to see them but the solitary station porter, who also manned the level crossing.' Henrik went on to tell me why security officials felt they could trust the locals to keep quiet. On a trip on a loch with an old Highland ghillie shortly before the first students arrived at Arisaig in late 1940, an Army official who'd been wrestling with the conundrum of how to maintain security in an area the size of Belgium remarked that 'a lot of foreigners' would be appearing in the coming weeks and months – and that 'strange things' would start happening in the surrounding hills and glens. The ghillie was told that the activity shouldn't be talked about and was then asked if he'd pass the word around. After considering this for a good, long moment, the ghillie told him that the people could be trusted to keep quiet. 'After all,' he said, 'we managed to keep Bonnie Prince Charlie secret here.' He'd made it sound as if the bonnie prince had been there yesterday, not 200 years earlier.

Occasionally, however, measures had to be taken to prevent the locals getting too close a look. One trainee used explosives for some off-syllabus fishing and ended up killing hundreds of salmon. These floated downstream, prompting questions from the normally taciturn crofters and villagers. A lot of diplomacy was deployed to permit SOE's trainees to blend back into the shadows.

When he did talk about his SOE training, Pop recalled that, though it was June, it rained continuously for 26 of the 28 days he was in Scotland. 'It was quite a tough course in very rugged country,' he said. No kidding. One of his contemporaries summarised it as 'trying to find our way by compass, stumbling over invisible obstacles, sinking into bogs and falling into gullies and ravines, whilst carrying tommy guns and 50-pound rucksacks'.

SOE's Group A paramilitary schools, the most important of which was the Arisaig complex, introduced the would-be agent to the basic skills they would need in enemy territory. In addition to physical training, these skills included silent killing, weapons handling (including the handling of foreign weapons), demolition training, map reading and compass work, elementary Morse code, para-naval training and boat work, and raid tactics. These skills would be 'topped up' further by parachute training at Ringway near Manchester and Group B training at Beaulieu, in the New Forest, where the focus was on teaching the student how to 'blend in', as well as methods of communication and the recruitment and handling of agents – i.e. indigenous 'sub-agents' controlled by the SOE-trained agents themselves – once inside enemy-held territory. The Group B courses also taught students 'specialist methods' such as how to pick locks and handcuffs. The fact that Pop didn't receive either Group A parachute training or Group B specialist training at this stage struck me as significant.

While it may have been indicative of the state of flux in which the SOE training syllabus found itself in the middle of 1943 – when, I knew, a more streamlined selection process had been introduced in the way Baker Street, the London headquarters of SOE, interviewed prospective candidates – it seemed to have been suggestive of something else: that the powers-that-be had *already* decided the role that they wanted Pop to play. The trouble was, at this point in their selection, no SOE recruits were told what they had been 'volunteered' for, let alone the specialist roles earmarked for them. All Pop ever said was that his training at Arisaig consisted of 'unarmed combat, considerable training on my own and pistol practice'.

Unarmed and silent killing was taught for part of the war by two ex-Shanghai municipal police officers – William Fairbairn and Eric Anthony Sykes, whose initials were given to the FS fighting knife that equipped, amongst others, the Royal Marines Commando force. Pop had a Commando knife at home and Will and I had played with it, along with the gun. It wasn't until now, however, that I realised that he must have acquired the knife while he had been in SOE.

It is evident from documents that have survived the war – including a manual for SOE instructors preserved at The National Archives at Kew – that any lingering impression derived by candidates that the organisation they had entered was for 'gentlemen' would have been dispelled after a day or two at Arisaig. An introduction to the silent-killing course informed students that this was a mode of warfare unlike anything they would have ever encountered before. 'This is war, not sport,' the instructor told every new recruit. 'Your aim is to kill your opponent as quickly as possible. So forget the Queensberry

Rules; forget the term "foul methods". Foul methods help you to kill quickly.'

By May 1943, background detail on the art of silent killing drew on intelligence culled from nearly three years of operations against the enemy.

Weapons training also introduced recruits to the Colt .45 and .38, as well as to the Sten gun, much favoured by Resistance groups on the continent, though considered unreliable by plenty of others. The recruits were taught to fire by aiming from the hip rather than the shoulder and by loosing off two initial shots at the target before firing further shots on automatic. This method became known as the 'double tap' and was later adopted by special forces all over the world, including the Special Air Service.

Demolition and explosives training saw recruits planting dummy explosives on local railways thanks to a cooperation agreement with the West Highland Line. The mantra behind the Demolition Course was that 'the demolition must never fail'. Training, therefore, was rigorous and included information on how a train moved on a track, types of track, how to disrupt a track with and without explosives, as well as suitable sites for derailment.

The West Highland Line was also co-opted by SOE in other ways. The one achievement Pop said he remembered at Arisaig was being taught to drive the Western Isles Express. 'You have no idea how difficult it is to stop a steam train in a railway station,' he told me in one of our early, tantalising discussions about SOE, 'or how tricky it is to align with the platform.' It took me a while to figure out why, in this intense and highly charged training environment, he would have been given time off to indulge some boyhood fantasy. Then I read that SOE spent time familiarising agents with the industrial sabotage targets they were expected to be deployed against. Factory visits were arranged in the UK, for example, that allowed agents to understand exactly where to plant their explosives. Did this mean that someone, somewhere, already knew that Pop would be tasked with blowing up trains when he deployed abroad? The answer must have been: yes. When using explosives, the two main methods were 'cutting charges' – usually using plastic explosive placed superficially to shatter a piece of track – as well as mined or buried charges to lift the track, causing the locomotive to derail.

The students were encouraged to develop their sense of hearing for night-time sabotage operations – 'as this, more than any other sense, must be relied on to replace sight, and the aim should be to achieve the acute analytical hearing of a blind man'. No detail was overlooked. When moving in enemy-held territory, students were taught 'field-craft' – 'the art of being like an animal in its own terrain'. Factors that needed to be uppermost in the minds of anyone moving along a route, their instructors told them, was to know enemy dispositions – guards; patrols; systems of communication; wires and the proximity of local troops; fixed features to be avoided, including roads, houses, farms and all skylines; the presence or absence of cover, particularly in the latter stages of approach to the enemy; and the position of the sun.

For raiding parties, attacks should be carried out against supplies rather than personnel, unless the latter were of great importance. 'The destruction of the German soldier is the job of the Army,' the manual said, 'and for the partisan to engage enemy troops is usually too risky a procedure.'

It is also noteworthy that a para-naval training unit had been established at a house called Swordland Lodge in Tarbert Bay, around 6 miles, as the crow flies, from Arisaig. In the early stages of its use, this facility was given over extensively to 'training men in the use of small boats for landing operations, as well as in attacks on shipping', according to a pamphlet (compiled by David M. Harrison) on SOE training I'd picked up in Arisaig. This responsibility, however, was quickly delegated to Gerry Holdsworth's unit at Helford in Cornwall – and certainly had been by the time Pop trained there.

In this way, after a month of instruction, Pop, and the 70 or so other members of his course, would have learned almost everything they needed to know to mount both offensive and defensive operations behind enemy lines. He would also have been told to have kept everything about what he had learned to himself – to divulge it to nobody. During the entire war – while precise figures are unavailable – it is calculated that almost 7,000 students went through SOE's preliminary and paramilitary courses. Of these, fewer than 500 were British, the remainder coming from occupied countries.

In a postscript to his month at Arisaig, Pop once related how he had had a remarkable meeting there – 'although,' as he said, 'I did not know it at the time'. He had met, he said, 'two immensely unassuming, nondescript people who seemed to be doing the same training as me, although they had two British military officers who escorted them very closely'. These two people, he said, were Czech and looked like old-fashioned bank clerks. 'I subsequently learned that a few weeks later they parachuted [to a location] some 50km from Prague, where they held up [Reinhard] Heydrich, who was head of Germany's secret police and Hitler's right-hand man.' The two Czechs had been sent in, he added, as Heydrich's assassins and ended up attacking him in his open staff car as his driver had slowed to take a bend. All of which was completely true, except for the fact that Heydrich was assassinated in May 1942, a whole year earlier.

There was never any suggestion that Pop came up with this episode to pep up his story. He didn't need to – and, in any case, as we all knew, any element of 'talking up' his time in SOE, or any other aspect of his life, was anathema to him.

As I flew home from Oban, and found myself thinking about this and everything else I had learned in Arisaig, the best explanation I could come up with was that he had unwittingly conflated a genuine meeting with two other trainee Czech agents – many passed through the Group A and B training schools throughout the war – with the men who had genuinely participated in Operation Anthropoid, the Heydrich assassination mission.

Anthropoid resulted, in June 1942, in the death of Heydrich from wounds he had sustained during the attack. It also resulted in the death of the assassins and vicious reprisals by the Nazis against the local Czech population. For me, Pop's encounter with Heydrich's 'assassins' was a reminder that I had come away from Arisaig with little idea still as to why SOE had recruited him. SOE, it was now clear, went for people it trusted or people who had been recommended by *someone trusted* under whom the would-be agent had served in his or her particular branch of the armed forces. But this wasn't the case with Pop. Pop had been serving in the Navy, as a lowly rating, and had been pulled out of active duty when an eye test revealed he was colour blind and been sent to work as an administrator – a pen-pusher – at Chatham Docks. And although he had spent a year as a student at Cambridge, he hadn't amassed the kind of contacts there – or anywhere else for that matter – that would have marked him out in SOE's books as a 'good egg'. Indeed, his tutor had dismissed the blue he had received for football at Cambridge as worthless – the only worthy blue, he told Pop, was a half-blue in chess. For his part, Pop claimed that he never worked that hard at Cambridge, but had found the freedom there 'marvellous'. It was at Cambridge, too, he said, that his love of music and books intensified.

I knew from my time at Arisaig, and from further research I'd undertaken, that languages were important, but Pop couldn't speak any of the languages of occupied Europe – he'd spoken German, which was certainly useful, but not as useful, if you're trying to blend in, as French, Belgian, Dutch, Norwegian, Danish or Polish. Given Cambridge's later reputation as a recruiting ground for spies, I sensed this must have formed part of the picture, but still felt I was missing something. If I was to stand any hope of understanding why my father had ended up in Monopoli, in December 1943, I had to delve deeper. Because if it wasn't about a language skill, if it wasn't about a social connection or some innate ability that had earmarked him for SOE while he'd served below decks on convoy duty, or, afterwards, while he'd shuffled pieces of paper across a desk, then it must have been down to something more basic.

It must have been about him.

Chapter 6

'A raw and callow recruit'

Londonderry, Northern Ireland, September to October 1942

Autumn 1942 coincided with one of the most intense periods in the Battle of the Atlantic. The Americans had been in the war for nine months. German U-Boats, initially concentrating on attacking convoys off the US Eastern seaboard, were switched back to attacking convoys in the North Atlantic towards the end of July. In this period of the war, the tactic employed by Admiral Dönitz, the head of the German Navy, was to hunt and destroy convoys using 'wolf packs' of U-Boats – groups of up to 15 submarines – that stalked by day and attacked by night. Allied losses in the Atlantic reached their peak in 1942. In the first six months of the year, 500 ships were sent to the bottom, most of them by U-Boats.

Able Seaman Bob Clark probably joined HMS *Fleetwood* in Londonderry, in Northern Ireland, in September or October 1942. Beyond the fact that *Gone with the Wind* had been showing at the cinema, Pop had been unable to remember anything about this landmark event – or Londonderry – when I'd asked him about it. He was conscious, however, that, despite America's recent entry into the war, Britain's very survival was under threat from the U-Boat menace, with supplies of food, fuel and raw material for the war reaching critically low levels. HMS *Fleetwood*, a Grimsby-class sloop, with the pennant 'L47' painted on the side of her hull, was to be one of the ships in the forefront of the battle – this at a time when the Allies had to fight 'blind' due to the fact that the *Kriegsmarine* had switched its U-Boats to a completely new Enigma key – Enigma being the coding system Germany used for its communications traffic throughout the war. Having been able to read previous iterations of the Enigma cipher – one of the biggest and most enduring secrets of Britain's war – the Royal Navy was now out on a considerable limb. With no inside track on German submarine movements, the Navy had to rely on tactical hunting methods – on ASDIC, an underwater direction-finding system, in particular – to track down and destroy the U-Boat threat. The North Atlantic, however, was a big haystack and the needles almost infinitesimally small.

With no details, I had been left to imagine what had gone through my father's 18-year-old mind when he first saw *Fleetwood*. He had barely left Cambridge and before that Highgate, his North London public school. In 1941, his final year there, he had been head boy and captain of the football and cricket teams. He had gone up to King's College, Cambridge, to read modern languages, but, after just a year there, he suddenly decided to join the Royal Navy. 'It didn't seem right to continue my personal education while the country was fighting for its very existence,' he'd once said. It appeared that Pop wasn't that fussed which service he joined, as long as he could take the fight to the enemy. 'I volunteered for the Navy, as opposed to the Army or the RAF,' he wrote, 'because at least I thought I would be sleeping in a bunk and maybe between sheets.'

This nonchalance was belied by the facts – that he'd joined the RNVR, not as an officer, but as a seaman, beginning, as all sailors did during the war, by going to a land-based training ship on shore. This establishment was HMS *Collingwood* at Fareham, near Portsmouth, where newly initiated recruits were divided into huts containing 30 people, from all walks of life, each hut being run and ruled by a Chief Petty Officer who had been in the regular Navy before the war. Pop said they did a pretty good job of instilling discipline, fitness and pride into the 'ill-disciplined and dirty' assortment of volunteers that pitched up at *Collingwood* for three months' intensive training.

Even so, upon his arrival in Londonderry, a bleak port in the forefront of the U-Boat war, and stepping aboard *Fleetwood*, looking suitably warlike in her blue and grey camouflage – 'Admiralty Light', as it was referred to by the Navy – it must have been a considerable shock and reminded me about his evident lack of connections: connections being the route via which so many had joined SOE in the early stages of the war. He quickly learned how to live, eat and sleep with 24 other sailors in the forecastle, a mess deck some 40 feet by 15 feet, set in the bows. *Fleetwood*'s duties were to provide escort duties for convoys, mainly on the Gibraltar and Freetown routes, the latter a more hazardous undertaking than it sounded, down to West Africa. He'd once told me about visits he'd made to Gibraltar at this time – and to Malta. *Fleetwood*'s service record shows that the bulk of his time with her was taken up with escorting convoys supplying the Allied troops that had recently taken part in the North Africa Torch landings as well as with the 43rd Escort Group, based in Gibraltar, on convoy escort duty in the western Med.

Having joined the Navy in the belief that it would be less rough and ready than the other services, life on board *Fleetwood* was anything but luxurious. For Pop, there would be little sleeping on a bunk, and none between sheets.

Towards the end of 1942, the new Commander-in-Chief Western Approaches, Admiral Sir Max Horton, started to use the growing number of escorts available to the British to reinforce convoys that came under attack. In contrast to previous practice, the new 'support groups' were not responsible for the safety of any particular convoy, giving them flexibility to roam as widely as they needed to kill U-Boats. They did this with standard depth charges and the new 'Hedgehog' weapon – an anti-submarine mortar that fired contact-fused bombs into the path of the ASDIC beam for greater lethality. Under the support group concept, corvettes and sloops were detached to hunt down submarines that had been picked up by aerial reconnaissance or identified by on-board high-frequency direction-finding equipment. While regular escorts had to break off attacks and remain with their convoy, support group escorts could spend as long as they needed – often days – stalking a U-Boat, waiting for it to run out of air and surface. In prosecuting this mission, in which the hunters often became the hunted, crews worked around the clock and lived more or less on top of each other. It was a world away from Highgate and Cambridge.

Pop's few notes on this period made it clear that he was helped by a mentor, a Petty Officer called Chapman, around 12 years his senior, who was in charge of the forecastle, the seething, sweat-filled hole in the bows of the ship that became Pop's home for the six months he spent on *Fleetwood*.

'Chapman taught me not only to be tidy and clean, which was absolutely essential in a confined space, but also naval language: "slide" for butter, "grit" for sugar etc. He also taught me how to live in a community... and with such patience and friendliness,' he said years later. 'I was a very raw and callow recruit.' In an interview that I found online, in which Pop reflected on his career in the City, he couldn't have been more fulsome in his praise of Chapman, who, though a pre-war regular, had been demoted due to his liking for the booze and for going on the occasional bender. On the Malta run, Chapman's experience and coolness came into its own when *Fleetwood* came under attack. Some of his crewmates, Pop told the interviewer, were good under fire, others not. Chapman didn't shout or scream at them – he just exuded a quiet authority. Pop then described how he'd seen five crewmen die. Asked how he'd reacted, he said he 'didn't think very much of it', adding he was able to set it aside, as 'he wasn't very imaginative'. This, I think, belied the truth. I believe it is more accurate to say that my father had always been good at focusing on what he needed to. When asked if, 50 years later, he ever thought of death, he told his interviewer succinctly: 'No, very rarely.'

In early 1943, Pop left *Fleetwood* to seek to qualify as an officer at an establishment called HMS *King Alfred* on the south coast, near Brighton, followed by a week at the Naval College, Greenwich. When he'd joined the RNVR, Pop received the dire news that he was colour blind. But in a piece of luck that was typical of him, they managed to lose his papers. At *King Alfred*, he almost got away with it again by memorising the lines of the sight-test after they were given to him by a fellow recruit. But it didn't take too long for the medics to catch up with him and Pop was told that he'd never go to sea in another warship, and that he would be given a supply-side job on shore. For Pop, who had left Cambridge to get stuck into the fight, and who for six months had already tasted action on the seas, the idea of seeing out the rest of the war from behind a desk came, he said, as 'the end of the world'. He was posted to Chatham Dockyard in Kent. But, shortly after he arrived, he had another piece of phenomenal luck – a 'man from the ministry' who came to ask if anyone at the dockyard had 'sailing experience'. Sensing his opportunity, Pop replied that he had.

SOE's Baker Street headquarters was a nondescript building above a branch of Marks & Spencer, not far from Oxford Street.

Pop never said much about the methods via which he came to be selected for SOE, although, over the years, others have – their stories told in papers held at The National Archives and in many books, all of which afforded me a very good and detailed sense of what he would have gone through.

I knew that he would, after a short wait, have been shown into an interview room, and that, following a brief chat with an official, in which it would not have been divulged for a moment what he was actually being interviewed *for*, Pop would have been subjected to a steady stream of tests designed to assess his psychological aptitude for clandestine work.

These so-called 'SAB tests' – for Student Assessment Board – had been crafted to probe reasoning ability as well as psychological make-up. They included the well-known Rorschach Test – the candidate's reaction to, and interpretation of, ink blots – and to his or her being shown a short film.

Both tests also had a further purpose: to get the candidates to start talking about themselves. The next test was dubbed the Thematic Apperception Test, or TAT, and was designed to probe a candidate's 'underlying motives, concerns and the way they see the world', according to archive records. This was based on their reactions – drawn out in the way they told a short story – to 'ambiguous pictures of people'. The rationale behind this was that 'people tend to interpret ambiguous situations in accordance with their own past experiences and current motivations, which may be conscious or unconscious'. In other words, without the candidate even knowing it, they were revealing hidden sides to themselves. One of the TAT pictures, now in the archives, showed a painting of a frightening-looking old woman poised to whisper something into the ear of a young, attractive-looking woman standing in the foreground. The TAT required the SOE candidate to make up a story about what the picture said to them. This needed to include details of the events that led up to the picture, what was happening in the picture itself, what the characters were thinking about and feeling, and the outcome of the story. For the interviewer, guidance was given that 'the subject must be made to talk about himself, but kept on the rails'.

The interviewer was looking at everything: people who fumbled with their hands or played with their keys were clearly ill at ease; the chap who started with a stream of questions or stared at the interviewer in an aggressive manner was patently nervous; and the untidy man was, more than likely, disorganised.

If the candidates made it this far, they were asked about their schooling and employment records and then about any special aptitudes they felt they had. Interviews had to cover how they felt about themselves and their achievements, their attitudes towards family, if they had any military experience or hobbies ('the good type is one that shifts from hobby to hobby', according to the guidance notes in the archives), reading ('check the contents of something [the interviewer] knows'), health ('does he get cold easily? Suffer from headaches? Stomach trouble (generally bad type)? Neuritis? (generally imagined illness)'). Finally, the candidate would be grilled over 'habits and routine (timekeeping, drinking, attitude to money, security, obeying orders)'. The normal procedure, interviewers were advised, would be to pass lightly over any normal answers and to go into detail only when a point arose on which the subject showed 'any weakness or strain'.

What would Pop have told them?

His background couldn't have been more normal or middle class. His father, my paternal grandfather, was an engineer from Newcastle (where he was apprenticed to Sir Charles Parsons, the inventor of the turbine engine), who'd come to London in 1900 at the age of 21 as an employee of a mid-sized engineering company called Mitchell Shackleton. At his digs, he met Gladys, my grandmother, a Somerset girl who'd come to London just before the First World War to attend the National School of Cookery and ended up driving ambulances for the Women's Volunteer Reserve. They got married and my grandfather worked hard, eventually buying a new semi-detached house with bow windows in a tree-lined avenue in East Finchley, North London.

Pop was born in 1924, a couple of years after his brother, Bernard. Gladys had been a large, warm-hearted woman; my grandfather, 17 years older than her, somewhat remote and imbued with what Pop described later as 'high standards'. Pop had a very happy upbringing; there was 'a help' in the house in the form of a lady called Maud – the daughter of friends of my grandmother's from Wells; fish was served on Fridays, Scottish potatoes on Mondays, and a roast, without fail, on Sundays. My grandmother, being religious, would go to church, taking the boys with her, but my grandfather, who had no interest in religion, doggedly stayed at home. In the evenings, there were singsongs around the piano, which my grandmother used to play, gatherings around a radio the size of a chest of drawers, and occasional trips to concerts and the theatre. On war being declared, Bernard joined the RAF and went to Canada for flying training. There, he fell in love with and married a Canadian girl. Bernard returned to Canada and settled there after the war. I learned that Pop, aged 16, had been in Canada on a trip to the Eastern seaboard (the heavily subsidised cost for schoolchildren had been thirty-five pounds) when war was declared and had been hastily bundled on a ship home, arriving back in England – and going straight to school – around a week later. I knew little else about his school years, beyond the fact he'd gone to Highgate Junior and Senior Schools in North London (which had been evacuated to Westward Ho! in Devon), had been very good at sports and, during the summer of 1940, had watched the RAF and the Luftwaffe dogfighting above London while he had played cricket at Hampstead Cricket Club. Having discovered the joy of reading from an uncle, who every Christmas gave him a book that was always just in advance of his supposed capacity to understand it, Pop immersed himself in non-fiction classics such as H.G. Wells's *A Short History of the World*. At Westward Ho!, he learned to love music from a teacher, a colonel in the First World War, who played his opera and classical record collection to Pop and a group of his friends on a wind-up gramophone on wet Sunday afternoons.

By chance, on passing the Houses of Parliament on 20 August, while back in the capital, Pop had managed to get a seat in the public gallery to hear Winston Churchill's 'Never in the field of human conflict' speech: his thanks, on behalf of the nation, to the RAF. One other point of significance, perhaps, and one his SOE interviewers may well have picked up on, was that in 1938, when he was 14, Pop had gone as an exchange student to Germany for six weeks. The family had lived in Düsseldorf, but had taken Pop on a short holiday to Bad Hönningen on the Rhine. While they were on the road, Pop saw rallies, a lot of uniformed men snapping Hitler salutes, and sensed, even at 14, that war was coming. The family's younger son, Kurt, then came back to spend several weeks with Pop and my grandparents in East Finchley.

The German trip would hardly have earmarked Pop as material for SOE – it was during his later school years, as well as his time at Cambridge, that he honed his German language skill; and, in any case, as I'd already concluded, a German language skill, at this point in the war, wasn't what SOE needed. So, if his education and naval record weren't significant factors in SOE's ultimate conclusion that Pop might be useful to its war effort, then it must have been something else – and here I fell back on what Pop had told me when the 'man from the ministry' had shown up at Chatham Docks asking for people with sailing experience. His answer – that he'd had 'extensive experience' was, in fact, a stretch. What it had actually amounted to was a summer 'mucking around in boats' on the Welsh Harp, a mile-long stretch of water in Wembley, five miles from Central London. At Arisaig, Pop had *not* gone on, as most of the other agents had, to the Parachute School at Ringway or the Specialist School at Beaulieu; he had been sent to the Helford River. What this in turn told me was that, in mid-1943, SOE was desperate for another kind of agent – one for whom naval backgrounds and 'para-naval skills' were the prerequuisite: an intimate knowledge of coastal inlets and inland waterways – *Swallows and Amazons* stuff. As with the eye test, Pop had bluffed his way again, but this time it had worked, because following his selection, and after what was clearly a successful four weeks at Arisaig, he was dispatched to Cornwall, where Gerry Holdsworth's unconventional 'naval circus' had been operating since the beginning of 1941.

Helford served as the base for an SOE naval unit, the 'Helford Flotilla', which, like the privateers that had operated from Cornwall centuries earlier, would harass and divert the enemy in a multitude of inventive ways. A cluster of requisitioned houses on a point of land where the Helford River meets Frenchman's Creek – a place brought a certain notoriety by Daphne du Maurier's eponymous novel – Helford was, and still is, nothing if not atmospheric.

Although established and led by Holdsworth, Helford's fleet of ragtag sailing and fishing boats was actually the brainchild of two brothers, Brooks and Robin Richards. This, when I visited Helford to try to get a sense of its impact and influence on Pop when he arrived there in June 1943, made the visit suitably poignant, because Robin, who had been unwell for some time, had died just a month earlier. Brooks was an RNVR officer whose ship was blown up by a mine during a sweep of the Channel in 1940. While he was recovering in hospital, he and Robin started thinking about how Breton fishing boats that had fled from France, and were now laid up in English ports in the Southwest, might be used for clandestine operations to and from Brittany. They wrote a paper and submitted it to the powers-that-be in November 1940. Both brothers were very experienced sailors, their father having taught them to sail at an early age. A boyhood affinity with 'mucking about in boats', in fact, would distinguish many of those who ended up serving with No.1 Special Force, SOE's covert operations unit in Italy. So, when Pop had invoked this to the man from the ministry, he'd pressed the right buttons.

The Richards brothers' paper had coincided with a similar idea from Gerry Holdsworth. In August 1940, the then-infant SOE had wanted to send a group of agents to Brittany. At the time, the Royal Navy had no resources to offer – motor gunboats certainly could not be spared – and so Holdsworth stepped into the breach by offering to drop them off using a Belgian yacht.

But after endless technical troubles – the engine kept failing – the operation never happened. Holdsworth wrote a report saying such missions were feasible, but that they would need to be supported by proper training and equipment. As a result, he was given the princely sum of a thousand pounds, told to obtain the necessary ships and personnel – and to find a suitable base.

With the help of his wife, Mary – who we now know would lend her name to 'Maryland', the codename for Monopoli (Mary also worked for Section D and had amassed skills in forging documents and demolition) – Holdsworth established his HQ at a house called Ridifarne, overlooking the Helford River. Mary was de facto in charge and, by all accounts, a woman not to be trifled with. One of the Flotilla crewmembers, while describing her as a kind-hearted soul, also said that she declined to be 'bossed about by a bunch of idiots'.

Most of Holdsworth's one thousand pounds was taken up with the purchase of two boats, one of which, a 60-ton yawl named the *Mutin*, would later sail with him, Laming, Long, Scott and Macintosh into Monopoli harbour in September 1943. *Mutin* had been built as a 'tunnyman' but used as a training ship for the French Navy. Holdsworth took her to Dartmouth and replaced her unreliable auxiliary motor with a German Deutz diesel engine. The engine was one of only two in the country that had made it across to England in a packing case shortly before the fall of France. Brooks Richards, by now fully recovered from his encounter with the mine, joined Holdsworth as his deputy, and training for operations started in earnest in 1941. The initial aim was to ferry SOE agents and supplies to France and return with agents and aircrew downed in enemy-occupied territory. It used authentic French motor fishing vessels – MFVs – that had made it across the Channel after the French surrender.

But what neither Holdsworth nor the Richards brothers had accounted for was the fact that SOE's mission was seen in other parts of Britain's covert intelligence and special operations community – most notably, the Secret Intelligence Service, MI6 – as an invasion of its 'turf'. Since the earliest days of the war, SIS had been based just down the coast in Falmouth with its own fleet of boats. Under the aegis of Commander Frank Slocum, the SIS unit had a fundamentally different objective from the upstart SOE, which had only come about during the war itself as an antidote to Nazi occupation. SOE was primarily about blowing things up and 'going noisy', but SIS was about clandestine surveillance and agent infiltration and extraction – operations that required a higher degree of subterfuge. As a consequence, each group viewed the other with a high degree of suspicion and considerable animosity.

'Gerry Holdsworth's main battle was not against the Germans, but against Slocum, who was supposed to be running all the clandestine traffic between the UK and northern France, and Gerry didn't like that at all,' one member of the Helford Flotilla recalled years later. 'In fact, if he could conduct an operation without consulting Slocum, he did.' Consequently, Slocum and Holdsworth battled each other for two long years – each more or less doing his own thing – but in the end the battle could not be sustained and it was Holdsworth who emerged the loser. It was decided above them that the two services would co-locate on the Helford – SIS moving its operations there from Falmouth – and that SIS, not SOE, would be put in overall charge. As Robin noted later, Holdsworth's reaction was to 'put two fingers up, get into *Mutin* and go off to Gibraltar to make a new career for himself in North Africa'. Although there was an element of pique here, he had a job to do. In the wake of the Allied landings, his task was to run missions to Tunisia, Corsica, Italy and southern France from the Algerian coast, exploiting the experience he had gained while at Helford.

That had been at the end of 1942 and had led nine months later to Holdsworth's appointment as the boss of No.1 Special Force in Monopoli.

Pop, as an officer at Helford, had been billeted in an elegant stone house called Pedn Billy, positioned halfway up a steep wooded hillside overlooking the river. When I visited Pedn Billy on a dank late spring afternoon more than 70 years later, it wasn't hard to see how this isolated part of Cornwall, less than 100 miles from the French coast, could successfully swallow up the comings and goings of the SOE/SIS armada of little boats. Sailing under French colours, and often spending several days off the French coast on their insertion and extraction missions, the MFVs of the Flotilla were constantly at risk of being stopped and boarded. Unarmed, except for the hand-held weapons of their crews, there was nowhere to run or hide. The crews of the MFVs knew that if they were caught by the Germans – dressed as they were in Breton fishing gear – they would be shot as spies.

At Pedn Billy, before he left for North Africa, Holdsworth introduced his successor, Lieutenant Commander Bevil Warington Smyth, to two of his most experienced officers: Lieutenant Tom Long and Sub-Lieutenant Robin Richards, the latter having joined the unit at the request of his brother, Brooks.

Warington Smyth would have met two other Helford stalwarts at the same time: Petty Officer Eddie Cauvain and Petty Officer William 'Faithful' Banks. Three of them were already known to me, Long having been one of the four para-naval officers Pop had met upon his arrival in Monopoli and Cauvain having jumped with Pop on the night of his fateful mission into enemy territory in November 1944.

And then, of course, there was Robin. After leaving Stowe School, Robin had entered the RNVR as an engineer cadet. In the first nine months of 1940, he'd undergone an apprenticeship in the workshops of the Tottenham and District Gas Company's Willoughby Lane Works, where he recorded in an interview for the Imperial War Museum, 'there was a lot of bad language and a lot of good workmanship'. It was here, Robin said, that he 'learned how to fit a cast-iron piston-ring in a steam-driven tar-pump'. When the offer of a place for an engineering degree at Cambridge came, he felt he would be stupid not to accept it. As was the norm in wartime, he did his two-year degree in the space of 18 months, his graduation coinciding with a plea from his brother, Brooks, to come and join the 'Holdsworth Circus' on the Helford River.

In October 1942, Robin found himself on one of SOE's first 'lardering' operations, which involved caching weapons for the French Resistance on isolated Breton beaches. The mission was led by Commander Ted Davis, one of Slocum's men, but the man who took the weapons ashore was the 29-year-old Lieutenant Dick Laming (whom I already knew to be Dutch-born and raised with an English father, a former British Consul in Amsterdam), another officer to whom Pop had been introduced upon his arrival at Monopoli. Laming's personnel file in The National Archives at Kew described him as a 'merchant seaman with considerable knowledge of South Africa, Western

Europe [and] the West Indies… who spoke Dutch, English, German, workable Italian, Kiswahili and Malay'. He was the nephew of R.V. Laming, the first head of SOE's N (Netherlands) Section.

In the aftermath of the Nazi invasion of the Netherlands, Dick Laming had spent several months ferrying agents in and out of the country on the so-called 'Scheveningen Ferry' route, named after the Dutch coastal resort where the agents were landed and exfiltrated. The runs ended when, one night, the Germans arrested the reception committee and almost captured the raiding party along with Laming's motor torpedo boat as it was idling off the coast.

In June 1942, Laming found himself at Anderson Manor in Dorset, the headquarters of the Small Scale Raiding Force, a commando unit under the joint control of SOE and Admiral Louis Mountbatten, the head of Combined Operations. SSRF's mission was to launch 'pin-prick' raids against German establishments on or close to the French coast – the idea being for them to waste considerable manpower defending a multitude of potential targets all along the Channel and Atlantic seaboard. Four months later, Laming was transferred to the Helford River, where his skills quickly became integral to SOE's 'lardering' operations for the French Resistance. But these missions, especially in autumn and winter, were not easy. During October, for example, three attempts were made to run half a ton of stores across to the nearby Île de Batz for burial, but all three failed on account of the atrocious weather.

One consequence of this was SOE's realisation that it needed to develop a better method for getting its personnel ashore in rough seas. To accomplish this, a vessel called the 'surf-boat' was developed – one of the first examples of the improved levels of cooperation between SOE and SIS following their co-location at Helford. This new-found fraternity should not have been altogether surprising, since the man appointed commander of the Inshore Patrol Flotilla, as the new joint endeavour was rebranded, was Nigel Warington Smyth, brother of Bevil Warington Smyth, Gerry Holdsworth's successor. The surf-boats were designed by Nigel and built by the Camper and Nicholson shipyard in Southampton, the first model being designated the SN1 (S for Smyth and N for Nicholson). They were designed to be lowered over the side of the parent motor gunboat – known within the Navy as an 'MGB' – beyond the line of rocks that demarcated the surf zone. The SN1's design allowed it to be rowed ashore in silence and under good control through the surf. Six oarsmen were required for a larger boat, two for a smaller one, with steering provided by a man at the back using a sweep oar over the stern. Trials at Praa Sands – around 10 miles to the west of Helford, a beach fully exposed to the raw power of the Atlantic – were carried out under the oversight of SIS's Deputy Director Operations Division's 15th Motor Gunboat Flotilla. These went extremely well; so much so that one of the officers of the MGB Flotilla, Guy Hamilton – who would become a film director for the James Bond franchise (as well as of the movie *The Battle of Britain*) – pronounced himself, according to Brooks Richards, to have been 'amazed at the amount of stores and bodies that could be piled aboard the 14-foot SN1 and at the same time ride smoothly with just two stout matelots at the oars'.

Immediately upon his arrival at Helford, Pop was assigned to Robin's MFV, along with Eddie Cauvain and William Banks – the two Petty Officers who would go on to serve behind enemy lines with him. But three weeks later, on 20 July, a message arrived from London informing Robin that in three days' time he and his crew – everyone, in fact, except for Pop, who was too raw a recruit to be allowed to go – would be 'heading north' to Glasgow in readiness to sail to Algiers, where, by now, Holdsworth had established his para-naval community as part of SOE's burgeoning presence in North Africa. The Helford logbook, which I'd located in The National Archives, recorded that, on 23 July, after three days' leave, Robin was back at Helford with his sailing orders.

The following morning, after a boozy send-off, Robin, Cauvain, Banks and a fourth member of his crew – Fred Albin – left by train for Glasgow where they would pick up a boat for the 10-day voyage to North Africa.

In later life, Pop mentioned that he had made a couple of trips to France and the Channel Islands while at Helford, presumably to drop agents there or collect them, but I could find no official record of this in the archives. On the night of 28 July, the Helford logbook stated that Pop led a mock attack on a burned-out house that masqueraded as an enemy headquarters and that he had done a 'good job'. His co-commander in the exercise was Peter Simpson-Jones, who three months later would ask specifically for Pop to be sent to Italy from North Africa to help SOE run its beleaguered boat operations along the Italian coast. The day after the mock attack, Pop was given a 'special briefing' by MI9, the intelligence unit tasked with organising the escape of POWs behind enemy lines; an organisation that was expert in escape-and-evasion tactics. But if all this sounded like a prelude to deployment, Pop was about to be disappointed. For a whole month, he languished with nothing happening. Then, on 29 August, he took part in an exercise called 'Saturation'. As the logbook stated: 'The plan for this exercise was to go up the river in rubber boats, land at a suitably deserted place, make a bivouac, spend the night in the woods and return at dawn after removing all traces of the camp.' At dawn, the logbook stated, 'the fire was got going again, tea was made, and preparations made for the return journey'.

On Sunday 5 September, plans were being made to sail MFV 2025 on the Tuesday morning to the Scilly Isles, which lie around 30 miles to the west of Land's End, with Pop's crew on board. These plans, the logbook made clear, were drafted purely to maintain morale amongst the crew.

Four days later, a week after the Allies invaded Southern Italy, he finally received his orders to sail for Algeria. From there, as I already knew, his journey would take him via Malta to Monopoli, where, more than anything, SOE wanted at this juncture of its war in the Med people who could 'muck around in boats'.

Chapter 7

'I have never felt so happy as when I was with you'

Monopoli, Southern Italy, January 1944

A photograph of my father taken shortly after he returned from his seven-day undersea voyage to Chioggia depicts a tall, striking RNVR officer with an unkempt beard, grown, no doubt, during the claustro-phobic operation on board the dangerously unseaworthy *Marea*. The beard, worn around the time Pop was celebrating his 20th birthday, lent him a piratical air that could not have been more at odds with the father I'd known or his public business persona.

But it did conform, I could see, to what I was beginning to sense was a very strong *corps d'esprit* amongst the small, close-knit group that had trained and sailed together on the Helford – and which, after transit from Algeria and Malta, was now ensconced in Monopoli at the forefront of SOE's plans for waging unconventional war in Italy and the Adriatic. But herein lay a big problem: how would I begin to tell this part of Pop's story?

In January 1944, Pop and Mop were both in Monopoli. Mop, as she'd told me by now, had already been introduced to my father. Her description of the man she had spotted, but paid little attention to, in the officers' mess following his submarine voyage, tallied with the photograph we had of him: tall, bearded and thoughtful after the mis-sion. But, after the passage of 70-plus years, my mother's memory wasn't what it was and, I knew, couldn't be relied on to provide the detail I needed to produce the narrative.

Pop made his jump into Northern Italy in November 1944 – almost 11 months after events that had seen them arrive, more or less at the same time, in Monopoli. What I did have were some scratchy notes on a series of boat operations that Pop undertook between Jan-uary and May – drawn from papers held at The National Archives, books like Brooks Richards's *Secret Flotillas* and the few words Pop had devoted publicly to the subject – and this was cause enough for concern. But for the period between May and November 1944, I had nothing at all, and with the recent death of my godfather, Robin Richards, I could not fall back on any members of the para-naval unit to help, as there were none still alive. I had placed an advertisement on the notice board in the Special Forces Club in the hope that someone, somewhere, might have some information. I had trawled the Imperial War Museum and The National Archives for all the available source material on this part of Pop's war. The notes were sparse on matters of operational history, but I had next to nothing on the circumstances in which he and my mother had met or the relationship that had formed between them.

One day, frustrated at having come this far, and with no prospect of overcoming the hurdle, I confided in my brother-in-law, John Comerford. The investigation, I told him, had hit a very thick brick wall.

'The letters may contain the kind of detail you're looking for,' he said.

We had met to discuss progress, or the lack of it, at the Special Forces Club – a setting, given the impasse, that now felt suitably mocking. It was just before Christmas. Club members were coming and going, clapping their hands and stamping their feet as they walked in from the cold.

The fire crackled in the grate in the room on the ground floor where John and I were sitting. I looked at him, thinking I must have misheard him.

'What letters?'

'Pop wrote to Mop almost every day they were in Italy,' he said. 'She told me. Just the other day. We were talking about your research and it just popped out.' He looked at me. 'I thought she must have told you about them.'

Mop told him that she had kept every single letter my father had ever written to her – including those he'd sent her in Italy – and that they'd been languishing in an old suitcase in the attic. Looking back, John said, she had most likely told him this by way of a confidence. Mop had told him she'd wanted to read the letters again, as a way of reconnecting with Pop after his death, but had not been able to bring herself to open up the suitcase.

John then articulated why this hadn't come to light before. 'Would *you* show what *you'd* written to *your* 19-year-old girlfriend to *your* children – especially if that girlfriend then went on to become their mother?' he said.

John, with my sister, Catherine, was due to see my mother in the next couple of days and I asked – as it had been John to whom she'd revealed the existence of the letters – whether he'd ask her if she'd share with me any that shed light on Pop's missing months – the January to November 1944 period when I had virtually nothing. John said he'd broach the subject with her and let me know immediately.

When I next went to see Mop several days later, there, sitting on the kitchen table, was a battered old suitcase. Without saying anything, my mother reached into it and handed me a letter. I looked at the date. There was even a time on it. It was written on 16 November 1944, at 1.30am, 30 minutes before the bomber from which he was to jump was due to take off.

I scanned the page until I saw this: *By now you must know how much I have enjoyed the last months in your company. Everything in the world goes right when I am with you. I have never felt so happy as when I was with you.*

I looked up. Mop was silent, but I could see she was close to tears.

I opened the suitcase and removed the green manila file that lay inside. I opened the flap. It was difficult to tell how many letters there were – some, I could see, were on writing paper, others had been scrawled on whatever Pop must have been able to find, tiny scraps, pieces of cardboard, official-looking message slips from the Naval Office where he'd worked... there was even some blotting paper jammed with notes written in pencil.

There had to be easily more than 100, maybe 150, individual pieces of correspondence. With the letters, the dozens of books on SOE's Italian war that I'd amassed, the archive research, Pop's Westminster speech and the five pages of handwritten notes I'd jotted down from all my conversations with him, I felt I was now in with a shout and could start building the narrative of the months leading up to the jump.

For security reasons, many of Pop's letters were undated. They contained no mission details, unless you counted the odd unintended clue (of which I was to find quite a few later). But on top of the research I'd already gathered, the letters were a treasure trove.

Close to the top of the pile (and, just to add to the confusion, they were no longer in correct date order) was a note that referred to a night out in Bari for dinner and a film. And it appeared to be a double-date involving Nancy and Robin, whom Pop referred to as 'Rob'. Yet it was clear that getting to Bari, which was around 50km away, wasn't easy, due to Mop's antisocial shift hours down at the Signals Office and problems arranging a lift. Pop wrote in one of his early letters:

> *Owing to all sorts of unforeseen difficulties with transport etc.,*
> *Friday is off, but Hilary [Scott] will take us in tonight as he has*
> *to go part of the way himself. He is leaving here at 7pm. This*
> *is awkward in a way for us, as we cannot manage dinner and a*
> *'flick', but would you like to come aboard and have high tea, say,*
> *around a quarter to six?*
>
> *I hope this letter gets to you all right and does not get lost*
> *in transit: I think the best way to reply is either a note through*
> *Peggy or ring up Peggy to give me an answer, as I don't know*
> *when I shall be in the office, and Peggy could leave a note.*

Peggy, Mop told me, was a secretary who worked in the Naval Office, where Pop worked with Hilary Scott, Robin and Dick Laming when they weren't on ops. Tea, she added, was a regular ritual on Pop and Robin's boat, the *Eduardo*, which they had turned into a de facto bachelor pad. Mop couldn't remember whether or not, in the end, they ever got to see the film.

I searched for any other correspondence that gave a clue to what might have happened after this, but there was nothing, except for an undated note – long before any romance blossomed – from Pop explaining that he had tickets for a play at Bari's theatre, the Piccinni:

> *I was so glad to hear you could come* ce soir; *arrangements*

*about it are now clarifying themselves (doesn't that sound stiff!)
and we have tickets for* Quiet Weekend *at the Piccinni. It is the
London company, so might be pretty good. Judging from usual
standards, the time, we should tell you, is a quarter past six. But
if you are a prompt type (which I trust you are), the time is half-
past!*

Quiet Weekend was a romantic comedy, a sequel to a popular 1941 play called *Quiet Wedding*. The play, especially when performed by a 'London company', would have been an opportunity for Pop, Robin, Mop and Nancy – weeks before my mother and father's relationship had blossomed into romance – to forget about the war for a few hours.

In the second half of January 1944, Pop was dispatched on the first of a series of missions that would see him going behind the lines for the first time by surface vessel. On 2 January, Dick Laming had delivered two agents on behalf of SIS/MI6 to an area just outside Porto San Giorgio, around 120km north of the German lines, which, following the fall of Ortona, were now demarcated on the Adriatic coast at Pescara – a key strategic port. Laming had done this in the *Seahawk*, another converted fishing trawler. The Dutch-born Englishman, who had reasonably good Italian, was in charge of the logistics in almost all operations involving the MS boats and their Italian crews, with whom – despite, or perhaps because of, flourishes like the stencilled cruiser HMS *Manchester* on one of the MS boats – he had by now developed a good working relationship. From early January, the MS boats had been running out of SOE's forward operating ports of Manfredonia (the nearest to Monopoli) on the Gargano peninsula; Termoli, just to the north of the peninsula; and Ortona, the scene of Laming's 'real boozy party' with Captain Black, which was the closest of the three ports to the front line. Laming used Holdsworth's old converted fishing boat, the *Mutin*, as a ferry to transport agents from Monopoli to the ports, from where they would embark on the MS/MAS boats to their destinations behind the lines.

'To me,' Laming said after the war, 'the Adriatic was a great picnic, and, on the main [beach] landings I made, I only played the role of figurehead.' This, from my observation of the missions he'd already undertaken and those that followed, was both modest and untrue, as Laming was normally in the thick of things – indeed, he took command of several missions out of Termoli during the next few months. However, after Pop's arrival, the record showed that Laming did leave as much of the actual 'boat work' as possible to his three deputies – Pop, Robin and Tom Long – and it was probably this that allowed Pop to take a leading role in a combined operation – dubbed 'Abberton' by SOE and 'QWQ 2' by 'A-Force', as MI9 operations in support of POW escape missions were sometimes known – on the night of 20/21 January. The mission, in two parts, required Pop to sail to the mouth of the River Chienti near Civitanova Marche, around 130km north of Ortona. This was SOE's first boat operation in this specific area from what I could tell, but would by no means be the last. The brief was first to drop four agents ashore, including an Italian general. The second phase, in the same location, tasked them with the delivery of another Italian agent and the extraction of a 'Captain Fowler', who was in charge of the exfiltration of 23 Allied POWs. The POWs were to come back in the boats with Fowler.

The operation was carried out in an Italian MS boat – MS65 – commanded by a Lt Di Vascello Pinotti. MS65, I read in a mission report at Kew, arrived at the pinpoint at 10pm, where Pop and the Italian waited for a recognition signal. In post-war correspondence between SOE's historian Christopher Woods and one of the Italians who went ashore that night, I discovered how 'Sub Lt R. A. Clark', who was 'in charge of 1SF's part in the operation', took a small landing party ashore in a rowing boat with the four Italian agents under tow in three rubber dinghies. After putting the Italians ashore safely, 17 of the POWs were piled into the dinghies and towed back to MS65. The dinghies were then paddled back to the shore, where the remaining POWs embarked and were then rowed back to MS65. Anchor was weighed at 11.05pm, with the MS setting a return course for Termoli, where it arrived at 3.15am on the 21st.

I was fortunate, and grateful, to have been provided with an account of this mission from the other side – by two of the evacuees. The account came via a highly knowledgeable researcher and writer called Annelisa Nebbia, who lived and worked in the area where the evacuation had taken place. In an account called *My Days At War*, a memoir written by a friend of hers, Ettore Damini, who, as a 16-year-old, had worked with A-Force as a translator – I read how Captain James Cameron, accompanied by Damini and four others from A-Force, had left the port of Termoli on the night of 15/16 December 1943, on a mission codenamed 'Sassoon'. Its objective was the recovery of 25–30 British ex-POWs hiding out in the Chienti and Tenna river valleys. After rendezvousing with the prisoners, five attempts by the Sassoon team to exfiltrate them from the beach and bring them back to Termoli had failed, mainly due to bad weather – one attempt, however, had resulted in the mission being scrubbed due to a damaged dinghy and the death by drowning of one of the POWs. It was Pop's attempt – the sixth – that succeeded in bringing them back. Captain Cameron, quoted by Damini, described how, soon after assembling the POWs on the beach, 'a shadow appeared to seaward… a fast Italian motor craft with an Italian naval crew and an officer from the Royal Navy [Pop was actually, of course, RNVR]. This time, there was no mistake. A string of rubber boats [as Cameron saw them] paddled in and took off all the prisoners in one lift. An interesting wait followed on the beach for the rear party, but nothing stirred, and the boats returned to take us off unmolested. A few minutes later, we were off to the south in a cloud of spray.'

Damini then recounted how, after disembarkation on the pier at Termoli, they were taken to a large room in a building on the harbour's edge, 'where they gave us hot tea with rum, biscuits and chocolate'.

Not all MAS/MS crews, however, were quite as dependable as Lt Di Vascello Pinotti's. In *Mission Accomplished*, David Stafford related how several members of another MAS crew had snapped Nazi salutes during a harbour-side inspection by their new Royal Navy allies. The Italian officers in charge had promised that there would be no repeats of this incident, but several British officers reported subsequently that, during covert missions in the dark of the moon, they felt distinctly ill at ease sailing near, and sometimes into, German-occupied harbours with only these not-so-lovable rogues to depend upon. Indeed,

Robin, in his IWM interview, said that on several occasions he over-heard his Italian crew, believing him not to understand a word they were saying, discussing what sounded suspiciously like the pros and cons of turning themselves (and possibly their new British allies) over to the Germans. Fortunately, this never happened.

On the same night that Pop sailed north in MS65, Laming had taken command of an operation called 'Speedometer', which entailed the infiltration of a No.1 Special Force sabotage team to derail a train. A week later, Laming was in charge of Operation 'Aberystwyth', in which he put five agents ashore near Pescara. Both operations were carried out on MS boats out of Termoli, with Laming responsible for navigation, getting the landing party ashore and for beach reconnais-sance. The operations were all carried out successfully.

At the end of January, Pop and Tom Long took *Mutin* to the island of Vis off the coast of Dalmatia. This was a trip of around 150km from the Gargano peninsula across a dangerous stretch of sea patrolled by German warships and fighter-bombers based in Italy and occupied Yugoslavia. Following the Italian armistice, the Germans and Croa-tians had managed to occupy every island in the Adriatic off the Yugoslav coast except for Vis, which became the headquarters of Yugoslavia's partisan forces under Marshal Tito. On 16 January, fol-lowing a directive from Winston Churchill for British forces to lend military assistance to Tito, a contingent of Royal Marines Comman-dos landed on Vis with orders to reduce pressure on Tito's partisans on the Yugoslav mainland by drawing off large numbers of opposing forces, composed mainly of the *Wehrmacht*'s 118th Mountain Divi-sion. The Commandos were led by 'Mad Jack' Churchill, a man with a fearsome reputation. Mad Jack led his troops into battle brandishing a sword and was the only man during the Second World War to have killed with a bow and arrow.

On 26 January, 10 days after arriving on Vis, Mad Jack led a series of raids on German positions and garrisons on the mainland and neighbouring islands, starting with an assault on the garrison at Milna on the island of Brac. Pop and Tom Long, I learned from *Secret Flotil-las*, were required to support this operation in the *Mutin*, the record stating that she delivered 'a much-needed' cargo of petrol and camouflage nets during a hazardous mission.

The Luftwaffe still had relative command of the skies in the eastern Adriatic and tended to strafe anything on the water. Pop had once told me that he was on a boat that was attacked by a German aircraft and that a man on deck had his head blown clean off by a cannon shell. Without ceremony, they had been forced to roll the body off the deck and into the sea, the boat's commander – unidentified by Pop or any other member of No.1 SF – having taken the decision that a mutilated body on deck would be 'bad for morale'.

From the diaries of one of the men on the Vis voyage – Fred Albin, the able seaman who had journeyed from Helford to Algeria with Robin – it was apparent that the sea between Manfredonia and Vis was heavily mined and that the trip could only be made under cover of darkness, due to the high threat from Me109s and Ju88s. This struck me as a true Devil's alternative in that sailing under the cover of darkness made it impossible to spot any mines that might be in their path. 'When it was dark, we'd let go and go alongside a quay, which was cut out of the rock,' Albin wrote. 'From around the corner would come these Yugoslav people… they were wounded. Some were old women. Some were children.' The *Mutin* took as many on board as it could before sailing them back to Manfredonia. I scoured Pop's letters to Mop to see if I could find any corroborating reference to this trip, but I couldn't, although Mop had clearly been on his mind while he was gone, because, on 7 February, as soon as he returned, she received a note from him which read: *Robin and I thought it would be rather wizzo if you would accompany us on an expedition to the Bari concert next Sunday.* Pop asked Mop to ask Nancy as well – no doubt at the request of Robin, who had also signed the note.

In amongst Mop's letters, I found a programme for the concert, with the date – 'Feb 13th' – scribbled on the back. Mop must have done this when she received the note from Pop. She'd written down 'Bob and Robin' next to it.

When I checked, I discovered that the 13th was indeed a Sunday. On the bill were Beethoven's 'Pastoral Symphony', Tchaikovsky's '1812 Overture' and Wagner's 'Ride of the Valkyries' – compositions that seemed a strange mixture of appropriate (soothing, the 'Pastoral Symphony'), apt ('1812', war) and not so fitting (Wagner, Hitler's favourite composer), given the time and the place.

Winston Churchill's prediction that an attack on Italy would constitute a relatively easy push into the 'soft underbelly of Europe' had, by the end of 1943, acquired more than a hollow ring to it: indeed, the phrase was starting to haunt him.

On 6 February 1944, Malcolm Munthe had established an SOE training base on the island of Ischia near Naples (where another SOE operator, Peter Simpson-Jones, had also established a small flotilla of MS/MAS boats for covert operations along Italy's west coast) – and had decided to make direct contact with the resistance movement in Rome.

This stemmed from an order issued late the previous year by Colin Gubbins, the head of SOE, that with the Germans digging in between Rome and Naples on the 'Gustav Line' – as this part of the Winter Line fortifications was known – No.1 SF was to step up the missions it was becoming increasingly good at: running stealthy boat operations in support of agent drops and pick-ups, sabotage missions and partisan liaison.

Munthe, I knew, had arrived in Monopoli late the previous year, biding his time over Christmas and the New Year while he waited for movement to pick up on the battlefront so that he could re-enter the fray. At the beginning of 1944, with the Allied armies facing the Gustav Line, it had become clear to both sides that the next big push would be for Rome itself, some 75km to the north. Field Marshal Kesselring, the Commander-in-Chief of Army Group C, had bolstered the hinterland between Rome and the Gustav Line with more than 20 of Hitler's best divisions – indeed, Hitler himself, sensing the battle that was looming, had diverted key reinforcements from the Balkans and France in anticipation of an Allied offensive. On Christmas Day, at a meeting of senior Allied commanders, chaired by Churchill near Tunis, it was decided that a bold move to outflank the Gustav Line was needed to outmanoeuvre and outwit the overwhelming defences that faced the Allies on the road to Rome. A plan was thus drawn up to land a large Allied force around 120km north of the Gustav Line at Anzio. This would coincide with a conventional assault on the Gustav Line by the troops dug in against it.

The landing took place on 22 January 1944 and to begin with was an outstanding success. By noon that day, the beachhead extended more than 7km inland. By nightfall on the 22nd, 36,000 British and American troops had been landed, as well as more than 3,000 vehicles, with only 13 of their number killed and 97 wounded. This was ascribed to the fact that local German commanders had been assured by their supreme headquarters, the OKW (*Oberkommando der Wehrmacht*), more than 1,500km away in Germany, that the Allies would not dare mount an amphibious landing in the winter months. German forces had thus moved troops back behind the Gustav Line, leaving just one company in the vicinity of the Anzio beaches. But this honeymoon period wasn't to last. By the end of January, German reinforcements had been rushed to the beachhead from Rome – including the 4th Parachute and Hermann Göring Divisions – and with mounting support from the Luftwaffe, the Anzio assault started to founder.

Against growing casualties, the Allies took the decision to halt the push from the beachhead altogether and consolidate their forces – by now numbering more than 60,000 troops – in and around Anzio. Kesselring, using the time to build up his reinforcements, now had 70,000 troops ranged against them and, by early February, these numbers had surged again to around 100,000 troops, with a similar number of Allied troops opposing them. The German counteroffensive started on 3 February with a massive artillery barrage, but, in the churned-up, waterlogged terrain, the German advance rapidly ran out of steam and soon ground to a complete halt. The battle of Anzio had now become a war of attrition, with territorial gains and losses on both sides becoming a nightmarish throwback to the battles of the First World War.

In early January, Munthe was briefed at Allied headquarters in Naples about the planned Anzio assault. He quickly abandoned his own plans for getting to Rome and booked himself on an Anzio invasion ship. His small group comprised Captain Michael Gubbins, General Colin Gubbins's son, and radio operator Corporal Bill Pickering, who had been plucked gratefully from the Monopoli Signals Office and the overbearing oversight of 'Oddjob'. The 22-year-old Michael Gubbins had a habit of humming a song that was doing the rounds at that time called 'Abdul Abulbul Amir', especially when he found himself under fire. He was a popular figure at Monopoli, despite, perhaps, the slight awkwardness of his relationship to the 'boss'.

The three of them, with two jeeps and a radio set, landed just north of Anzio and gave themselves the ambitious target of reaching Rome within a week. This looked increasingly unachievable as the Anzio breakout faltered.

In the meantime, Maryland had sent a signal to all resistance elements in Rome to throw everything they had at the Germans. With the Allies bogged down on the Anzio beachhead, however, the resistance initiative was brutally crushed by the Germans and all its signalling equipment captured. With no communications channels now open between the Allies and the partisans, Munthe determinedly avowed to break out of the beachhead and get to Rome so that contact could be re-established. He found an Italian, a Roman, who claimed to know a route that would get them to the capital.

The guide, having just returned from another recce, was being held in a cave just their side of the front lines by a detachment of Irish Guards, who provided food and shelter for him while they waited for Munthe and Gubbins – by now minus Pickering – to arrive.

The pair set off to the cave, heading towards the weakest point in the lines, which, by chance, was held on the Allied side by Munthe's old regiment, the 6th Gordon Highlanders. They reached the position during a lull in the fighting and stopped for a moment or two to catch their breath. Munthe recalled in his official report how 'it was Sunday afternoon about four o'clock and quite peaceful and so sunny, I remember, that we lay on the grass to eat our rations'. Gubbins started to read a letter he had just received from home.

Deciding to make their move, they jumped into a ditch beside a road that ran close to a dilapidated church belfry (which, owing to its resemblance to an industrial chimney, was dubbed 'the Factory') and, in the knowledge they were out of sight of the German positions, which were so close they could have whistled them a greeting, they began to creep towards the cave held by the Irish Guards. As they approached an intersection marked by a 12-foot-high cross, Munthe, still in the ditch, knocked a dead branch, which rolled away to reveal a German staring at him. It took him a second or two to realise that the soldier was dead. It appeared, from the waxy complexion of his skin, that he had been killed within the last day or so. They promptly jumped out of the trench and were halfway to the crossroads when a heavy machine gun opened up on them from the Factory. As they dived for cover, they realised that, in the time it had taken for them to receive the message from the Irish Guards, the lines had shifted and the cave where their contact was waiting had been overrun by the enemy. 'Suddenly,' Munthe wrote, 'the Moaning Minnies started' – 'Moaning Minnies' being a nickname for *Nebelwerfer*, German multi-barrelled rocket launchers. With the 'Minnies' exploding all around them, they jumped into a slit trench around six feet from the one they had just abandoned – and Gubbins started humming 'Abdul Abulbul Amir'. A shell landed directly in the next trench, blowing the German and the dead branch into the air. According to Bill Pickering, who detailed the engagement in *The Bandits of Cisterna*, Munthe heard the whine of another incoming mortar. There was a deafening explosion and he felt a violent pain in his chest. When he opened his eyes, Gubbins was lying on his back, dead, his eyes wide open, his helmet blown off and with blood all over his tunic.

Despite his own injuries, Munthe attempted to drag Gubbins's body out of the trench. Two stretcher-bearers then appeared, but both were hit as they tried to drag Munthe to safety. Doctors later told him that a photograph of his girlfriend in his breast pocket, contained within a metal frame, had saved his life. For Munthe, however, one of the outstanding figures of SOE's campaign in Italy, the war was over. A shell fragment had buried itself in the left side of his skull, threatening the sight in his left eye. His recommendation for the Military Cross, which he was later awarded, testified to his 'inspired leadership and to his contempt for danger'. Alan Ogden, in *A Spur Called Courage*, related that his bravery 'masked a deep sensitivity which meant that the deaths of men under his command weighed heavily on him throughout his life'. He later became a pacifist.

On receiving word of Michael Gubbins's death, Pickering had to communicate this news via Naples to London, which meant telling his father, the head of SOE. 'Michael had been one of the kindest, most courageous young men I had met and my eyes filled with tears as I sent my coded dispatch,' he said.

The manner in which General Gubbins received the news in Baker Street has been detailed by David Stafford. The general had just returned from another inspection of SOE's Mediterranean operations. The officer on duty had placed the telegram marked 'Deepest Sympathy' in his in-tray on top of some operational files. Normally, Gubbins's secretary would have been at work before him. But, on this particular Monday, the general was at his desk early in order to work on some papers before a chiefs of staff meeting that afternoon, action in the Mediterranean being at the top of the agenda. He found the telegram on his desk and opened it. 'Overwhelmed by grief and remorse,' according to his biographers, 'he steeled himself to attend the meeting.' General Gubbins's contribution to the discussion, they observed, 'could only have been perfunctory'. Of his son's death, Gubbins wrote poignantly in some correspondence after the war that it had been 'totally useless'.

Chapter 8

'I've got Monopoli blues – I've had Monopoli properly…'

Southern Italy, February 1944

Mirroring the frustrations of military planners over the stalemate at Anzio, an atmosphere of ennui permeated the Naval Office at Monopoli in the weeks following Abberton, Speedometer, Aberystwyth and the mission across the Adriatic to Vis. Operations could only be undertaken during the 'dark of the moon' period in any given month. This meant two or three nights of high adrenalin followed by weeks of boredom. *I think I shall start a graph showing the ups and downs of one's morale*, Pop wrote to Mop in mid-February. *It seems to be made of meteoric rises followed by perpendicular descents.*

The Naval Office wasn't the only part of No.1 Special Force that was feeling the strain. A non-commissioned officer (NCO) waiting to go into enemy-occupied territory had gone berserk during this period, shooting and wounding a sergeant. The incident had taken place in the other ranks' mess, a hall in the middle of the town. When someone had run breathlessly to relay the news to the officers' mess that the NCO was still holding a group of soldiers at gunpoint, one of the first there to hear the news was Charles Macintosh. Macintosh, who had been deputising for Holdsworth in all matters relating to air and land operations since his arrival on the *Mutin*, had just received orders that he was being transferred to a forward Army unit in anticipation of a breakout from Anzio. Macintosh had never settled into his administrative duties in Monopoli and had welcomed the development, though, sadly, it had come about through the death of Michael Gubbins. There were some initial concerns that Macintosh's deep inside knowledge of operational matters at No.1 Special Force represented a risk were he to be captured, but these were dismissed by Holdsworth, who recognised Macintosh's need for action as something that ran in his blood.

It was inevitable, then, that Macintosh would be the one to respond to the NCO who'd run amok. When he got to the sergeants' mess, he found the wounded sergeant lying on the floor and the NCO standing over him, still brandishing his gun. In the corner, to the right of the entrance, was a group of other ranks – all under threat of being shot if they made a move. The NCO was holding another sergeant hostage, his pistol pointed at his temple. Macintosh kept the gunman talking and eventually got close enough to him to be able to grab his weapon. The NCO's hostage then hit him with a big bunch of keys he'd been holding and put him out for the count. 'It was not the first time that a long wait for a drop into enemy territory proved too much for a sensitive type,' Macintosh observed. Soon afterwards, he left for the front.

Mop and Pop, meanwhile, settled into several tedious weeks of routine. For Pop, this meant getting down to paperwork, which he hated; for Mop, it meant shift work at the Signals Office under the gaze of 'Oddjob'. The only possible diversions were trips into Bari and Taranto, but, from Pop's letters, getting there was clearly problematic. *I shall be leaving around a quarter to two and can be back anytime after half–past five,* he wrote to Mop during this period. But in a second note, delivered a few hours later, he did an about-turn: *I can't go to Taranto after all – it's quite a long story of pitfalls. The glimmer of light is that I shall in all probability be going tomorrow. How does that suit?*

Pop promised to secure transport from his boss, Hilary Scott, whom he referred to affectionately as the 'Old Dad' (at that point, Scott was coming up to his 38th birthday, ancient indeed), and he held out the hope that it might be a jeep. But, from his next letter, it was clear that they never made it out of Monopoli, because, scribbled on naval message paper, Pop wrote he was sorry to hear that Mop had been taken ill – and that he hoped she would be well again by the next day, *for I shall be looking forward to seeing you then.*

He signed it. *Love, Bob.*

As soon as Mop was recovered and back in the Signals Office, Pop wrote again: *My Dear Marjorie, I'm bored – yes again – in fact, my morale chart has suddenly sunk.* He referred to a visit by her to the Naval Office – brief, but long enough for them both to enjoy some conversation over a cup of tea. Many years later, Pop was asked in an interview whether he had fallen in love with my mother at first sight and he replied that he hadn't. Their love, he told his interviewer, had grown out of a special friendship forged by the circumstances in which they had found themselves. Be that as it may, a few days later, as Pop's interest in my mother evidently increased, I learned from his letters how he had offered to meet her after her shift at the Signals Office 'armed with a bottle of gin'. When I asked Mop about this, she said this was exactly what had happened – and that this was how their courtship developed over the next few weeks: the two of them sitting on the harbour wall, drinking gin and talking for hours into the winter nights. It was thus, she told me, that she and Pop got to know each other and began to fall in love.

In addition to these al fresco meetings, they used to meet at 'socials' in the mess and for singsongs around the piano. On these occasions, they would congregate in the company of Hilary Scott and Alan Clark, two of the 'originals' who had sailed into Brindisi with Gerry Holdsworth on the *Mutin*.

Clark – an Army major and no relation to my family – was a gifted songwriter and the source of numerous satirical tunes about No.1 Special Force and its unusual complement of characters. For these gatherings, which could often go long into the night, they were accompanied by an Army captain, Edward Renton, who before the war had performed at Glyndebourne as an operatic director. Renton was another *Mutin* 'original'. It wasn't hard now for me to picture the scene – Renton waving his arms as he conducted, Hilary Scott playing the piano, with Mop, Pop, Robin, Nancy and Alan Clark singing at the tops of their voices. The scene was extraordinarily vivid, in fact, except for one detail. One day, I asked Mop what they used to sing. She couldn't remember, she said. Too long ago. Then something shifted and I saw her turn towards the window. For a moment or two, she said nothing, but then some words started to come. They had been written by Alan Clark, she told me.

The song, she remembered, had been called 'Monopoli Blues':

I've got Monopoli blues, Monopoli blues

I'm blue – I'm through; this isn't the life I'd choose
I've got Monopoli blues, Monopoli blues
Oh Lord, I'm bored and I don't like Monopoli booze

I sit drearily in the mess
Life doesn't strike me as good
I'd like to see the FANYs
But they couldn't care less
And I don't see why they should

I've got Monopoli blues – I've had Monopoli properly
I've got Monopoli blues…

At the beginning of March, in preparation for the new 'dark of the moon', Pop received word he was about to deploy on a new round of missions. *What I really wanted to say in my none too eloquent and all too clumsy way*, he wrote to my mother, *was to thank you very much for the time I have had during the last fortnight. I think you stood between me and the madhouse.*

A few days later, Pop and Robin sailed up the coast in the *Eduardo*, joining Dick Laming at Ortona, where Laming had been based for a couple of weeks in his role as supervisor of the MS/MAS fleet at their forward operating locations. Ortona was the staging point for the three missions that had been assigned to them over the nights of 19/20 and 21/22 March.

Both 'Aintree/Avonmouth', which were combined into a single mission, and 'Ampthill', scheduled for two nights later, were sabotage operations, the first that Pop was to undertake. They were to take place a short way inland from the mouth of the Chienti River – heavily defended territory – and already familiar to me from the mission that Pop had undertaken on the night of 21/22 January.

A description of the defences in the area had been provided by Ettore Damini, the 16-year-old translator with A-Force whom Pop had plucked off the beach that night: 'The Germans were in the major centres such as Macerata, Ascoli, Porto Civitanova etc. and the patrols moved frequently along the coast, that is, along the railway and the coastal road towards Pescara, on which troops transited by night directly towards the front [which was then] on the Sangro [River]', several hundred kilometres to the south. These convoys, Damini reported, were frequently shelled from the sea or machine-gunned from the sky. 'The most inland areas,' he continued, 'were entrusted to the control of the fascists and the Carabinieri, who were minimally efficient, disorganised and lacking in motivation' – but dangerous, nevertheless. 'With a telephone call or a rocket they could at any moment call in the Germans, whose promptness and methods, on the other hand, were well known to all.'

Under the original plan, the Avonmouth agents were due to land two hours after the Aintree insertion mission, but it was decided that the two missions should be combined so as to minimise the danger each posed to the other as soon as they 'went noisy'.

For the first mission, Laming and Bob were joined by a new face, Lt Roy Taylor. Taylor *(pictured)* was an Army officer, who had been in the Lincolnshire Regiment before joining SOE. Short, stocky, with brown hair and grey eyes, like so many other recruits to No.1 Special Force he had been familiar with boats and the sea prior to the war – what set him apart, however, was the fact that he had been a world-

class athlete. Between 1935 and 1939, he had distinguished himself as a big-game fisherman in Bermuda, his birthplace, and before that had been in the swimming and diving teams that had represented the island at the British Empire Games in Canada in 1930. Thirty-three by the time he arrived in Italy from Massingham, Taylor was dispatched directly to the naval section and deployed on the Ortona mission a few days later.

The raw archive account of the merged operation that took place on the 19/20 had MS56 casting off from Ortona 'in fine weather' at 6.53pm, shortly after sunset. With Laming as skipper and Pop once again in charge of the landing party, it headed out into the Adriatic and turned north, all members of the crew keeping their eyes peeled for E-Boats and other enemy activity.

Fortunately, they encountered none and, at 12.40am, arrived off the pinpoint around 800m from the town of Senigallia, 30km north of Ancona. This was deep in enemy waters. Throttling right back, Laming manoeuvred the torpedo boat as close to the shore as he dared, exploiting MS56's key feature: its submerged, low-noise exhausts. When the engines cut completely, Pop then readied the landing party. This consisted of eight agents, six of whom were listed in official documents at Kew as 'saboteurs'.

Fifteen minutes after the two dories were lowered over the side, they set off for the shore under Pop's command. What the precise targets were is unclear. It is possible that the Aintree target was a train as Pop once told me he had witnessed at least one train destroyed by charges during a boat mission. There is no official word, however, of what the mission achieved.

By 1.30am, both operations had been completed with the two dories safely back alongside the parent torpedo boat. Ten minutes later, MS56 commenced her return voyage and, around five hours after that, re-entered Ortona harbour, berthing alongside a fuel ship. Aintree is billed as the last 'body' operation by the Maryland naval force – which signified to me that some of the 'bodies' that night must have been stay-behind agents. This is supported by Brooks Richards in *Secret Flotillas*, where the 'cargo' that night is listed as 'sabotage *instructors*' with a side note that they were to link up with 'Marcasite', a W/T radio station established in the region the previous year.

Two nights later, Pop slipped out of Ortona again and this time headed for Porto San Giorgio, around 12km south of the previous target. For this mission, he was accompanied by Robin and Roy Taylor, with Laming skippering. The boat was once again MS56. Amongst the crew was Fred Albin, the able seaman who had accompanied Pop on the trip to Vis, and Eddie Cauvain, a Helford old hand who, I knew, would later parachute with Pop behind the lines. In his diary, Albin recounted what was expected of them were they to be left behind. 'If you couldn't get back to your [dories], they said you had to come back to [the landing point] every other night for six nights and wait to be picked up. If you hadn't been picked up, you had to make your own way across German lines.'

Each man was given seventy-five pounds in lira, a flask of rum, a first-aid kit and an automatic pistol with two clips of ammunition. Typically, on a sabotage mission, Albin wrote, an MS boat would take them to within a quarter of a mile of the shore, with at least one dory packed with the equipment they would need for the operation. 'If we were doing a bridge, we needed twelve 75-pound canisters of ammonal, the same explosive used in a depth charge. For railway lines,' Albin said, 'we'd use 808 plastic cutting charges and we'd cut the line in half either side of the fishplate where the railway lines were joined.'

On this particular night, the 21/22 March, they were tasked with blowing up a railway line (not the bridge that is listed as the target in *Secret Flotillas* – Robin and Pop's own sketchy account of the attack made this aspect at least of the mission quite clear). The official account held at The National Archives in Kew for 'Ampthill' lists the dories being lowered at 10pm, while the MS boat was still some way out at sea – this to minimise any chance of their being heard from the shore. The parent vessel then dropped anchor at 10.50pm.

At 11pm, the landing party, this time under the command of Robin, left for the shore. Laming remained on MS56 as the officer in charge of the Italian crew. In Robin's report, also held in The National Archives, he stated that the landing party of eight made shore at 11.15pm. 'Several lights were seen on the coast road during the approach,' he reported, 'but the weather was calm, with a light onshore breeze and surf rolling up the narrow shingle beach.' While Robin's demolition party proceeded to the railway, which was around 100m inland, Pop and Taylor were left in charge of the dories, which had been pulled up on to the beach just ahead of the surf line.

The demolition party then started to prepare the charges. They were not helped by the fact that a road ran parallel to, and 40m from, the railway line. Every so often a military truck would rumble past, forcing the saboteurs to take whatever cover they could find. The traffic, no doubt, would have unsettled the nerves of the demolition party, but would, I felt sure, have been even tougher on the constitutions of Pop and Taylor, who, guarding the dories on the beach, would have been unable to tell what was happening at the track. I had to remind myself, too, that the entire coastline was on standby for further amphibious raids of the kind that had enabled the Allies to capture Termoli and Ortona. Porto San Giorgio and Civitanova were in the thickest part of the German defences and would have been crawling with troops on high alert. For Pop and Roy, therefore, every second that the demolition party was out of sight would have seemed like an eternity. On a beach that was all but blacked out, except perhaps for the odd star and a few headlights on the road, they would have seen nothing. Over the sound of the surf, it would have been almost impossible to hear a sentry's footfall until he was on them.

At the railway line, the party worked as quickly as it could to set the charges. In order to apply the plastic explosive to the tracks, they first had to clear a large amount of pebble ballast to expose the rails and the fishplates that joined two tracks together. 'Explosive 808' looked like green plasticine, had the same general consistency and smelled strongly of almonds. It was SOE's explosive of choice for missions of this sort. Robin handed over a 'pencil' detonator and checked his watch. It was coming up to midnight.

Pencil detonators were colour coded to denote different time delays, which could range from 10 minutes to 24 hours. The British 'Number Ten Delay Switch' was the pencil detonator most commonly used by SOE and was typical of the 'back room' ingenuity that underpinned so many of its 'gadgets'.

A brass tube with a copper section at one end, it contained a glass vial of acid – usually cupric chloride – beneath which was a spring-loaded striker under tension held in place by a thin metal wire. The timer was started by crushing the copper section of the tube. The action broke the vial, which released the acid, which then ate into the wire. When the wire parted, the striker shot down the hollow centre of the tube, hitting the percussion cap at the other end of the detonator and setting off the plastic charge. Number Ten Delay Switches were so reliable that the anti-Nazi conspirators who tried to kill Hitler in July that year insisted on using a captured SOE time-pencil over a home-grown detonator. 'The five-hour time pencils were fixed at 0000 and the party left the beach at 0003, returning to the MS at 0018,' Robin relayed in his post-mission report. They waited at anchor 'in the hope of shooting up a southbound train, which might be stopped by the charges' – the detonator having a secondary mode that allowed it to be triggered by a passing train.

Laming kept MS56 at anchor for a further 40 minutes, waiting for a train to appear, but none did. This was probably just as well; if they had opened up on it with the MS boat's armament, it would have alerted their position to every German boat and shore battery in the vicinity. At 1am, Laming throttled up the engines, weighed anchor and set course for Ortona.

On the way back, there was a minor emergency when one of the two dories, which were being towed alongside, started to take in water. Cauvain jumped into the dory and saved it by replacing a rope that had snapped between the stern and a cleat on MS56. Cauvain was later praised for his 'skill and presence of mind'.

They made harbour at Ortona, Robin's report concluded, at 3.55am.

In my desire to learn more about these missions, I had been working with a number of researchers to see if there was anything more that could be gleaned from official sources. One of these researchers had written to Dr Roderick Bailey, a Wellcome Trust Research Fellow at the University of Oxford, and an expert on SOE (as well as the author of several books on SOE and Italy). Dr Bailey, in amongst several pointers to some further official sources I needed to check, furnished a detail that possibly shed altogether new light on the nature of these missions, as well as providing a reason why Pop had been so reluctant to speak to me, or anyone else, about them.

Dr Bailey said that he had personally conducted several of the interviews of No.1 Special Force personnel who had been involved in the boat missions – interviews now held at the Imperial War Museum – and that the recordings, if I hadn't already listened to them, represented a vital resource.

I had made extensive use of these interviews, Pop's amongst them, but the key point was contained in Bailey's postscript, which pulled me up short.

'I also interviewed Robin Richards for the IWM,' he wrote. 'He and Bob Clark were together a lot. Robin was a really lovely chap. It was he who hinted at a story, which I was unable to get Bob to talk about – of an encounter between Bob and a German soldier on an Italian beach one night. *I got the impression that Bob may have had to kill him…*'

These beaches, even before I'd received Dr Bailey's tip-off, were integral to Pop's story – but there was a wider dimension to them as well.

The two operations that Pop had undertaken by MS boat thus far had been to the same area: Civitanova Marche, the site of the first agent drop-off and POW extraction mission, and Porto San Giorgio, the site of the second demolition operation, were both located on a point of coastline between two river mouths. The more northern of the two, at Civitanova Marche, was where the River Chienti joined the sea; the second, at Porto San Giorgio, was where the River Tenna, 15 or so kilometres to the south of it, also flowed into the Adriatic.

In addition to these missions, Robin and Dick Laming had made at least one trip to the same area before Pop arrived in theatre. *Why?*

I went back to the letters to see if Pop's correspondence with my mother shed any further light on this. On 20 April, he wrote to let her know that he was intending to go to Bari on Sunday afternoon to do 'a good time Charlie'. *Will you be a good time Caroline, as I thought we might go to the Sunday afternoon concert. Does that appeal? Or do you think it rather dreary? My only other suggestion is that we could walk – a little further than last time – along the coast towards the castle.* This, I knew, was an SOE facility located a few kilometres south of Monopoli on the coast. Later on in the note, he teased her about an attempt to *bring back your RAF type last night* – a reference to an RAF crewmember who was down behind enemy lines, waiting to be rescued; Mop and Nancy having jokingly and flirtatiously hinted to Pop and Robin that 'RAF types' were more glamorous than the dishevelled sea dogs of the para-naval force. Another letter, two days later, revealed his utter frustration with life in the Naval Office and made reference to the fact that in a week's time, in normal circumstances, he would have been sitting finals at Cambridge. Another letter talked about a singa-long in the mess with Alan Clark. This same letter, however, also told how, earlier that afternoon, Pop had had an 'enjoyable walk', in which he'd gone down to the port and had much 'fun and games' putting together a collapsible canoe. *How much I prefer doing that to pushing a pen or imitating pushing a pen in this office.* This reference to 'fun and games' at the port was a clue that he was preparing for another mission, the most important of his war to date. I knew that in May – less than a month away – Pop was due to undertake a mission in a col-lapsible canoe and that it was set to involve one of the more uncon-ventional military units to grace the Italian theatre of operations, in a list where irregular units were in long supply: 'Popski's Private Army'. All of this I knew from my research, but the revelation from Dr Bailey that Pop might have killed a guard in the vicinity of Civitanova – coupled to No.1 Special Force's curious, quasi-magnetic attraction to the beaches near the Chienti and Tenna river mouths – told me that I needed to weigh the data in situ and visit Civitanova for myself.

Chapter 9

'On a hair trigger'

Civitanova Marche, March 2016

Modern Civitanova is a port town three hours' drive from Bologna's international airport. Soon after checking into my hotel, which was located in the middle of an industrial park around a kilometre from the sea, I decided to head for the beach to see if I could find the mouth of the Chienti. It was after dark and raining when, following my sat-nav, I got as close as I could and parked up beside a low wall separating the coast road from the beach. Tired from the journey, and soaked from the rain, part of me was tempted to forget the whole thing and head back to the hotel. But the better part of me pressed on. Being here in March, at the dead of night, would, I hoped, give me a sense of what it must have been like for Pop on this same stretch of beach at the same time of year.

This was no tranquil, picture-postcard Mediterranean resort – the waves did not lap the beach here; they pounded it. And with the wind and the rain in my face, unable to rely on my sight and my hearing, I began to feel a little vulnerable. I had no idea if I was alone or if there were people out there, watching me, waiting. Even with the ambient light from the town, I could barely see 10 feet in front of me; in Pop's day, in the dark of the moon, he'd have been able to see even less. The noise of the shingle beneath my feet was drowned out by the sound of the waves – had I been a German guard, I realised, no one would have heard me until I was on top of them.

Is this what had happened? Here, or along the coast, maybe? Had Pop been surprised by a guard? As I stood on a spit of sand and shingle where the Chienti met the sea, I thought back to my time at Arisaig and the silent killing methods taught to Pop and his fellow students. Had my father, as detailed in the SOE instruction manual, had to attack from the rear and thrust his knife into a man's kidneys? Whether he had or hadn't, what had it been like for him, barely 20 years old on that first boat mission, rowing agents ashore and POWs back to the boat? It had been hard enough for me to find, and I'd had GPS at my disposal. How had Pop and the MS crew managed to navigate here?

And again, I asked myself, *why here?*

The following morning, I drove 15km down the coast to Porto San Giorgio, the scene of Pop's railway sabotage mission, and close to his 'Popski beach reconnaissance', the mission he would undertake next. The point where the Chienti River met the beach was overlooked by a 15-storey block of flats. The beach was strewn with broken bottles and there was evidence of old campfires.

It wasn't raining, at least, but the wind was blowing hard, driving the slate-grey clouds inland. The only other person on the beach was a woman sifting the shoreline for driftwood. Now, in the daylight, I struggled to see Pop here – this despite the fact that I had followed the railway line most of the way from Civitanova, the same railway line where Robin and his team of demolition experts had planted their charges, while Pop and Roy Taylor had guarded the dories they'd pulled up on to the beach. The line was exactly where the archive accounts had said it was: set back between 50 and 200m from the beach and running parallel to it – a highly exposed target.

Porto San Giorgio, this part of it, at any rate, had changed beyond all recognition since the war. This wasn't the case, however, with the place I drove to next. From an account I'd read in the definitive story of Popski's Private Army – the autobiography of the man himself, Colonel Vladimir Peniakoff – I had managed to pinpoint what I felt confident was the exact location of the beach landing, 'a point on the coast one thousand yards south of the Tenna River'. Choosing a spot overlooking another shingle beach, distinguished by a set of posts on which several cormorants were drying their wings, I parked the car, pulled out my laptop and opened up my notes.

'No.1 Demolition Squadron PPA' – as Popski's Private Army was more formally known – was an 80-strong group of British special forces that had distinguished itself during the North African campaign in a series of operations behind the lines, its primary task being the destruction of General Rommel's fuel supplies. It was led by the colourful Major – later Lieutenant Colonel – Vladimir Peniakoff DSO, MC, who had been born, as noted earlier, in Belgium to Russian-Jewish parents in 1897. After studying at Cambridge and becoming an ardent Anglophile, Peniakoff served with the French Army in the First World War. He then joined the British Army in the Second World War, taking on the role of an Arabic translator in a unit called the Libyan Arab Force Commando (LAFC). Learning tactics from the legendary Long Range Desert Group, he developed an aptitude for special operations and transformed the LAFC into a highly effective fighting force. When the LAFC was disbanded, Peniakoff formed No.1 Demolition Squadron. It earned the nickname 'Popski's Private Army' due to a British inability, or perhaps a bloody-minded refusal, to pronounce 'Peniakoff'.

PPA was amongst the first British military units to arrive in Italy. Soon after landing at Taranto, it was given the job of intelligence-gathering and partisan support. It consisted of three fighting patrols, each composed of 18 men in six heavily armed jeeps and a mobile tactical HQ. PPA quickly added parachute missions, mountain warfare and amphibious operations to its roles and capabilities – and it was in the latter capacity that it was to cross paths with Pop. Sometime in late April or early May, Pop was briefed on a mission codenamed 'Anon' that required him and Robin to pilot a pair of two-man canoes to a spot close to the mouth of the Tenna. The mission differed from earlier ones in that it was designed to pave the way for an amphibious landing by PPA. A beach reconnaissance was altogether different from the agent drops and sabotage ops Pop had undertaken before.

As before, it had started with a departure in an MS/MAS boat from a forward operations harbour – Termoli, I learned, this time – with the boat approaching the target area as close as its crew dared before deploying the canoes. These were two-man canoes that would allow Pop and Cauvain in one, and Robin and Taylor in the other, to take shore samples and depth soundings that would feed into Popski's plans for the beach landing itself.

As with most of the missions handed to No.1 Special Force, it all happened very quickly. Pop had written to Mop the night before departure to say that he had 'done all the things he ought to have done' and that the only thing he had forgotten – and this was meant as a joke – was his 'last will and testament'. He also loaned her his watch for safekeeping, ostensibly because hers was being repaired, but the jollity, I could see, hid a deep anxiety on his part. At one point, he apologised that his writing in bed was worse than usual, blaming his nerves. The next night, he set sail in the *Eduardo* for Termoli, arriving there on 13 May. There, he wrote to Mop again. *Roy [Taylor] is opposite me, writing on deck. Robin arrived at Termoli an hour before us.*

At Termoli, two nights later, they picked up MS64, the boat that would take them north. MS64, as far as I could tell, was skippered for the mission by Dick Laming – just the man you'd want for an operation like this – a safe pair of hands. According to a report on 'Anon' in SOE files at Kew, the canoes were put over the side around half a mile from shore. Mk1 canoes were assigned, the kind that had been employed so effectively by commandos in Operation Frankton, the raid on German shipping in Bordeaux in December 1942 made famous by the post-war film *Cockleshell Heroes*. Chequered dipsticks were used for depth sounding. Plotting the location of the sandbars was laborious work – every reading had to be jotted down in a heaving and rolling sea. The use of torches so close to the shore was out of the question, so the party was equipped with a simple but ingenious invention: luminous hemispheres the size of golf balls that were held up to the pads so they could see what they were writing. The balls could also be used to signal the mother craft when they paddled back out to sea. A No.38 Mk3 portable radio set was used for communication between the canoes and MS64. The radio, in its canvas carrying-bag, was fixed between the two canoeists. The operator whispered into a microphone; instructions from MS64 were received over headphones.

Paddling to within a few hundred metres of the shore, the two canoe parties split up. Robin went to the north end of the beach to collect a sample of the shingle, while Pop moved a short way to the south to take his depth soundings. These details were all contained in the mission report. Around a kilometre from where the Tenna met the sea, the river – little more than a stream when it wasn't swollen by winter rains – opened out into a muddy flat around 150m wide. Here, the slow-moving water divided into rivulets, each dropping its silt on to a series of sandbars that ran parallel to the shore. Only the sandbars nearest the beach were visible. The others, at varying depths, needed to be plotted meticulously to allow Popski's landing craft to make it safely to shore. I looked up and could see some of the sandbanks – the first of them marked by the posts on which the cormorants sat. The combination of being here with information supplied by the wartime post-action reports was extraordinary. With very little imagination I could begin to see exactly what had happened on this beach 72 years earlier.

Either side of the river mouth, I could tell, Robin would have been able to see the silhouettes of a number of houses. There would have been no lights. The area, like everywhere else they had landed clandestinely, was on high alert for incursions such as this. He and Taylor would have paddled slowly towards the shore, a point where the last visible sandbar, the nearest to the beach, met the gently rolling waves. Riding the canoe on to the shingle, Robin would have hauled himself out of the craft and quickly collected his samples.

When he had finished, he and Taylor would have then paddled back to MS64, taking depth soundings as they went. Pop, meanwhile, had closed in on his section of shoreline a few hundred metres to the south. On this particular night, the report said, the sea was calm and the waves lapped gently along the shoreline. Everything was going to plan until, suddenly, Pop and Cauvain spotted figures on the beach. They stopped paddling and turned the canoe nose-on to the movement to minimise their silhouette against the horizon. Seconds passed. They scarcely dared to breathe. What had they seen? Squinting through the gloom, Pop was able to resolve what looked like an anti-aircraft gun. As they held the canoe steady, both he and Cauvain were agreed: the men on the beach were a flak crew. The emplacement was a few hundred metres from where they were supposed to take their soundings. Thirty seconds passed. Then a minute. They had half-expected to hear a barked command, rifles being cocked or, at any moment, to be blinded by a searchlight. But, as their nerves settled, they knew that if they had been spotted, something would have

happened by now. With slow strokes, they began once again to pad-
dle towards the beach. With one of them keeping close watch on the
gun emplacement and the soldiers, the other took the soundings. Pop
had once told me that the Germans' capacity to do everything by rote
had been an advantage when working behind the lines. He knew,
effectively, that if a patrol passed, it would be back exactly 30 minutes
later – on the dot. The report stated that the first sounding was taken
15m from the shore and the last approximately 800m from it. By then,
they were almost back at MS64. As soon as they had been picked up
by Laming, they stowed the canoes and MS64 was reversed slowly
towards the beach under the power of its stealthy propulsion system,
taking one last depth sounding 650m out from the shore, while the
entire crew kept a steady watch on the gun emplacement. They were
on a hair trigger to give it everything they'd got if the alarm went up.
When they had finished taking the final reading, Laming inched the
throttles forward and they headed back to Termoli, where they lost
no time in reporting the size, depth and position of the sandbars and
the composition of the beach's gradient: one in seven.

I closed the laptop and looked back out to sea, my eyes following
the path MS64 had taken back to Termoli. Being here had allowed me
to draw one important conclusion. If Pop had had to kill a guard, it
had not been on this beach – and it hadn't been at Civitanova either.
Both were shingle beaches. The rubbish-strewn beach at Porto San
Giorgio was an altogether quieter stretch of shore – the only location of the three where you'd have had some forewarning of a guard's
presence. And the accounts had been quite clear. At Civitanova, Pop
had landed agents and taken POWs off the beach back to the waiting MS boat. There had been no hint in the post-action report of an
incident. At the Popski beach, he and Cauvain had remained in their
canoe throughout the mission; that much was evident, too. That left
Porto San Giorgio, the mission in which he and Taylor had guarded
the dories on the beach while Robin's demolition party had planted
explosives on the track. Call it my imagination, but there had been
something about the place; somewhere I could picture Pop's war having changed in a heartbeat – from operations in which 'mucking

around in boats' had been the kind of adventure he'd always craved, to something that had left a shadow, one best never to speak about.

A month later, on 14 June, a single landing craft tank (LCT) made its way in the pre-dawn light towards the spot that Bob and Robin had reconnoitred. On board were Royal Marines Commandos of 9 Commando charged with picking up 150 POWs who had escaped and congregated in the Ancona area. Accompanying the Commandos were a dozen heavily armed jeeps of the PPA as well as Major Vladimir Peniakoff, Popski himself.

What happened next bordered on the catastrophic. The aim of the landing was to deposit Popski and the jeeps on to the beach, the patrol then linking up with a 'foot party' of PPA that had made its way to the landing area previously – some having arrived overland, others having been landed nearby by boat. The men, numbering around 70 altogether, would then move off into the open countryside in the jeeps, gathering intelligence on German troop movements stirred up by the Allies' summer offensive, which had commenced the previous month, after troops that had been dug in south of the Gustav Line had managed to link up with their colleagues in the Anzio pocket. With this combined force breaking out on 23 May, the Allies met little resistance all the way to Rome, which fell on 5 June. After this, the Germans retreated north in what at first constituted little better than a rout. In the ensuing chaos, Popski had calculated that his force would have plenty of opportunities for mischief – blowing up bridges and shooting up German columns: classic Popski operating tactics. The mission was codenamed Operation Astrolabe.

But what no one had factored into this plan was the extent to which the roads would be jammed by Germans retreating to new defensive positions as the Allies' summer offensive rolled northwards. Captain Robert Yunnie of PPA, who had landed in the area two nights previously by boat, had passed word back that the landing area was straddled by two distinctive pine trees – but whether these trees were ever identified as markers in Pop and Robin's report is unclear; it certainly seemed doubtful, based on what happened next.

Yunnie, accompanied by two PPA 'patrolmen' and two Italian partisan guides as he waited for the LCT to hove into view, signalled that the landing could go ahead; this despite the chaos of retreating Germans all around them. Yunnie, it seemed, was reluctant to cancel the mission; this, he felt, being a decision that should be left to Popski. In the resultant confusion, and realising that the tactical picture as they had envisaged it had changed, Popski took the decision to scrub Astrolabe. But he had left it too late. Charging in towards the beach, the LCT had hit a submerged sandbar and ground to a jarring halt. An escorting motor torpedo boat (MTB) also hit a sandbar, but managed to refloat before retreating 300m offshore. This was at 11.30pm. Too far from the shore to disembark his jeeps, Popski walked up to the road, which at that point was around 600m from the beach, and found an entire convoy of German trucks inching its way steadily north. He also spotted machine-gun posts on the bridges and had been told by Yunnie and the partisans with him that Porto San Giorgio was crawling with Germans, as well – all of them unaware of the landing party that was stuck fast on the beach. Realising their situation was hopeless, Popski gave the order to abandon ship and for everyone to make their way back to the waiting MTB. This was no simple matter as the LCT had 73 heavily armed commandos on board. In his book, Popski gave a minute-by-minute account of how he managed to get the soldiers back to the MTB: by taking the tyres off his vehicles and using the inner tubes as life jackets. He linked each man to a rope and, using a small boat, towed 11 of them at a time from the LCT to the MTB 300m offshore. This was painfully slow work and he only just managed to get the last man off the LCT by first light, when the Germans realised what had been taking place under their noses. The jeeps and the landing craft, however, were irretrievable and had to be destroyed. Captain Yunnie and his party declined to be taken and, in staying behind, operated in the immediate rear of the retreating enemy for several days. According to his citation recommendation at The National Archives, he caused 'considerable confusion' and managed to overpower a German demolition team that had been about to blow up a bridge, preserving it as a vital river crossing for the advancing Allies. For this, he received a Military Cross (MC).

Two days later, PPA set off in replacement jeeps for those it had lost in the LCT, this time travelling overland. Moving northwest towards the Umbrian capital Perugia, the small force – by now reunited with Yunnie's party – crossed the 5,000-feet-high Sibillini mountain range, one section of it being so steep that it could only be negotiated by the jeeps reversing up the slopes, after the loads had been removed and manhandled by the men. The Germans on the other side were taken by complete surprise, the patrol capturing the town of Camerino and handing it to local partisans to hold until the arrival of the main Allied advance. Quite what happened on the 'Popski beach' remained unclear to me, but it seemed that somewhere between Pop and Robin delivering their report – filing the results to the appropriate authorities – and the landing itself, critical information had been scrambled, lost or ignored.

Poignantly, the two pine trees earmarked by Yunnie as markers for the landing are commemorated today by a pair of cypress trees standing on each side of the entrance to the PPA memorial at the British National Memorial Arboretum.

After the beach, I drove inland, heading for the hilltop town of Fermo, about 10km from the coast. In an attempt to discover why SOE had been so fixated on this area above all others it could have chosen along the Adriatic coast for its infiltration and sabotage missions, I had come across a website for an organisation called the Escape Lines Memorial Society – this, extraordinarily, thanks to a tip-off by my neighbour, Reg Francis, who knew all about it.

ELMS was dedicated to preserving the memory of people across Europe who had helped Allied POWs escape during the war, as well as commemorating the POWs themselves. The organisation had come to my attention because one of its groups was dedicated to the so-called 'rat-lines' – POW escape routes – in the Tenna Valley. After the armistice, SOE, in its SIMCOL operation – its first experience of missions behind the lines – had assisted A-Force/MI9 in rounding up as many of the POWs that had escaped as it could. There had been two major camps in the Tenna Valley: Camp 59 at Servigliano had held around 3,000 prisoners; Camp 70 at nearby Monte Urano around 8,000. There were so many POWs at large after the armistice that not all of them could be scooped up in the SIMCOL operation. As a result, many had stayed in the area, working as farm labourers, or in some cases joining up with local partisan groups. Many yet, however, had joined the rat-lines that had been set up specifically to allow them to get back to their own lines, with two ports being used for the exfiltration operations: Porto San Giorgio, the scene of the railway demolition op, and San Benedetto del Tronto, around 20km to the south. 'There can be little doubt,' the ELMS website said, 'that many of our fathers would not have survived had it not been for the bravery and humanity of local Italian people, and we owe their descendants a huge debt for what they did.' ELMS singled out one particular home as having been a key safe house for POWs awaiting evacuation. This house was called the Villa Salvadori and it was a name that was already familiar to me. Pop had spoken to me on a number of occasions about a man he had served with in SOE called Max Salvadori. Max, I had learned, was an Anglo-Italian of British nationality who'd volunteered to serve with the British Army and was accepted to join SOE in early 1943. The Salvadori family had been passionately anti-fascist and Salvadori himself had been arrested before the war by OVRA, the Italian secret police, for seditious behaviour and been sentenced to 10 years in prison. Pressure from an English cousin secured his release, but only on the condition that he agreed to go into exile. Max farmed for three years in Kenya and then secured a teaching job at a university in upstate New York. There he continued to maintain contact with Italian anti-fascists via groups that had settled on the US East Coast. After joining SOE, he gave invaluable political advice to Gerry Holdsworth at Massingham before engaging in active operations on the mainland, where he became a frequent visitor to Monopoli.

Under the name 'Max Sylvester' he organised the escape of Benedetto Croce, an anti-fascist liberal philosopher, from the island of Capri and was invited by the British to help in rebuilding a new Italian government when Rome fell, as it had done a few days before the Popski beach landing.

And here was his family home, the Villa Salvadori, at the heart of operations to bring escaped Allied POWs to safety. Max's mother, the

ELMS website explained, had been integral in helping many groups of escapers reach pick-up points on the beaches where I'd just been – 'an operation,' it said, 'fraught with danger due to the proximity of German troops, frequent bad weather and the difficulty in obtaining a boat to take the evaders out to a waiting vessel'. Didn't I know it! In a further twist, the ELMS website mentioned how a descendant of Countess Salvadori, Clara Muzzarelli, had helped numerous descendants of the escapers retrace routes taken by their fathers and grandfathers. I had tracked Clara down to an address in Fermo, which I thought might possibly be her house, but found nobody home. Turning to leave, I'd had the good fortune to bump into her on the way back from a trip to the shops. We swapped stories over the next two hours. By the time I left, I had two invaluable pieces of information. First, the reason why Pop kept coming back time and again to the region was clear – SOE had familiarity with the Tenna and Chienti valleys via the network of contacts it had made through the SIMCOL operation. Second, SOE had an even stronger link through Max Salvadori, a man who would bind even more directly to Pop's narrative in the weeks to come.

Chapter 10

'What next?'

Monopoli, May 1944

Pop had been back in Monopoli for just a couple of days when, according to his letters, he received orders that he was to be on the move again – this time overland. His letters revealed his frustration at being unable to spend any time with Mop; at one point, he let her know how jealous he'd been of Roy Taylor, because Taylor had bumped into her in town. *I hope the watch works now and that you won't have to disbelieve mine anymore,* Pop wrote to her. He had taken to calling her 'Half Pint', a reference to my mother's slim, diminutive stature. The tone told me just how much his affection for her had deepened while he'd been gone on the Popski mission.

Between Mop's unremitting shift work and the post-mission debriefing for Popski, Pop had been packing for a trip 'up country' with his boss, Hilary Scott, leaving no time in which to see her. The reason for this trip was hard for me to decode, but seemed to be linked to the unfolding strategic picture, which had shifted dramatically in the preceding weeks. On 11 May, the Allied troops that had been dug in for months south of the Gustav Line on the west side of Italy had begun their summer offensive, eventually breaking through on 15 May. Racing towards Anzio, they'd met little resistance, as many of the troops facing them had been withdrawn to Rome. Meanwhile, on 15 April, Gerry Holdsworth had sent a note to SOE headquarters informing his superiors that he was 'taking the opportunity of the naval section's reduced programme this non-moon to send AM11 by air to report to you'. AM11 was code for Hilary Scott. On the agenda, in the clipped telex-like style of the message, was an instruction for Scott to discuss 'future possibilities para-naval work Mediterranean' and the recommendation that he should 'also see the latest para-naval equipment'. It ended with the advice that Scott was expected to arrive 'about the 20th'. The message suggested the destination was London,

not Massingham. If this was the case, what could have been so important that it required the presence of a man with a small force under
his command – five officers, two dozen seamen and a ragtag flotilla of
boats?

What is clear is that by April 1944 the first phase of SOE's work
in Italy, in particular its infiltration of teams of Italian 'organisers' and
W/T operators to establish contact with known resistance elements,
was drawing to a close – and from the available evidence, and with
the benefit of hindsight, it was equally clear that discussions were now
starting to take place within the higher echelons of SOE over 'what
next'. Since mid-April, as was evident from Holdsworth's 15 April
message to HQ, SOE had been looking for new assignments for its
para-naval group. Upon Pop's return from the Popski beach, Hilary
Scott, his boss, I had learned from oral testimony provided by my
godfather, Robin, at the Imperial War Museum, had at long last found
one. 'We became amateur soldiers,' Robin relayed to the IWM. 'We
were taken out of our black naval battle dress and put into khaki' – a
relief, he went on to note, as, in the minds of the partisans, black was
the colour of the *fascisti*.

The 'up-country' expedition mounted by Scott and Pop, which
departed Monopoli around 20 May, was an attempt to justify a land-
based combat/reconnaissance role for the para-naval force. While ill-
documented officially, I had the advantage of being able to track it
unofficially via Pop's letters, and to make some judgements on what
it was trying to achieve. It almost certainly involved linking up with
local partisans, eventually in the Ancona area, the next strategic port
on the Adriatic to fall into Allied hands. By late May, Maryland had
successfully infiltrated multiple teams of 'organisers and W/T operators' – all of them Italian – to make contact with 'known resistance
elements', as a report in SOE's official archive called them. After eight
months of this activity (the strategy was first formulated at Massingham), these teams were 'sufficiently developed', the report continued,
to allow Maryland to start infiltrating 'British Liaison Officers'. These
BLOs were SOE personnel who would help organise the 'resistance
elements' into a cohesive fighting force.

The resistance groups were many and various, but broadly comprised Communists, Liberals, Social Democrats, Christian Democrats and Socialists – groups, in fact, reflected in Italy's diverse political arena today. They went at the time under names such as 'the Garibaldini' (Communists), the 'Action Party' (Social Democrats) and the 'Autonomous' group, the only one that was non-political. While the broad strategic picture may have been opaque to both Pop and Hilary Scott in May 1944, their tactical objectives would have been clear. The intention at this point, according to SOE's official history of the Italian campaign at Kew, 'was to acquire the largest possible coverage of Northern Italy by British Missions' (BLOs). Their 'up-country' trip, therefore, was most likely an attempt to see what was achievable; and, with pressure on him to re-role the para-naval force to justify its existence in Italy, Hilary Scott might even have shared what was at stake with Pop prior to their departure.

Pop, of course, could share none of this with Mop – certainly not in writing. *I am in the process of trying to pack my things, discovered in the corners of the room, and put them tidily into a case,* he scribbled to her just before leaving. *The result can scarcely be classified an unqualified success.*

I hope it's a good party tomorrow night and be good, as at the other times, and don't do anything I would not do! It's going to be an awful long time to the twenty-sixth without you, Half Pint, but I hope the time will take wings.

After the Anzio breakout and the liberation of Rome, the Germans, in disarray, began a fighting withdrawal towards Bologna, 300km to the north. It was in this fluid fighting front that Pop and Scott found themselves, roaming an area north of Ortona and south of Ancona: a strip of land 160km long and 40km wide, bordered to the west by the Apennines and to the east by the Adriatic. The front was poorly defined and troops on both sides frequently found themselves encircled one moment and encircling the next. The key Allied objective, however, was the port of Ancona, 40km north of Civitanova, the area Pop – and I – had got to know rather well thanks to his boat missions.

On this fast-moving battlefront, it was scarcely surprising that there was radio silence from my father for several weeks – or at least from his letters.

On 10 June, he managed to send a letter to Mop that read: *Your two letters arrived via Dick Mallaby today, owing to our whereabouts being too hidden.* Mallaby's mention was significant, as he was something of an SOE legend. He had been dropped into Lake Como the previous summer as part of SOE's initial operations in Italy, only to be captured. But, after sweet-talking his way into Italian military headquarters in Rome, he had ended up helping to negotiate the Italian armistice via a link provided by his radio set to Massingham and Eisenhower. Since then, he had been in Monopoli helping to train Italian agents in W/T procedure, where he would have been in close proximity to Mop.

Hearing, I felt sure, that he was headed north into 'bandit territory', she would have considered Mallaby a safe pair of hands for conveying a message to Pop. In the same letter, Pop told my mother that he had been 'languishing ill for the last two days'. He also indicated that he was thoroughly browned off with his new role: *I am wasting time here. It is now almost three weeks since we left.* He signed off with an apology for the paltry number of letters he had been able to write – there being *no such thing as a post office around here.*

Pop's letter back to Mop had gone unanswered. Unknown to him, she had caught a ride with a group of FANYs to Rome and was amongst the first female Allied troops to enter the city. It was an extraordinary, exhilarating 24 hours, she told me, and close enough to the liberation, just a week earlier, for them to have been swept off their feet by grateful and enthusiastic Romans. When she arrived back in Monopoli, she found Pop waiting for her. He was suffering from a mystery illness, exhausted and in dire need of rest.

Quite who ended up prescribing it was not clear, although it was almost certainly the avuncular Hilary Scott, who, by now, had witnessed the positive effect that my mother was exerting on his young protégé (or perhaps the subtle reverse of this, that without Mop Pop might have been rather lost) and appeared to have given the relationship his blessing. In any case, Pop was given several days off to recover and Mop was allowed to go with him.

Though not officially 'together', they set off on the three- to four-hour journey to Ravello, near Naples, ending up – and staying separately – at the Villa Cimbrone, a magnificent house on the cliffs overlooking the sea in what would become, soon after the war, a very fashionable resort on the Amalfi Coast. In an enlightened move, Gerry Holdsworth had started a 'leave rota' that allowed the men and women under his charge to stay there – an antidote, he believed, to the many pressures they were increasingly having to endure.

As David Stafford observed in *Mission Accomplished*, the villa had huge comfortable rooms with private baths and had once been a haunt of the Bloomsbury Group and a 'secret trysting site for Greta Garbo and the English-born American conductor Leopold Stokowski during their grand love affair before the war'. To a 20-year-old naval officer and a girl whose horizon had been bounded by the grey skies and drab streets of wartime Britain just six months earlier, their time together on the Amalfi Coast would have had an unreal, dreamlike quality about it.

Soon after their return to Monopoli, Pop, not wholly recovered, penned Mop a short note on an envelope, perhaps the only piece of paper he could find: *To Marjorie. Avec la memoire de sept journées très heureuses. Bob.*

When they returned to Monopoli, Mop returned to the blacked-out world of the Signals Office and Pop to the *Eduardo*. In the space of time they had been away, they had become the subject of tittle-tattle amongst the other FANYs. Writing to Mop in mid-June, Pop was clearly irritated by the gossips and people who wanted to see the relationship fail. Amongst them, sadly, was Nancy, upset that Mop wanted to spend her spare time with Pop instead of with her. Others seemed to think that they were too young to have embarked on the kind of passionate relationship they were now tumbling into headlong.

At least Hilary is on our side, Pop wrote. *Maybe we are young, but I know what I want.* My father made no bones that he wanted to be with her.

Things were not helped by the fact that they were both now unwell. Pop was still suffering from the mysterious illness that had afflicted him on his trip up country, but Mop had gone down with something worse – sweats and a high fever – symptoms that were soon identified as malaria. She was transferred immediately to the 98th General Military Hospital in Bari. Pop made the hour-long drive to the town to visit her and, on his return, and clearly upset at seeing her in the grim surroundings of a military hospital ward, wrote: *It is only a few hours since I saw you, but already it seems like a decade. For God's sake do not be too long in that awful place.* And then, encouragingly: *The best news I have had comes from the ever-charming Hilary, who says that malaria should only be a matter of a week. I do so hope that he is right.*

Malaria and jaundice – often from septic mosquito bites – were rife in Monopoli, even though Southern Italy was considered to be free of malaria-carrying mosquitoes. Scott, it turned out, was right and Mop *was* back at Monopoli within a week. She was plunged back into the dim, airless world of the Signals Office. Surrounded by disapproval from her FANY colleagues, she had effectively been sent to Coventry. And Pop had gone again. He had been redeployed up country, where the fighting for Ancona was intensifying.

On the night of 12/13 June, a little over a week before Pop ventured north again, Major John Henderson, a name I had not previously come across, was dropped behind the lines near the town of Appignano, 20km to the south of Ancona. Henderson was accompanied by an Italian Army lieutenant and his radio operator – their task: to link up with the partisans and the Italian liaison mission codenamed 'Marcasite' to coordinate an attack with the British Eighth Army on Ancona. Marcasite, set up by SOE, had been operating in the region since the armistice. Henderson, who was fluent in Italian and had worked before the war in Turin, had joined SOE the previous October and had only just arrived in Monopoli when told that he was going behind the lines.

With a hornet's nest stirred by the Allies' summer offensive, Field Marshal Sir Harold Alexander, Commander-in-Chief, Allied Armies in Italy, had been conscious of the need for organisation in a theatre of operations that at times must have resembled utter mayhem. This was particularly true of the Adriatic sector. Partisans with their different political allegiances were permanently on the point of fighting each other as much as they were the Germans. The Corpo Italiano di Liberazione, CIL, a 24,000-strong unit of Italian Army regulars, which had been formed into a national 'Liberation Corps', was gathering between Termoli and Ortona to lend its support to the British V Corps, part of the Eighth Army. But CIL was short of proper weaponry.

On 16 June, Polish II Corps, under General Władysław Anders, was brought forward from British Eighth Army reserve to relieve V Corps, with direct orders to take Ancona. The port – for months the epicentre, along with Civitanova, for so many of the clandestine boat ops by the para-naval force – was deemed vital to the Allies' logistical needs, which were struggling to be supplied by the west coast port terminal at Anzio and its eastern counterpart in Pescara – Pescara being a few kilometres up the coast from SOE's forward operating MS/MAS base at Ortona. On 17 June, Gen Anders was given command of the entire Adriatic sector, allowing the rest of the British Eighth Army to concentrate its offensive on the western, inland side of the Apennines.

Hopes were still high just a week after Henderson's infiltration that Ancona could be taken with a force of 500 well-armed partisans and a British parachute battalion dropped just outside the city. But General Anders's push north quickly ran into stiff German opposition, forcing him to postpone his attempt to take the city, initially to 4 July and later to the 17th. In the midst of all this, the parachute assault was cancelled and Henderson, finding his command post overtaken by the Allied advance, had no choice but to return to Monopoli to report on all the frustrations. It was into this melting pot of uncertainty and confusion – somewhere in the hinterland around Ancona – that Pop and his boss now found themselves. On 22 June, Pop managed to scribble a note to Mop that he had spent the first two days of the trip 'huddled in a PU'. The PU, I recalled, was the troublesome Morris Commercial tactical communications truck that had so vexed Captain Scott-Job upon its arrival in Italy the previous year. But things were about to get a great deal worse.

Later that day, Pop was summoned to return briefly to Monopoli to be given what he later described to Mop as 'devastating news'. The

men of the para-naval force were all being offered a straight choice
– evidence in itself that the attempt to re-role them to the kind of
mission he now found himself in had failed: they were either to volunteer as BLOs for behind-the-lines operations or be sent to the Far
East. Upon hearing this – most likely from Holdsworth or his deputy
Dick Hewitt – Pop went to see Mop, only to find that she was sick
again. He told her he had already made his decision: he would remain
in Italy to be with her. Within the hour, he was heading north again.

What a nightmare yesterday was, he wrote to her on 23 June when he
was back at the PU. *I was almost shaken by the news.* A few paragraphs
later on, he said: *Why don't you go on leave, if you get the chance; it will
do you the world of good, for yesterday you did not look full of the joy of
spring.*

This wasn't altogether surprising. When I next saw Mop, I asked
her – had the malaria come back again? No, she told me. It wasn't
malaria this time, but jaundice. But this, she told me, hadn't been the
real issue. Quite simply, everything had started to overwhelm her.
Meanwhile, the pressures in the Signals Office – the W/T work that
she detested – had become too much.

To her, the alternative Pop had been offered was no alternative at
all. Had he gone to the Far East, she might never have seen him again.
But by volunteering for BLO missions behind the lines, he might be
captured or killed. 'Looking back on it, I think I had some kind of
breakdown,' she said.

Barely a week after returning from Ravello, Mop was soon heading
there a second time, only this time not to the Villa Cimbrone, but to
the infinitely grimmer surroundings of a 'rest camp'. Not wanting to
worry my father, she had kept the news from him, knowing he had
enough on his plate.

In the midst of soldiers, mostly young guardsmen, injured and
burned out by battle, she saw a different side to the war. 'There was
none of this business about it being a privilege to die for one's country,' she said. 'They were all absolutely terrified by the prospect of
going back to the front line.'

Pop wrote that on the evening of 23 June the defective PU had broken down in Vasto, a coastal town halfway between Termoli and Ortona. Two days later, having completely given up on it, he and Hilary transferred to a 15cwt (UK hundredweight) truck to continue the journey north. They spent the next night in the house of a local countess in 'newly won territory', which told me they were by now close to the scene of his Popski beach reconnaissance at Civitanova. *Hilary*, he wrote, *played the piano*. I wanted to know: where was this house with the piano and the countess? As it had been in an area I had become familiar with, albeit a little bit, from my visit, I started to obsess about how I might find out. It didn't seem, though, as if I'd have much luck, Italy being brimful of countesses – as well as villas with pianos. Two days later, Pop wrote to Mop that it was now almost a week since Hilary and he had departed Monopoli, but there was still no word in any of his letters – as you'd expect – regarding the nature of the mission itself. It seemed highly probable, however, that it had been geared towards investigating alliances with partisan groups in the taking of Ancona.

Our destination is not in our hands yet, Pop wrote. Indeed, the long-planned assault on Ancona had not even begun. Polish troops had become bogged down in the face of fierce resistance as they'd tried to cross the Chienti between Civitanova and Macerata, a hilltop town with commanding views from its picturesque centre across the plain to the sea. Macerata was the last major hotspot of German Resistance before Ancona. By this point, the *Mutin* had been sailed north to offer base and logistical support from harbours just this side of the front line. On 28 June, Pop wrote that he was writing to her from the *Mutin, kicking his heels with a truck as our home and generally finding bed to be rather hard*. It was clear that he didn't know that Mop had collapsed – or that she was back in Ravello; and it was probably just as well. *My life has been centred around the back of a truck on a very bumpy road, as dusty as the Ravello journey, but this time I have not had the charming company*, he wrote. He was clearly missing my mother very much: *I wonder when we will see each other again. It cannot be too soon. We can only hope.*

The following day, the Germans evacuated Macerata, paving the way for its occupation by CIL troops, which by now had moved to support the Polish assault on Ancona. Soon afterwards, Henderson and Mallaby arrived in Macerata to meet with the partisans in order to make an assessment of the operational lessons thus far – lessons that might be useful in the drafting of plans for the widespread insertion of BLOs into Northern Italy. *I almost had the opportunity to come back on a flying visit to Monop*, Pop wrote to Mop on the 29th, the day that Macerata fell. The only thing that had stopped him, he added, was the fact he wasn't sure where Mop was. *I thought you might either be on leave or on shift in that frightful five to midnight*, he said. He knew nothing of her breakdown or of her being sent to Naples to recuperate.

I was sent here to be with Hilary and I do not think he approved of my going back, Pop said in the end.

Hilary, it turned out, had driven into Macerata for a meeting with Henderson and Mallaby. They were joined, I'd read in an account of this meeting, by Max Salvadori – and, at that moment, the penny dropped.

The villa where Pop had stayed – where Hilary had played the piano – could only have been Villa Salvadori. The countess had been Max's mother.

After their meeting, Scott concluded in a handwritten note to Holdsworth that Henderson was 'not ideal' for liaison missions, being too abrupt and off-hand to deal with the partisans effectively. It was his assessment and Salvadori's assessment in general, however, that much useful experience had been gained from the close cooperation of a British Liaison Officer with the partisan units. Another conclusion, according to David Stafford in *Mission Accomplished*, was that the 'higher authorities' within the Allies' command structure had lacked any policy on the disarming and dispersal of bands of heavily armed partisans once a major town or city had been captured from the Germans. These partisan bands, especially when infiltrated by Communist elements, the British held, became as dangerous in the aftermath of the capture of a city as they had been useful before it.

Scott gave his handwritten note to Salvadori to deliver personally to Holdsworth, and Pop took the opportunity to hand him a note for my mother at the same time, telling her: *Max is off to Rome where he will post this for me.*

With the capital now in Allied hands, Salvadori was in fact due to meet with Harold Macmillan, Churchill's personal representative in the Mediterranean and the future British prime minister. Macmillan had come to Rome to persuade Salvadori to assist British efforts to rebuild the Italian political system – the subtext being that the system itself would have to be one that was approved of by the British. Salvadori would end up telling Macmillan that he preferred to stick to active resistance until all Italy was free.

On 8 July, with Polish forces now poised to take Ancona, Pop wrote to Mop from 'A Comfortable Resting Place' – a location he later identified as a villa close to the front line, which I now knew as the Villa Salvadori:

> *Darling Marjorie – I started to write a letter to you almost a week ago, which has now been torn up owing to antiquity… My fortunes have been fluctuating considerably – on several occasions, either alone or with Hilary, there have been opportunities for our temporary return, but as yet, darling, no luck at all; and how I regret it.*
>
> *We cannot complain about our life here, for it is very lazy, comfortable and luxurious. In this house we are quite spoiled – always eggs for breakfast, which has generally been at half-past nine…*
>
> *Yet, despite all this 'wizzo' living, I cannot say I have been content – all these new experiences are as nothing when I am missing you. It is now over a fortnight since the last time I saw you for five minutes and God knows when the next five minutes will be.*
>
> *How many of my past, illegible epistles have you received, posted from all corners of Italy?*
>
> *There was a Polish padre staying with us in this house and one day he went to bury some of the killed of his regiment and got blown up by a land mine. It is amazing how the news of the*

sudden death of someone you had been talking to a few hours earlier affects you.

Without any feeling of emotion, I heard of the casualties in Normandy... But somehow this one man, more than the five thousand killed on the second front, made me sit up and realize how very little we control our lives. How awful was the air hanging over the mess where he had been living...

I really must stop now, so until God knows when, all my love, Bob.

The main thrust for Ancona began a week later. Following a series of flanking manoeuvres, British and Polish troops cut off the German defenders from the northwest, driving them back towards the sea and from there into a retreat north. At 2.30pm on the afternoon of 18 July, Polish troops entered the Marche capital and moved rapidly to secure it. It had been a long and bitter fight. In a postscript to the Ancona campaign, Hilary Scott entered the city soon after its capture to meet with the partisans who would help set up its civil administration following the German withdrawal. Pop remained at the Villa Salvadori because he, too, had succumbed to jaundice and had become unfit to travel. He had lost weight and described himself in a letter to Mop on 20 July as feeling 'lost'. The others – Scott, Henderson, Mallaby and Salvadori – had all moved on, leaving him to recover alone. He hoped, he told my mother, to be back in Monopoli within a week.

This proved to be an accurate forecast – but what was also clear was that my father's return to Maryland coincided with a turning point in the mission of No.1 Special Force and especially for its para-naval contingent.

Within a few days, Hilary Scott would be sent back to Britain, his job in Italy done. With insufficient work for an active force of MS/MAS boats and support vessels, the 'fleet' – such as it had been – was effectively disbanded. The *Mutin* continued to serve as an administrative support vessel until such time as she headed back to England, which she eventually did in November.

The *Eduardo* was shipped to Taranto for a refit – one that would include at long last the provision of some much-needed deck armament.

Mop, recovering from the jaundice and nervous exhaustion that had seen her sent back to Ravello, returned to Monopoli, where she was reunited with Pop. She was told, to her immense relief, she would no longer have to work in the W/T section of the Signals Office; that her new task would be encoding and decoding inbound and outbound signals; a role, with her maths background, as well as temperamentally, to which she was better suited. Pop remained concerned for her health, begging her at one point *not to be a gubbins* and get sent back to the military hospital in Bari. This concern was particularly touching, I thought, given his own state of health, which remained precarious. He would spend the next three weeks in Monopoli recuperating.

Of the original members of the para-naval force, the only officers of the 'Helford Crew' to remain behind on active operations were Pop and Robin. Dick Laming returned to the UK via Massingham (it was Laming who would sail *Mutin* back to the UK, a trip he completed in November) and Tom Long found himself engaged on other duties. Roy Taylor received orders that he was being sent to Australia via the UK – I learned later that, on his transit through Britain, he would end up paying a visit to my grandparents, giving them some first-hand news of the girl their son had fallen in love with; his letters home having made it clear that my mother was someone special.

Gerry Holdsworth, meanwhile, had departed Monopoli to run SOE's Italian operations from Rome, leaving Dick Hewitt, his deputy, in charge of No.1 Special Force. Captain Teddy de Haan, a former trainee manager at the Savoy, was now appointed as Hewitt's deputy.

Uppermost in the minds of Holdsworth, Hewitt and his new second-in-command was how No.1 Special Force could best support the conventional war, drawing, in particular, on lessons learned in the liberation of places like Ancona and Rome. One immediate conclusion was that BLOs, with their knowledge of the local geography and partisan groups, were ideal problem-solvers in the complex environment of a recently liberated zone or city.

It was this lesson that provided the germ of an idea for how No.1 Special Force could best be employed in the uncertain months ahead; the idea being that BLOs should be dropped behind the lines to prepare for these conditions *ahead* of the enemy's withdrawal, as opposed to afterwards.

This thought – although only rudimentary at this stage – would be honed into the plan that would see Pop re-roled from a paramilitary to a fully fledged agent tasked with a range of missions in the heartland of the enemy.

Chapter 11

'No rules, nothing barred, all-in'

Monopoli, August 1944

In early August 1944, there was growing optimism amongst Allied military planners that fascist forces in Italy were nearing the point of collapse. During the summer offensive, the Allies had broken through at Cassino, breached the 'Hitler' and 'Gustav' lines, broken out of the Anzio beachhead and captured Rome. For almost two weeks, according to the official report by the Supreme Allied Commander Mediterranean, General Sir Henry Maitland Wilson – delivered to the Combined Chiefs of Staff and written immediately after the war – the enemy had been driven steadily northwards. Until, by 13 August, Allied forward troops were established on a line from the mouth of the Cesano River on the Adriatic through the mountains to the Ligurian Sea north of Pisa, where they found themselves up against a new and even more formidable German defensive fortification, the 'Gothic Line', which stretched from Pisa in the west to Rimini, roughly 80km north of Ancona, on the Adriatic.

With the liberation of Rome, the Allies turned their attention to the political structures that would need to be put in place in the vacuum created by the German withdrawal. Resistance groups – and this applied to most of Italy's major cities – were generally divided along familiar political lines, with particular concern amongst Allied planners over the influence of the Communists. As soon as they had reached Rome, the Allied powers moved to prevent the return of the king, eventually forcing him to hand power over to his son, Prince Humbert of Savoy, with the promise of a post-war vote on the future of the monarchy – a vote which resulted in its abolition in 1946.

Badoglio also resigned as prime minister and was replaced by Ivanoe Bonomi, who fronted a government comprising all the anti-fascist parties.

Within days, the new government approved a plan for the creation of a supreme military command for organising Italian Resistance, a body that shortly also assumed the mantle of the coordinating authority for all the political and military activities of the resistance movement in the north. Its mandate, however, became exceptionally difficult to implement in practice.

On 15 August, American and French troops launched an airborne and amphibious invasion of southern France, codenamed Operation Dragoon. The priority in Italy at this time, Maitland Wilson said, was to 'give the greatest possible assistance to Overlord [the D-Day landings in Normandy that had taken place two months earlier] by destroying or containing the maximum number of German formations in the Mediterranean'. The diversion of forces from Italy to deliver the assault on southern France 'placed a severe brake on the speed of our advance northwards through Tuscany, which by 13 August had practically come to a standstill,' he reported to the Combined Chiefs.

'Before it was possible to resume our forward movement it was necessary to regroup and readjust zones of armies and lesser formations,' Maitland Wilson said. Between the optimistic assessment at the beginning of August and the more downbeat appreciation of the position in the middle of the month, SOE had been tasked with devising a contingency plan in the event of a sudden German military collapse. This was focused on the strategically vital northwest – on a region roughly the size of Switzerland that is described by the provinces of Lombardy, Liguria and Piedmont. The plan postulated that a rapid German military withdrawal would follow an exit route northeastwards to Austria.

The SOE contingency strategy was known as the 'Rankin Plan' and covered a range of scenarios that were envisaged within a general and rapid German withdrawal. 'Rankin A' was projected as a static period in which German morale would collapse prior to a withdrawal order; 'Rankin B' was seen as the withdrawal period itself, during which retreating Nazi formations would be attacked and harried all the way by the resistance movement; and 'Rankin C' was projected as the immediate German post-withdrawal phase.

Given the problems encountered in and around Rome, Ancona and

Florence, which looked like being the next major city to fall, the Allies were most alarmed by the prospect of 'Rankin C' conditions – the chaos that would follow a German withdrawal before the arrival and stabilising presence of Allied troops. The main worry was the harm that heavily armed partisans might inflict on each other in the chaos following the enemy's departure.

Thoughts at this time of Spain and the civil war that had ripped it apart less than 10 years earlier were never far from the minds of Allied planners.

As David Stafford has made clear in *Mission Accomplished*, SOE's general conclusion was that, given the proper authority by the Allied leadership, SOE BLOs would be able to help 'significantly' via Rankin with a range of post-withdrawal tasks: from preventing the Germans sabotaging basic infrastructure, assisting in the rounding up of German and partisan weapons, harassing the enemy's retreat, preventing fascist atrocities and arranging local armistices. On the civilian side, they could help restore law and order, assist in the distribution of food and supplies, find re-employment for disbanded partisans and, with the support of the British Foreign Office and US State Department, do whatever needed to be done to foster the flowering of democratic institutions – as long as they were well disposed to Britain and America. Against this backdrop, a new face, Flight Lieutenant Christopher Brock of the RAF Volunteer Reserve (RAFVR), was drafted from SOE's Naples station to run Rankin planning. The ultimate version of the plan was that SOE should establish missions in the major northern cities of Milan, Turin, Trento and Genoa and sub-missions in the main provincial capitals. British and Italian teams already in the area would serve as the basis of the plan, supplemented by three wholly new missions equipped with radios, 13 'reinforcing missions' as well as another five to take over from existing Italian groups.

A number of initial conclusions about the type of person that needed to be dispatched into northwest Italy for Rankin missions almost pre-ordained that my father would be amongst them. A decision was taken not to brief personnel already in the field as it was felt that communicating the intricacies of Rankin would be too complicated as well as too risky over the radio. Another stated that No.1 SF should send in as many of the 'right sort of chaps with communications' as it could get its hands on – a directive that pointed unerringly towards men with the background experience of Pop and Robin.

On 25 August, all those who'd been handpicked for Rankin missions were summoned just outside Monopoli to the Castello di Santo Stefano for special briefings on what was expected of them as Rankin BLOs. Their duties, as briefed to them that day by Hewitt, de Haan and Macintosh – who had returned briefly following the capture of Florence to share his experiences there – were divided broadly into 'destructive' and 'constructive' operations: the former in support of the Allied armies marching north; the latter working with the Allied Control Commission, the body tasked with post-conflict administration, in post-withdrawal areas. Pop and Robin were amongst those who gathered at 'the Castle', as did fellow Helford old hands Eddie Cauvain and radio operator William 'Faithful' Banks. They found themselves in a large gathering and were told they would be joining the Rankin Plan in one of the 'reinforcing' capacities. There was an urgency to the proceedings that saw them poised for rapid deployment – ready to be dropped behind the lines within weeks. From the middle of the following month, Cauvain noted later that he was 'standing by for operations in the field'. In his personnel file at The National Archives, he recorded how he 'trained in parachute operations from 1 September for about ten days' at SOE's battle school at the airfield at San Vito dei Normanni, 10km outside the port city of Brindisi.

Banks was on the same course and Pop and Robin were likely to have been too. Pop had joked to my brother, Will, and me a couple of times that one of the reasons he felt drawn to operations behind the lines was due to the presence of a glamorous Italian *partigiana* at San Vito dei Normanni, with whom he received parachute instruction. My brother and I, however, knew that our mother would have given her a good run for her money. Pop maintained a variation of the line he'd given me as a child that parachuting was no harder than jumping off a 12-foot wall – that he'd turned up at San Vito at 11 in the morning and by four had made his first jump. All in all, he made around 10 practice jumps. Mop, as she'd once told me, had been invited to watch him make one of them, but the weather, which, according to Pop's letters, had turned stormy, thwarted this on more than one occasion. *It is probably just as well that you did not come tonight as the jumping was postponed due to wind*, Pop wrote to her. *However, all is well for Friday. We can eat out and then return to Para School to see me do our night jump around half-past nine.*

Mop finally got to see him jump in mid-September and recalled it when I spoke to her about it as a bittersweet experience. 'Behind the smiles and relief that he had landed in one piece, from that moment on I was just waiting for him to be dropped behind the lines,' she said. When we had returned to Monopoli shortly after Pop died, we had driven out to Brindisi to see if there had been anything left to observe of the wartime airfield – and to our amazement there was. The runway had long since been ploughed over, but it was still a military installation of sorts. When we pulled up at the gate and were stopped by a military guard, I was told it was now a storage depot. The depot was run by the UN, and given over to humanitarian relief operations, an appropriate echo of its wartime role as the airfield from which the Rankin teams – whose own brief was to prevent Italy descending into chaos after the German retreat – had taken off on their missions to drop behind the lines.

With the launch of a further Allied offensive on 25 August against the Gothic Line coupled with a string of Allied military successes throughout the early part of September, that day – the day when he would drop behind the lines – must have seemed very close. Pop, for his part, was trying to juggle his training commitments at 'the Castle' with moments when he could see Mop.

In addition to operational briefings, there was training at the nearby 'battle school', which Bill Pickering, the man who had had to radio the news of Michael Gubbins's death to SOE headquarters, described in *The Bandits of Cisterna*. Pickering detailed how his unit had been readied for life behind the lines 'by learning to sleep under the stars and [conjuring] up a five-course meal from a hedgerow'. Pickering also related how theory would be put into practice through exercises that saw them dropped without money into the foothills 150km away, with orders to return to Monopoli as quickly as possible, living on their wits without any form of assistance from Allied troops.

During this period, Pop wrote to my mother about the life that he saw them sharing after the war. Always methodical, he told her that he wanted to be able to look her father in the eye when he asked his permission to marry her and her father asked him back if he had the means to provide for her. His plan was to work for four years on 'Civvy Street' – at what, he wasn't quite sure yet – so he could save enough money for him to answer honestly: yes.

On 15 September, Pop told her that he was unable to come into Monopoli that evening as he had suddenly learned that his departure was 'imminent'. He told Mop that, 'all being well', he would probably fly on the Tuesday – four nights from then – adding: 'strict security!' That would leave Sunday, he said, as the only day for a party before he left for the airfield at San Vito and clambered into the aircraft that would fly him northwards.

It was reassuring for me that, after the spat with her FANY colleagues that had contributed to her spell in hospital in July, Mop's friendship with Nancy had been rekindled – Pop, in his letter, saying that she was invited too.

The next night, a big storm hit Monopoli. Robin and Roy Taylor, according to Pop's note to Mop that day, had departed the Castle – Taylor back to England; Robin to hospital, as now he too had succumbed to illness. Compounding the sense of gloom, Pop reported that someone had stolen the 500 Player's No.3s that Mop had entrusted to his care for safekeeping. Pop didn't smoke, but she did. He hoped that she would forgive him for not taking better care of them. As he wrote, he described to Mop how the doors and windows were banging throughout the old building – and, all told, the weather seemed to have dampened his morale. For the first time, his fears over what might lie in store for him surfaced in his writing. He must have been counting down the hours to the moment he jumped – now less than three days away:

I have been thinking of all the red letter days since January – the only record of time – and they all seem to have been spent with you: Ravello, Sunday afternoon at sea, parties and many others. Everything goes well until one gets to the question of where do we go from here? A greater uncertainty than the future can scarcely be imagined. God knows what will happen to me, when I shall come back or where to.

Pop, at only 20, would have been made aware by his briefers of the environment he would be parachuting into and the uncertain fate that awaited him were he to be captured. While there were conflicting views on the status in enemy eyes of SOE agents operating behind the lines, BLO personnel preparing for Rankin would have privately given little chance to their survival, owing to the increasingly unpredictable and brutal behaviour of the Germans and Italian fascists as the Allied armies pushed them back towards the Swiss Alps.

At Arisaig, Pop's instructors had devoted whole sections of the course to familiarising students with German interrogation methods. SOE manuals – in particular, one entitled *How To Be An Agent In Occupied Europe* – attested to the fact that the Gestapo could be expected to detain a suspect for as long as it took to obtain a confession. Here the watchwords were: 'No rules; nothing barred; "all-in".' Every effort, the manual stated, would be made to make the prisoner feel ill at ease both physically and mentally. Techniques employed to get prisoners to crack would include: wholly or partially stripping them, beating them up and threatening them with the firing squad. They could expect 'bully types', smooth types who would put sharp, concise questions to them and friendly types, offering food, cigarettes and other inducements to speak. The good cop/bad cop routine, but far more brutal. Is this what Pop had been put through – perhaps in the little stone hut that Henrik Chart had pointed out to me in front of Arisaig House, when I'd visited it months earlier?

In reality, the manual said, prisoners could expect their interrogators to circle back to the same question, suggestions that they had been let down by their friends and colleagues, and signed false 'confessions' from compatriots. To counter these and other techniques, students were taught to watch out for stool pigeons in their cells, the attentions of friendly warders and hidden microphones. When questioned, they were advised to speak slowly, clearly and firmly, not to answer simple questions immediately and to hesitate with more difficult ones.

Overall, instructors said, they should create an impression of 'being an averagely stupid, honest citizen, who was trying his best to answer questions intelligently and to deny everything you cannot explain'. SOE agents were occasionally issued with lethal 'L-tablets', because the organisation's leadership knew that there were limits to what the human body could take under torture. There is no evidence, however, that anyone at No.1 Special Force was provided with L-tablets for their missions behind the lines.

In the early autumn of 1944, the Allies estimated there were around 150,000 partisans in the hills and plains of Northern Italy, supported by 18 British and 15 Italian liaison missions – a number that, with hindsight, was wildly optimistic, but which reflected the growing confidence of the resistance movement in their fight against the Germans and Italian fascists. These resistance fighters, as Pop would have been briefed at the Castle, were made up of groups of differing political allegiances and were generally not well armed. This lack was of great concern to some Allied planners as they contemplated the bitter autumn and winter months ahead. Lord Selborne, the British minister responsible for supporting resistance efforts on the European continent, wrote to Churchill in October to voice his fears over what might happen should air-dropped supplies to the partisans in the north dwindle any more than they had already. 'Winter will be a hard time for the partisans and if we cannot send them the reinforcements and supplies they need, we shall be depriving ourselves of a valuable weapon, crippling our existing missions and laying numbers of Italian communities open to fearful German reprisals.'

This, in fact, had been happening ever since the armistice. Allied intelligence files were already filled with a disturbing number of accounts of reprisals and massacres involving Italian civilians and, as the Germans retreated northwards, their number and incidence were steadily increasing.

A particularly brutal and infamous example followed a bomb attack on a ceremonial procession of German Army and SS units in Rome on 23 March 1944. The bomb killed 30 soldiers and injured more than 60. Hitler immediately ordered reprisals – the shooting of 10 Italians for every German death. Three hundred and thirty-five locals, as well as political prisoners and Jews, were rounded up and transported to the Ardeatine Caves, a complex of ancient Christian catacombs southeast of Rome. The interior of the caves was lit by burning torches as the prisoners were dragged inside. Each was then forced to lie on the pile of those who had died before them before they too were shot in the back of the head. The youngest was 15; eight others not yet 18. The Germans' policy of executing 10 Italians for every German or fascist soldier killed by the resistance became enshrined within their reprisal doctrine as the German Army retreated to the Gothic Line.

By late summer, in a reflection of the optimism within Allied circles that the Germans were on the point of abandoning Italy altogether, attacks by partisan groups on German and Italian fascist military formations intensified.

Where their successes resulted in territory cleared of Germans or Italian troops loyal to the Fascist Republic – the Repubblica Sociale Italiana or RSI that had been established in north Italy in response to the armistice – many of them declared these areas 'free republics' in unilateral acts that infuriated the Nazi leadership. To counter these successes, Kesselring began to flood Liguria and Piedmont – the provinces in which SOE was intending to concentrate a high proportion of its Rankin BLOs – with more than 20,000 battle-hardened troops. These came from the *Wehrmacht*'s 34th Infantry Division, just returned from the Eastern Front and including pro-Nazi volunteers from several southern Soviet republics, and, on the RSI side, Black Brigades and Cacciatori degli Appennini, a unit dedicated to mountain warfare.

Throughout August, a series of clashes took place between partisan groups and fascist forces in the hinterland around the port of Imperia on the Ligurian coast. On the 17th, having failed in an attack against a partisan group in a valley just to the northwest of Imperia, the fascists rounded up and killed 24 local civilians, including two priests and 13 farm labourers who had been out cutting hay on the lower slopes of the valley. On 4 September, the Free Republic of Pigna was declared in the same area, provoking a swift fascist response. In their drive towards Pigna, German troops and Italian fascists surrounded a group of several hundred partisans who had been hiding out in a forest near the town of Rezzo in a mountainous region between Imperia and the town of Mondovi, just across the provincial border in Piedmont. The fascist forces – made up predominantly of experienced German infantry and artillery units – installed two heavy guns on a nearby hilltop and started to pummel the partisan positions, forcing the latter to counter-attack. The counter-attack was successful, allowing the partisans to break free of the cordon and regroup. At the beginning of October, a heavily armed fascist fighting force attacked the Free Republic, causing the enclave's collapse four days later. This event marked the start of a strategic retreat by the partisans across the mountains into Piedmont. Six partisans who were caught in the retreat were shot in the local town a few days later.

Heavily depleted, short of ammunition and with large numbers of walking wounded, the main partisan force descended on the isolated village of Fontane, a few kilometres south of the town of Mondovi, where they spent the next three weeks recovering and regrouping. The Mondovi district itself had been the epicentre of much partisan activity since the end of the previous year. In the weeks after the armistice, bands of soldiers from the area, most of them experienced mountain troops, returned home after years of fighting and disappeared into the surrounding hills and valleys before the Germans could round them up and put them into camps. Buoyed by strong support from the local populace, which was predominantly loyal to the king and the Badoglio government, these soldiers became the nucleus of the partisan movement in the Mondovi area. Politically, a number of these groups pledged their loyalty to Communism, but predominantly the partisans in the region were determined to remain 'Autonomous' – that is, free of any allegiance to a particular party.

Mondovi, as I knew all too well from our close ties for many years to the Curetti family – Sergio being the boy who had taken care of my father the night he dropped on nearby San Giacomo (landing in a tree and breaking his ribs) – was the area I needed to focus on; the mountainous Alpine area in which Pop would operate with the partisans for the best part of three weeks, as well as being the area in which he would be held following his capture, until his transfer to the jail at Turin. Geographically, the region was well suited to resistance. To the south of Mondovi – an ancient citadel on top of a hill with a new town built below it – lay a series of valleys spread out like the four fingers of a hand into the snow-capped mountains. It was in these valleys – the Val Pesio, the Val Corsaglia, the Val Ellero and the Val Casotto – that the partisans began to form themselves into fighting units in 1943–4 and to mount sporadic, but increasingly daring, attacks on the Germans. These soon attracted the attention of resistance leaders from the big northern cities, who arrived in the area during the autumn and early winter to provide organisational expertise.

What had started as a movement with little cohesion in late 1943 represented a real threat to the Germans by early 1944, prompting them to launch increasingly ferocious reprisal operations in the Mondovi area as soon as the first spring snow melts came. These culminated in vicious skirmishes and battles in the Val Casotto in March, resulting in hundreds of local civilians being rounded up, tortured, deported to Germany and killed. The Val Casotto battles were triggered by a new German tactic for flushing partisans out into the open – so-called *rastrellamenti* (singular: *rastrellamento*) or 'rakings'.

In an attempt to prevent further resistance, the Republican government dispatched to the area a former Black Brigade 'action squad' from Milan, the 'Ettore Muti' Mobile Legion (Muti, an Italian aviator and fascist politician, had died in a skirmish following his arrest the previous August), which established itself in the Val Casotto in the spring, hunting down, arresting and killing anyone in the area it suspected of resistance. In the summer of 1944, after a two-month lull in the fighting, the valleys were once again the scene of attacks and counter-attacks between the resistance and the occupiers. By September, spurred on by Allied victories to the south, many partisan units were able to push back into the valleys as well as into the Langhe region to the west. It was to these forces that the badly mauled Ligurian partisans made their way in the wake of the collapse of the Pigna

Free Republic to the south. By early November, the entire region to the south of Mondovi was seething with partisan activity.

What the resistance badly needed to be effective, however, was weaponry, which, by the late autumn, was in drastically short supply – a reflection of the condition experienced by Italian 'regular' forces, as earlier evidenced by the poor readiness state of CIL forces to the south and east.

The Germans' 34th Infantry Division along with hundreds of Cacciatori degli Appennini, meanwhile, chose Mondovi to garrison their forces as they prepared for action against the growing numbers of resistance entering Piedmont. One BLO, writing after the war, provided a cold assessment of the way in which the 34th and its Italian fascist partners went about hunting down partisans during this period. 'It can generally be said,' he stated in his report, 'that all captured partisans were inhumanly tortured before being killed.'

In planning for Rankin, SOE had decided in its wisdom that my father and his team would be dropped into the hills just to the west of Mondovi.

By September 1944, SOE was operating 33 missions in Northern Italy – the closest to Mondovi being one codenamed 'Flap' in the Langhe region. Others may have been geographically close as well, but due to the mountainous terrain were to all intents and purposes unreachable. Pop's party would be geared to operating on its own. It was little wonder he had allowed doubts about his safe return to surface in his letters to Mop. He was heading for exactly the kind of uncharted terrain – its dangers posed by occupying German and fascist forces and the twisted loyalties of the local population – that his briefers had warned him about in the preceding weeks.

Chapter 12

'Just cancel the op'

Monopoli, September 1944

The Rankin missions were ready to go in late September 1944, but, just as Pop and his comrades were preparing to depart, there came a shift in the strategic military picture. The Allied offensive that had commenced on 25 August came to a juddering halt with the capture of Rimini on 21 September.

The offensive had achieved remarkable successes – it had resulted in Eighth Army's breaking the Gothic Line, crossing the Apennines and reaching the Po Valley, home to the cities of Milan, Turin, Modena and Parma – but they had come at an enormous cost. As David Stafford observed in *Mission Accomplished*: 'The promised land of the plains quickly turned into "a green nightmare of rivers, dykes and soft water meadows", across which ran thirteen major waterways that formed formidable barriers against Allied armour.'

What was initially viewed as a lull was to turn into a postponement to offensive operations that was to last throughout the winter. On top of this, the weather had turned and looked like being obstinately bad into the autumn. As a result, the order came through from headquarters that the Rankin missions were to be put on hold. Brock, the RAFVR planner for the operation, proposed sending in the Rankin BLOs on other missions pending the resurrection of the Rankin brief. These operations would take the form of 'regular' SOE missions behind the lines: coordinating partisan attacks, ensuring partisan missions were in line with wider Allied military objectives and that the resistance movement was properly supplied with weapons during the coming winter. Brock also envisaged the BLOs adding 'anti-scorch' duties to this tasking. It was feared that the Germans would employ a 'scorched earth' policy as they withdrew from the industrialised cities and that if this were implemented on a widespread basis it would bring the country to its knees. This fear was summarised in a note

Holdsworth had written to Hewitt on 26 August: 'It appears that if the Germans succeed in totally destroying the white power [electrical] network in the north of Italy, this country has just about had it politically and economically for at least ten years to come.' He went on to reveal that SOE had been asked by American elements within the ACC – the post-war-focused Allied Control Commission – to do 'absolutely anything we can' with its partisan allies to avoid the destruction of basic infrastructure assets, if necessary, fighting 'to the death'. The fear uppermost in the minds of the British and Americans was that loss of basic utilities such as water and electricity would trigger the unrest that would, quite possibly, spark civil war.

Pop greeted the development with disappointment, even though it meant precious additional days, perhaps longer, with Mop. *The morale is not exactly soaring*, he wrote to her on 25 September, the day Rankin was postponed, *as we have just had another chap put into the party – a major who will be in charge.* The 'other chap' was Major Duncan 'Huffy' Campbell, a 30-year-old veteran of campaigns in Sudan, Egypt, Abyssinia and Libya. His personnel file at The National Archives recorded that he joined the Argyll and Sutherland Highlanders in 1933 and went on, as 'a somewhat restless spirit', to serve under secondment with the Sudan Defence Force before ultimately ending up in North Africa, where he fought with distinction, winning two MCs. Before arriving in Monopoli, Campbell *(pictured)* had been in Greece and Cairo, where he had become engaged to a FANY and signals planning officer at headquarters – before travelling back to the UK in a Sunderland flying boat. After a short spell of home leave, and a frustrating lack of cooperation from Baker Street on news regarding his next tasking – beyond the fact that it would be somewhere behind the lines in north-west Italy – Campbell decided to take matters into his own hands. A few days before he had been ordered to report to Monopoli, he had an appointment for two o'clock at Baker Street at the office of 'a certain captain', as he referred to him in an unpublished memoir written many years after the war. The meeting was to arrange the travel papers that would allow him to get to Italy. By 2.30pm, the captain still had not turned up and Campbell found himself becoming more and more impatient. As the minutes ticked by, and judging that the secretaries knew what his transport orders were anyway, Campbell suggested they finish off the paperwork and let him get on his way. Somewhat to his astonishment, they agreed. With the papers safely in his hands and still with no sign of the offending SOE captain, he turned to one of the secretaries before leaving the office and said: 'Where the devil is your officer anyway?'

'He hasn't got back from lunch yet,' she replied, barely lifting her eyes.

'This sort of thing tended to confirm the fighting man's opinion of the staff,' Campbell noted in his memoir.

Major Duncan Campbell was a highly regarded, brave and skilful officer steeped in old-school military values. He did not suffer fools gladly and, by his own testimony, had a tendency towards impatience – a characteristic that, in a no less honest appraisal of the mission he was about to lead behind the lines, would raise the stakes against it from the instant that it hit the ground.

The mission, No.1 Special Force had determined, was to be code-named 'Clarion' and would consist of a six man team. Campbell would lead it with Captain Colin Irving-Bell, an Italian-speaking regular officer of the Royal Norfolk Regiment, as his deputy. Irving-Bell had at the last minute substituted for another Italian-speaker, Captain Robert Bentley, who had been posted to Maryland from a job with Civil Affairs in the Tripolitania region of Libya. Bentley was removed from Clarion for reasons that would emerge later. My father, as a sub-lieutenant, was the next most senior member of the team.

The three officers were supported by a corporal named Stephens and the two Helford old hands, Cauvain and Banks. They were to be dropped into the Langhe, the hilly area west of Mondovi. Pop's experience of land/sea missions would have been useful, if not vital, if it came to a need to supply the partisans in Liguria and Piedmont by sea. This, it seemed, was the primary rationale for Clarion's inclusion of an experienced three-man para-naval team.

Clarion's reception party was the nearby 'Flap' mission, which was led by an SOE BLO called Major Neville Darewski, who had been in-theatre for several months. Darewski, who had adopted the *nom de guerre* 'Major Temple', was the 30-year-old son of a Polish-born music hall composer and an English actress. His job was to build and fortify links with the resistance movement in western Liguria. Flap was one of several missions designed to support the US/French-led invasion force that had landed on the French Riviera on 15 August. The idea, ambitiously, was to link Italian and French partisans in cross-border operations against the Germans in the High Alps. These operations, which were organised not by SOE but by another Massingham-based unit tasked specifically with assisting the Operation Dragoon invasion force, were unsuccessful, but did help to underpin the mission foundations for Clarion. Operating alongside Darewski were partisan formations – around 3,000 men in total in the late summer of 1944 – under the command of Major Enrico Martini, codename: 'Mauri'. Mauri *(pictured p.159)* was an ex-'Alpini' and a colourful character. Forty years old, built stockily, with piercing blue eyes and an affected dress-style, he moved 'always with a personal bodyguard of handpicked young men', according to one contemporary eyewitness account. Bill Pickering, who had earlier, and more prosaically, described these same partisans as looking as if they had emerged from an 'end of war jumble sale', noted that 'Mauri's polite but assertive manner singled him out from his men, who obviously adored him.'

One man named Carluccio Dalmasso – a sprightly 89-year-old when I met him on one of my several trips to Mondovì, but little more than a boy when he joined the resistance – had served for a while as one of Mauri's bodyguards in 1944. Like many of his fellow *partigiani*, Carluccio *(pictured p.160 between Tim Clark and Sergio Curetti's daughter Daniela)* had joined the resistance, he said, because he was young, impetuous and looking for adventure. This, however, masked a number of reasons for taking up the fight against the Germans and Italian fascists. Men and boys like Carluccio generally faced three choices: deportation to Germany to work; recruitment by the fascists; or joining a partisan unit. Many chose the latter because they were starving and there was a perception in the towns and villages that the partisans were better able to live off the land. 'So, I went into the mountains in December 1943 to try something new,' Carluccio told me – to begin with in the mountains close to Mondovì and later in the Langhe, where food was in marginally better supply.

Initially, there was little to no organisation amongst the partisan groups, or within them, and Carluccio professed to hardly knowing one end of a rifle from the other. It had needed a man like Mauri, he said, to pull the disparate bands together and instil in each the discipline that would be needed to engage the Germans. With the armistice, Mauri had left his position with the Italian General Staff and made his way to Piedmont, where he professed his desire to fight against the German occupation. Captured soon after he arrived there, he was imprisoned in a concentration camp in Tuscany, but quickly managed to escape. Returning to the Mondovi area, he moved rapidly to establish and command the 1st Group Alpine Division, an 'Autonomous' unit that operated independently of the CLN, the Committee for National Liberation, which represented the six main anti-fascist parties: the Communists, the Socialists, the Christian Democrats, the Labour Democrats, the Liberals and the Action Party. The CLN, and its Milan-based northern sub-group, the CLNAI, the Committee of National Liberation for Northern Italy, was opposed to the king and the Badoglio government. Mauri, on the other hand, was a Badoglio supporter and Autonomous military units, including his 1st Group Alpine Division, wore blue or 'Badoglian' scarves as a sign of their allegiance. By March of 1944, Mauri's units were at last ready to fight.

The 1st Group Alpine Division operated on the Piedmont–Ligurian border and, under Mauri's leadership, was divided into a number of sub-units – called 'divisions' and 'brigades' – that operated in the valleys to the south and the west of Mondovi. Two key units were the 4th Alpine Division under Colonel 'Alessandro' – Pier Alessandro Vanni – and its subordinate unit, the 15th Val Casotto Brigade under Lieutenant Ezio Aceto, which had been based in the suburbs of Mondovi until driven into the countryside by German attacks; and the 3rd Alpine Division led by Captain Piero Cosa, whose headquarters was in the village of Prea, close to Rastello, in the Val Ellero south of Mondovi. Carluccio initially joined the Val Casotto before moving into the Langhe, linking up with Mauri's leadership organisation and becoming one of his bodyguards. Mauri, he said, operated a flat organisational structure, with no more than 20 people acting as the 'organisers' of the divisions under his command. The term 'division' obscured the fact that in the early stages of his resistance operations some of them barely contained 100 men.

Before he'd left Bari, Darewski – a.k.a. 'Temple' – had been told by de Haan that his brief for 'Flap' was to ascertain the character and fighting potential of Mauri's partisans, as well as their needs for arms, supplies and instructors. If the character of Mauri and his men was anything to go by, the situation in the Cuneo sector, at least, looked encouraging. But they had had a real time of it.

Soon after Mauri's partisans had become fighting fit in March 1944, the Germans launched their first *rastrellamento* up the Val Casotto; this after the partisans had started to attack German vehicle movements on the Turin–Savona road. Different partisan units trained in different skills and missions – the Val Casotto's was in attacking garrisons and capturing German weapons. It was only now that the Germans began fully to appreciate that men they'd initially branded as 'criminals and bandits' presented a serious threat to their security. The *rastrellamenti* were devised to restore order and the rule of law.

The first *rastrellamento* was so fierce that it took the partisans by surprise. 'The Germans destroyed everything,' Carluccio told me, as I sat and drank coffee with him in the piazza of the old town of Mondovi,

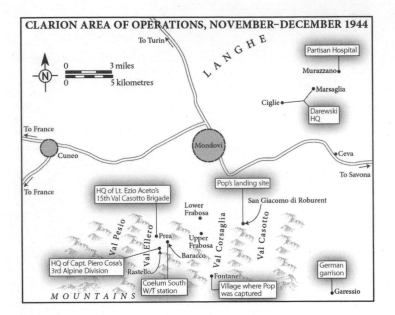

Map 2

'hitting us so hard that for a while we lost our "identity".' In effect, by burning, destroying and killing anything in their path, the Germans removed the Mauri organisation's ability to act as a unified fighting force. The whole team disbanded. Mauri fled to the Langhe. Many partisans defected to the Republicans and Carluccio was betrayed and captured. He managed to escape, he told me, but for eight days wandered the valleys south of Mondovi 'with nothing other than snow to eat'.

From the Val Casotto, the Germans consolidated their victory by sweeping through the three neighbouring valleys, clearing each systematically. From a fighting force of 800, the Val Casotto was reduced to 40 men. In all, 200 partisans were killed in the German operation. But, bit by bit, as the Allies fought their way northwards and it became clear that the German position in Italy was ultimately untenable, Mauri managed to regroup, helped by many defections from the Republican fascists. During the summer, attacks against German columns and garrisons gathered pace again. In late September, the weather worsened, airdrops into the region dwindled and then started to dry up altogether; and the Germans launched a new series of aggressive anti-partisan operations. These were not as comprehensive as the *rastrellamenti* of the March–April period, but were highly disruptive nonetheless and only added to the uncertainty back at Monopoli about Clarion's departure date.

As usual, we never know ten minutes in advance what our future is going to be… so about tomorrow I can only say I'll be with you when I possibly can, Pop wrote to my mother on 25 September. Maybe if it was a decent day, he suggested, they could go for lunch in Bari. He had recently heard that he would not be charged over an incident in which he had run the *Eduardo* aground in Bari harbour. Hilary Scott, who had been a lawyer before the war (and would offer Pop a job at Slaughter and May after it), had been able to work his magic with the authorities. The officer in charge of the port, a man named Michael Verey (whom Pop came to know well in his City career after the war), had taken the view in any case that there were more important things to worry about in a war (I'd been told about this by Pop after a chance remark in which I mentioned I'd been talking to Verey's son, David, at a work meeting). The lunch, therefore, would be by way of a celebration – something to keep the morale up during the interminable waiting. In early October, and still with no news about Clarion's 'go' date, Pop also had a long lunch with Robin, in which they discussed the mission to come. Robin, at one point during the summer, had also been picked for a BLO mission, but, due to the fact that he had been taken ill, had found himself posted to a different type of operation, one that was more in keeping with his para-naval background – he was to become, to all intents and purposes, Pop's link to the outside world.

No.1 Special Force had decided to establish a small naval base in southern France from which to support its missions in northwest Italy, in particular those in the western part of Liguria and especially those in the province of Imperia, the coastal region south of Mondovi. The unit, dubbed Detachment 20, was part of a broader SOE plan to find alternative ways of infiltrating 'bodies' and supplies into the northwest due to the fact that aircraft were in increasingly short supply. Such aircraft that were available for drops, as the Clarion party knew only too well, had been prevented from delivering men and materiel by excessive demands on the supply system, the appalling weather and the hazards posed by the mountainous terrain. A check at The National Archives on the activities of 148 Squadron, the RAF unit based at Brindisi that had been assigned to drop SOE agents behind the lines, revealed just how bad it had become. In the first week of November, three out of seven missions had had to be scrubbed due to bad weather. The other four hardly went any better. The unit reported that it was having problems bringing into service the Short Stirling, recently converted from a heavy bomber to the para-dropping role. Its Handley Page Halifaxes, the standard four-engine bomber converted to SOE and supply drop missions, had suffered recurring engine problems, meanwhile, forcing several to turn back, one to ditch in the sea off Vis following an engine fire and one more to crash land close to its target.

Through his meeting with Robin, Pop would have learned – if he had not already done so – why Captain Bentley, Clarion's original second-in-command, had been withdrawn from the mission and been replaced by Colin Irving-Bell. Bentley, it turned out, had been sent to Det. 20 in Nice to evaluate the practicalities of leading a mission into Liguria by sea. And while no official records have come to light, it appeared that at least part of the Clarion mission objective was to explore the possibilities of opening up an inland supply route from Imperia, a seaport between Nice and Genoa on the Ligurian coast, and the hinterland around Mondovi. Robin, exploiting all the experience that he and Pop had built up during the winter and early spring in their MS/MAS boat missions with Dick Laming, would be tasked with responsibility for the seaborne in- and exfiltrations. After the war, Robin would provide a colourful description of the set-up at Det. 20, which 'installed itself in a very comfortable villa near the coast, complete with all the mod cons, a lift from the first floor to the ground floor and personnel to run our private motor cars...'

How would my godfather have felt, I wondered, about Pop's selection for Clarion and his own dispatch to the less threatening surroundings of southern France? His brother, Brooks, writing in *Secret Flotillas*, considered Robin most fortunate to have been unwell when selection took place – otherwise, he wrote, he probably would have suffered a similar fate to Pop.

From my own relationship with Robin, who had been the best of men, I knew that he would have been deeply upset that he and Pop – the firmest of friends after their initial meeting at Helford, months of boat missions, living and socialising together at Monopoli, and the Popski beach reconnaissance for which they would both be awarded the DSC – had been split up in this way.

Not that Robin would be having an easy time of it. German direction-finding equipment installed along the Ligurian coast meant that any Allied vessel entering its littoral waters would be a highly vulnerable target – and missions involving agent and supply drops between France and Italy in the final stages of the war indeed proved fraught with danger. But there was something appropriate, which no doubt Pop and Robin also felt, in the fact that they would remain linked – even when Pop was behind the lines – via the Det. 20 supply operation. In a letter that Robin would take with him to southern France to secure the cooperation of forces on the ground for Det. 20, Allied headquarters made it clear that he was 'thoroughly experienced in the type of work involved' and that his 'sparring partner', as they referred to him, 'Sub Lieutenant Clark, RNVR', should make it a priority to 'establish a direct W/T link' between them as soon as Pop had installed himself amongst the partisans in and around the Langhe. This would ensure that the Nice–Liguria supply route ran as smoothly as possible in the weeks and months ahead.

Writing to Mop after his meeting with Robin, Pop said:

> *We disagreed over lunch about extremes. Robin held he got more out of life by not having peaks and pits of morale, but rather keeping a steadier graph. I still think he is wrong and he thinks I am, so we did not get very far. I think that if one's morale is too steady, there are no highlights to remember.*

What struck me as ironic when I read this was that, to anyone who knew him post-war, you couldn't have found anyone more inclined to a 'steady graph' than my father.

Sensing that the order to jump was close, Pop spent the evening checking and double-checking the equipment he would take with him.

Following Hitler's 1942 Führer order that all special forces would be treated as partisans and shot, SOE BLOs dropped in uniform – not that this was deemed to be any form of protection in the event of capture. To ward against the bitter cold, agents jumped during winter wearing two pairs of socks, battledress trousers, a flannel shirt, a short-sleeve woollen vest or woollen sweater, a windcheater, web belt, holster, ammunition pouches, a magazine holder and a water bottle. He also had a scarf made of parachute silk with a map of north-west Italy printed on it – his emergency escape chart if he needed to go on the run. Years later, Pop would donate one such scarf to the Imperial War Museum. In his rucksack, which might have weighed as much as 60 pounds, he carried a spare shirt, three more pairs of socks, a pair of gloves, medical kit, shaving kit, a blanket lined with parachute silk, a sheepskin coat and a ground sheet. His 'personal kit' included binoculars, a map case, a Bowie knife, a torch with spare batteries and bulbs, candles and sewing kit. The weapons he would take with him comprised a 9mm Sten gun, a semi-automatic pistol with 40 rounds of spare ammunition – the Beretta, I imagined, that Will and I had played with as children – two hand grenades and four spare Sten magazines – with 160 rounds altogether, if you counted the fifth magazine in the Sten. His medical kit included an iodine pencil for disinfecting wounds, plaster dressings, laxative pills, bismuth subcarbonate against dysentery, multivitamin tablets and the stimulant benzedrine carbonate in the event that he needed to stay awake. If he was given a cyanide pill – the lethal L-pill he had learned about in his training at Arisaig – as many of his counterparts were in France, there was no mention of it. If he did get into any trouble, he wouldn't even be able to talk his way out of it, as his Italian was still pretty rudimentary. 'I could tell someone how to strip a machine gun in Italian,' he once told me, 'but that was pretty much the extent of it.'

And then, before anyone even knew it, the mission was on. On 10 October, the Clarion party was ordered to the airfield at San Vito dei Normanni.

The aircraft from which they would jump was, of course, a Halifax of 148 Squadron (SD), the SOE 'Special Duties' squadron. Considering range to be more important to SOE operations than firepower, the RAF had come up with a 'BII' version of the bomber that provided it with extra fuel for the long missions north. To reduce drag – and thereby increase its range – the aircraft had streamlined engine nacelles (a modification that was giving trouble, judging from the surges and engine fires that plagued No.148's Halifaxes at this time, as recorded at The National Archives) and a faired-over, metal nose in place of the forward gun-turret. The mid-upper turret had also been removed leaving only the rear guns for defence against night fighters. Parachutists and stores exited the aircraft via a hatch on the floor of the fuselage. In addition to the engine problems came others. One account at Kew, particularly tragic, detailed an incident in which a Lysander on a mission to land three agents behind the lines had been shot down by an American P-51, the American having misidentified the Lysander as an enemy aircraft.

In a lull before take-off, most probably in the dispersal area, where they would have carried out a final check of the kit they were taking with them, Pop sat down and wrote a letter to my mother:

When you read this, you and I will be an awful long way apart in miles, but not in our thoughts. I suppose many times you have heard me say how much I wanted to get away, but I am sure you must realise that it is only a professional reason and that, the more I am with you, the happier I feel. For, during the last couple of months, everything has seemed so much brighter…

Darling, you have changed the last few weeks from what might have been extreme boredom to the happiest days.

Once again – for what he thought would be the final time – Pop sought to console my mother by talking about his four-year plan for their future – the plan that would culminate in his asking her father's permission to marry her:

> *Four years – let's hope it might be much less – is an awful long time, but I am sure it will be worthwhile. What makes me happier still is that you agreed with me… that we should wait until times are cooler and more settled.*
>
> *I will be back soon and I only look forward to the time when we can be together again, darling; to a time when shifts do not mean a thing and operations do not exist.*
>
> *These days will come and so, until then, God bless and all my love to you, my darling. Bob.*

They were driven out to the two Halifaxes waiting in the darkness. The time was a little after ten o'clock. Two aircraft were needed to transport the large quantity of stores that would drop with them. The six members of the group wore quilted khaki jumpsuits with their parachutes strapped to their backs as they boarded the aircraft. The team divided – Campbell, Irving–Bell, Stephens and Banks in one aircraft; Pop and Cauvain in the other. Why the team split unevenly in this way was never explained. Pop and Cauvain took up their positions on the small, uncomfortable seats on either side of the fuselage. A strong smell of petrol, mixed with oil, sweat and leather, permeated the air around them. The stores containers for the weapons and other supplies that were dropping with them were secured close by. The Halifax taxied out to the threshold of Brindisi's long runway. After running up the engines, the pilots pushed the throttles to the stops, filling the length of the fuselage with noise and vibration. Moments later, the aircraft rumbled down the runway. Within 30 seconds it was clawing its way into the night sky.

Pop, Cauvain and the crew would have tried as best they could to settle down for the three-hour flight, although any thought of sleep was out of the question. Due to overwhelming Allied air superiority, the chances of their running into a German night fighter were remote, but the further north they flew, the edgier, inevitably, the crew would become. The hazards, as I already knew, and of which they would have been only too well aware, were many.

Approaching the drop-zone, the pilots reduced their altitude to around 800 feet, even though there were mountains – their soaring, jagged peaks dropping away into ravine-like river valleys below – 10 times this height all around them. With little ambient light to navigate by, the prospect of ploughing into a mountain-ridge was a real concern – many aircraft had already suffered just such a fate. Only the previous month a Halifax had ripped into a mountain near the town of Biella between Milan and Turin, killing all on board. The pilot circled the area, banking the Halifax in a series of tight turns in an attempt to spot the signal fires lit by Darewski and Mauri's partisans. Everybody peeled their eyes, straining through the gloom. There was no sign of any lights below.

After several minutes, and still with no lights to guide them, they discussed what to do. All of them would have been conscious that their presence was attracting unwelcome attention on the ground. If they stayed any longer, the fear was that they would attract night fighters as well. Without the signal fires, there was no possibility of continuing. For this reason, reluctantly, they turned for home, landing back at Brindisi shortly after 5.30am, more than six hours after they had taken off. What had gone through Pop's mind as the wheels of the Halifax had greased the tarmac? Alan Clark, the composer of 'Monopoli Blues', had written the words for a song that must have conveyed much of the frustration he felt. I had found them typed out on a sheet of paper amongst his letters to Mop.[1]

> *The 'Joes' were ready, the stores laid on,*
> *By twenty-three hundred the boys should be gone.*
> *There's been months of planning and standing by,*
> *Lots of hard work and many a sigh.*
> *Training finished to the perfect pitch,*
> *Clothes fixed up to the very last stitch,*
> *Hours of conference (oft heated to boot)*
> *To see if the boys would go in by 'chute';*

1. 'Joe' was SOE slang for 'agent'.

Then after a drink in the local pub –
'Capitano, we thinka we go in by sub!'
Cracks sent out and the field prepared,
Every precaution for fear they be snared,
And landing should find, at the end of a gun
Instead of Antonio – Heydrich the Hun.
In fact, there was nothing that had not been done.

By nineteen hundred the stage was set.
No! One more hurdle had still to be met.
A major decision had still to be taken
If the faith of the 'Joes' was not to be shaken.
The problem that faced them was how they could get
The 'Joes' to the Airport where they would be met
By the 'plane that would take them for a very long ride;
Would eventually drop them on the other side.

Now the show was a special one, very high grade,
And the 'Joes' felt like heroes (tho' very self made).
They wanted a car (a saloon car in fact),
And 'twas here that the brains of the T.O. were racked.
Proverbial time marched proverbially on,
The sun gave place to a full moon that shone
On a world steeped in war (its problems are many),
But a car was not found. No! There just were not any.
'My car! Oh I say! My very dear fellow,
I'm off to a show starring Ivor Novello.

'Business and pleasure don't mix – that's my motto
I'm taking a FANY to dine at "The Grotto".'
And others approached had similar reason
Why their cars simply could not be spared in the season.

'We're shopping in BARI very first thing tomorrow;
If it's not back by then, there's none I can borrow,
The Morris? You say that that's not a runner –

Then the answer, old boy, is to use a three-tonner.
What? The job is a special? Why, who ever knows
What's likely to happen to a 'plane load of "Joes"?
Well, if that won't do – oh! Bother this shop;
Damn the "Joes" and the car; just cancel the op.'

Chapter 13

'Rastrellamenti'

Monopoli, November 1944

In the immediate aftermath of the 'mission abort', Pop occupied himself with long walks in the countryside around San Vito as he and his fellow officers, Campbell and Irving-Bell, debated the likely fate of Clarion. They remained in Brindisi on standby to go again. Three more times in October and early November they flew, but on each occasion the mission was scrubbed due to bad weather over the Langhe or their inability to spot signal fires from the air.

Pop's frustration was tempered by the prospect of seeing Mop again, even though he knew they would have to face up to the torture of another goodbye. But Mop had been sent away for operational training, leaving him upset that he had been unable to get to see her before she left. *I was awake at five and thought of you getting ready,* he wrote to her from Brindisi. *I was awake at six and thought of you going, and I have been thinking of you ever since.* To distract himself, he went to see two films in Bari, *I Married a Witch* (with Fredric March and Veronica Lake) and the Hitchcock thriller *Shadow of a Doubt.* He received a letter from his parents describing how Roy Taylor, who had visited them while he was in transit to Australia, had been able to tell them about life in Monopoli and the girl that he had fallen for – and he was pleased to note that, from everything they had heard, their reaction was favourable. On 27 October, a 'day of business' in nearby Taranto came as a welcome distraction. Pop recorded in a letter to Mop that he had had an enjoyable lunch at the naval mess with Ben Levy, *who*, he revealed, *still persists in calling me 'Duckie'.*

I was keen to know what the colourful-sounding Levy had wanted to discuss. In the book *Selling War* by Nicholas John Cull, there was a reference to the 'playwright and future MP Ben Levy' having been a member of SOE's covert propaganda wing, SO.1, and archive papers at Kew revealed that 'from the earliest days of SOE work (in) Italy, close liaison had been maintained with the PWE on the dissemination of suitable propaganda in support of the campaign'. The PWE was the Political Warfare Executive, a clandestine government department tasked with the dissemination of white and black propaganda in occupied countries. The staff for the PWE came mainly from SO.1. Since June, they had been broadcasting a special programme to the resistance with material supplied largely from information received from British and Italian liaison missions in the field. BLOs were expected to inform the PWE liaison officer at Maryland about rumours circulating in their area of operations, particularly with a view to 'black propaganda' opportunities – a ready winner being some good old-fashioned spin to the undeniable truth that Italian women were cavorting with the German Army of occupation. Pop's lunch with Levy would have undoubtedly touched on ways in which Clarion might have been able to help the PWE with its propaganda; the more so as Clarion was poised to head into northwest Italy at a critical juncture in relations between the Allies and the partisans.

Throughout 1944, the resistance movement had frequently been called upon to mount a last, all-out effort to defeat the enemy – now, even though the main military offensive had halted, it was being asked to do so again, this time at the onset of winter. While the Clarion team commuted between Monopoli and Brindisi, waiting for the call to fly back to Piedmont, a delegation of the Italian National Committee of Liberation for Northern Italy, CLNAI, visited SOE's operations in Bari, Brindisi and Monopoli to discuss the situation. SOE recognised, as Churchill's Minister for Resistance, Lord Selborne, had pointed out a few weeks earlier, that it was essential to increase the supply of arms, ammunition, food and clothing to the partisans 'if they were to survive a second defensive winter campaign'. At the same time, it was trying to disguise the fact that reduced airlift – due to the weather and the demands of the Yugoslav campaign, where an operation to liberate Belgrade by the Soviet Red Army, Yugoslav partisans and the Bulgarian People's Army was reaching its climax – would place an enormous constraint on their ability to get large-scale supplies to the partisans in the months ahead. Ironically, as David

Stafford pointed out in *Mission Accomplished*, this period saw a brief resumption in the delivery of air-dropped supplies. On 12 November, Mauri, the flamboyant commander of the partisans around Mondovi, received a large drop arranged by Darewski, a.k.a. 'Major Temple'. At midday, in clear blue skies, Mauri reported in his memoirs, 'a huge Halifax approaches... so low that the pilots can be seen waving'. Mauri described how a 'shower of parachutes – white, green, yellow, red, blue – could be seen falling to earth'. Elsewhere in the region, further drops from more than 30 aircraft rained down, causing a huge surge in partisan morale; this despite the arrival of the first heavy snows of winter, which threatened the collection of the containers that were scattered across the countryside. Carluccio, who had left Mauri's command structure by now to rejoin a fighting unit in the valleys, remembered the drop when I spoke with him about it. After months of increasingly bold partisan attacks, culminating in the establishment of the 'Free Republic of Alba' on 10 October in the Langhe, it was clear, even to him, that the Germans would not take these attacks lying down, and that a fresh series of *rastrellamenti* were in the offing.

The Germans received help from an unexpected quarter. In an announcement that would be described by SOE after the war as a 'terrible miscalculation', the day after the drop to Mauri, on 13 November, General Harold Alexander, C-in-C, Allied Armies in Italy, broadcast a message over the BBC that came to have huge repercussions for the resistance movement, as well as for Clarion itself. The so-called 'Winter Directive' was a reversal of all previous Allied messaging. Broadcast openly by the BBC, it informed the partisans that due to the change of season, and the inability of the Allies to deliver needed weapons and supplies until the weather improved, they should cease all large-scale offensive operations until the spring.

Had No.1 Special Force received any forewarning of this, it would almost certainly have moved to stop the broadcast going ahead. But headquarters drafted and transmitted it without consulting anyone and SOE perceived it as a disaster. 'Almost overnight,' SOE's official history noted after the war, (the partisans') instructions changed from 'last all-out effort' to 'go slow'. To add to this, it reported, 'the receipt of this directive corresponded almost exactly with the granting of an amnesty to the "rebels" by Mussolini's government'. In the despair and confusion that followed, the BLOs on the ground – people like Darewski – were hard put to control the partisans and 're-orientate' them to this new policy. As a result, many resistance formations broke up and there were desertions to Mussolini's Republican forces, formed the previous year from former Army units still loyal to the fascist cause and Italian pro-Nazis recruited by the Germans in the wake of the Italian surrender.

Switching sides in this way was more often than not prompted simply by the urge to survive – without basic provisions, starvation in the snow-bound villages in the remote valleys outside Mondovi was a real possibility. Within hours of the Winter Directive going out, Holdsworth – minded no doubt to do something to restore balance on the ground – ordered that the Rankin missions should be sent in as soon as possible. Neither Pop nor Campbell, the Clarion mission commander, recorded official responses to the Winter Directive in any of their private papers or correspondence after the war, so it was impossible to know what they had felt at the prospect of parachuting into a region where a swath of the population, feeling abandoned by the Allies, was now predisposed against them. They would undoubtedly have put their faith in their training as well as in the professionalism of the friendly forces waiting for them on the ground: Mauri's partisans and Darewski's 'Flap' mission that was helping to coordinate them.

They were also, as was by now clearly apparent, desperate to go. That night, sensing that something was 'up', Pop wrote a letter to Mop from the officers' mess in Brindisi, urging her to send the photo of herself she'd been promising him for weeks. He told her that he would try to call her on the 'crackling Battle School phone' (in Brindisi) as it is 'far too long since I saw you'.

On 13 November, as Carluccio and others had feared, the Germans launched their second series of major *rastrellamenti* in the Mondovi region. They had been well prepared for the assault even as the large drop of supplies and multi-coloured parachutes that had so delighted Mauri had rained down from clear blue skies the previous day. Over the next three days, artillery barrages inflicted heavy casualties on Mauri's men. In the village of Castellino, close to Mondovi, 10 hostages taken by the Germans in a roundup of local civilians were summarily executed. Many houses were burned to the ground. Darewski had set up camp in a large villa in Ciglie, near the village of Marsaglia, which was roughly 12km to the northeast of Mondovi. On a nearby area of flat land the partisans had managed to create a landing strip big enough to take a C47 Dakota transport or a twin-engined B25 Mitchell bomber. It was into this area that the Clarion party had been directed to jump. Darewski's party would be on the ground to meet it.

On the morning of the 15th, the German assault suddenly turned on Ciglie, forcing Darewski and his partisans to retreat in a small uncovered lorry to safer ground. A female partisan, Lucia Boetto Testori, who was travelling with them, later reported to Bill Pickering what happened next. 'We set off towards Marsaglia, hearing the shells exploding ever closer,' she told Pickering. 'The enemy had broken through our lines in several places.' At Marsaglia, she continued, Darewski had had some matters to attend to. While the lorry waited, its engine running, he hung around outside the partisans' storehouse, chatting to a local commander. Everyone on the back of the lorry started to become anxious as the shells landed closer and closer. The lorry was parked in the corner of the square next to a stone wall. Deciding he could wait no longer, the driver began to edge the lorry down the street that led out of the village towards relative safety. Urged by the passengers to jump on board, Darewski ran down the street and tried to get up on to the tailgate, but he missed his footing and was left hanging on the side of the vehicle as it continued to rumble down the street. Suddenly, an oxcart laden with straw swung around the corner. The lorry driver, with nowhere else to go, swerved into the stone wall, crushing Darewski between it and the vehicle. Darewski survived, but was badly wounded and in unbearable pain. They drove to a partisan hospital in nearby Murazzano, but still finding themselves under attack moved on to another hospital at Cortemilia. It was there, early in the afternoon, that Darewski died of internal bleeding. The news of his death was communicated by radio to another SOE agent, Lieutenant Colonel Selby Cope, who had been operating as a BLO in Cuneo, a short drive west of Mondovi, since mid-September. Cope had reached the end of his assignment and was due to fly out with the rest of his team in a Lysander in the next few days. He made his way to Murazzano as quickly as he could, gathered up Darewski's personal belongings and flew them back with him to Monopoli.

One member of Cope's party remained in situ. Corporal Williamson, a W/T operator from the Royal Signals, established himself in a house between Baracco and Prea in the Val Ellero, in a valley south of Mondovi. The W/T station was given the codename 'Coelum South' – a random combination of words, it appeared, given that *coelum* was Latin for 'heaven' and there never had been a 'Coelum North'. It was unclear why Williamson had stayed behind, but it was a decision that would have major implications for both Pop and Mop. Coelum South would be, for a short time, at least, Pop's only link to the outside world. For whatever reason, SOE remained ignorant of Darewski's fate until after Cope's arrival back in Monopoli.

In the meantime, the Clarion mission had been given the green light to go again. On 16 November, the six members of the team made their way to the airfield and readied themselves to jump for a fifth time. This time, Pop had been assigned a different pilot. This pilot told him that he had had an unblemished record of bundling the agents or cargo within his charge out into the slipstream.

At two o'clock in the morning, my father sat down and wrote his last letter to my mother:

> *My Darling Marjorie,*
>
> *Today looks like being the big day, and so at last it really seems as if we shall be parted. The waiting had become so long and the false alarms so frequent that I had given up the idea of ever saying goodbye.*
>
> *Maybe it is just as well, in that goodbyes like ours are too tantalising, because I should never have known how to leave you.*

So, it is left to a meagre letter in which to say farewell for the time being, and my poor hand can make no satisfactory effort…

By now you must know how much I have enjoyed the last months in your company. Everything in the world goes right when I am with you. I have never felt so happy as when I was with you, darling, and how the intervals between seeing you have lingered.

But I go away now, laden with happy memories of things done in your company and the hopes of many more in the not-too-distant future.

It is now two o'clock and we leave at half-past, so, as there will be a good deal of flap after that, I have half an hour of peace.

There is nothing very much else to say, for you must know how much I shall miss you and how much I love you, Marjorie. I hope we shall not be separated too long, but, anyway, I long for the next time, darling.

If you listen to 'Flap', you will hear that we got there OK. After that, it's Bill Banks…

My words are too inarticulate, so goodbye for now, my darling. I love you. Bob.

He made his way out to the aircraft. As usual, the Clarion team split into two parties – he and Cauvain and a load of stores in one aircraft, the rest of the group in the other and within minutes they were in the air.

Three hours later, 800 feet over the drop-zone, the crew of Pop's Halifax spotted fires on the ground and he and Cauvain jumped.

The operations record book for 148 Squadron recorded that on the night of 16 November, '14 Halifaxes were detailed to undertake night operations to Northern Italy'. It went on to say that it had been a 'most unfortunate night', because only six aircraft succeeded in dropping their loads. 'Six did not receive the correct signal from the ground and returned their loads to base. Another returned owing to bad weather, whilst the other was forced to return owing to mechanical trouble.' This, however, was not the whole story.

There are two stories behind the signal seen by Pop's Halifax crew. One is that it was a signal fire that had been lit by a band of partisans who were waiting for supplies to be air-dropped to them some 40km to the south and east of Pop's intended drop-zone. Instead of dropping into the flat space of the real drop site in the Langhe, close to the airstrip that Darewski had built for C47s and B25s, Pop and Cauvain had pitched into the night over a mountainous valley some 20km to the south of Mondovi. Seconds after they exited the Halifax's dropchute, the static lines attached to the aircraft snapped their parachutes open. But, in the slipstream, the lines of Pop's canopy became twisted and his parachute failed to deploy properly. Unable to see the ground that rushed at him, he hit a tree – a good thing in retrospect, as it may well have saved his life – but he landed heavily, breaking several ribs. He was so badly hurt, in fact, that when he tried to get to his feet to walk, he couldn't.

Years later, Pop said that the signal on the ground that had been spotted from his aircraft was, as it turned out (and somewhat more prosaic than the account above), a priest burning rubbish at the bottom of his garden and that this was where he had landed. After the priest had dragged him into his house, he muttered something Pop understood as: 'You can't stay here.' And in a state of great agitation, he then took off into the night. For Pop, anxious moments followed.

He had no idea whether the priest had gone to fetch help or the Germans. Fortunately, it was the former in the shape of a 16-year-old *partigiano* called Sergio Curetti, who was with the 15th Val Casotto Brigade, commanded by Lt Aceto. Aceto's had been the unit based in the suburbs of Mondovi that, a few weeks earlier, had been driven into the valleys south of the town by one of the numerous fascist assaults that had culminated in Darewski's death. Curetti's group had been told by an emissary of Aceto's – a lawyer named Verzone, closely linked to Mauri's group, who had been acting as a go-between for the partisans and the Committee for National Liberation in Turin – to wait in the village of San Giacomo di Roburent for a delivery of supplies. Supplies were supposed to have been dispensed to Aceto's unit by partisans operating in the Langhe – where most of the drops were targeted – as well as by the 3rd Alpine Division, which had set up operations in the nearby valley of San Ellero. Inevitably, however, due to the fierce rivalry amongst these groups, even under the supposedly unified command of Mauri, units tended to cling to their supplies. For this reason, it struck me as entirely possible – given what happened next – that the 4th Alpine decided to mount an unauthorised bid for its own airdrop. Verzone had brought word with him that there was to be an airdrop of stores from a number of Allied aircraft over the coming nights and that Curetti and his colleagues were to prepare signal fires for the arrival of the supplies. One of the signals was in the shape of an 'L', the other an 'S'.

After Sergio Curetti tracked my father down in the early 1990s, our two families had remained in touch. In my next port of call, a visit to Mondovi to get a better feel for the territory around the town that my father had dropped into, I met up with the Curettis again and we talked about the circumstances under which Pop and Sergio had met. Sergio had died several years earlier, but had written a book, *Meglio di niente* ('better than nothing'), which had not been available the last time I had visited – when I'd first come over to meet the family with Mop and Pop. The book was invaluable in filling in key details. It described how, for several days in mid-November, Sergio and his comrades had waited for the supplies to arrive, but none had come. They had all but given up, when, in the small hours of the morning of the 17th, they had heard the unmistakable drone of a multi-engine aircraft. Curetti had started to leap to his feet to run to the edge of the village to light the fire, but his unit commander stopped him, saying that the aircraft was approaching from the wrong way – Verzone, the lawyer, having indicated that the plane would come from a different direction. They had listened as the plane had circled before it eventually peeled away to the south. In the midst of an argument about the rights and wrongs of the intelligence they had been given, they heard a second aircraft approaching. This time, there was no discussion: they rushed out, lit the fires and received a series of flashes in response from the plane.

Despite some original ambiguity over exactly who had lit the fire spotted from Pop's aircraft, what can be said to have happened with certainty is that Lt Aceto's unit had been expecting supplies – authorised or not – and had got less than it had bargained for, because, instead of arms and food, it got Pop and Cauvain. The Halifax containing Campbell's party, not seeing fires on the ground, had circled the area and returned home. It is more than probable that this was the first aircraft that Sergio and his group had heard. In any case, it was amongst the six aircraft that did not receive the correct signal and which, according to the 148 Squadron operations book, returned their 'loads' to base.

Cauvain was luckier than Pop in that he made a good landing. He located Pop around the same time that Sergio and his group showed up at the priest's house. The Italian related later that he was struck by the size of the 'injured officer'. 'He was very tall,' he wrote, 'a real giant.' For a while, Pop recounted in a mission report filed after the war, which is now at The National Archives, the locals stood around debating what to do. Then they picked him up and, together with Cauvain, carried him to the village inn, along with the container that had dropped with them. In it, Sergio wrote in his book, 'there was a nice sheepskin jacket, a shotgun of a kind I'd never seen before and lots of underwear'.

Lucky him, the Italian thought – as he'd been wearing the same pair for months! Noticing Curetti admiring the gun, Pop asked if he'd like to keep it.

Unaware that the other aircraft had turned back, Pop explained in his halting Italian that a search of the surrounding countryside had to be made for Campbell's party and the stores that had dropped from both aircraft. Cauvain led the search and, by 9.30am the following morning, they had tracked down all 12 packages from their Halifax. As Sergio observed, the packages contained a 47mm anti-tank gun without any rounds, some rounds for a mortar, but no mortar, some more shotguns, some Stens, a lot of plastic explosive, some clothes, some corned beef, plus cigarettes and chocolate.

During the night, Lt Aceto arrived to greet San Giacomo's new guests. As Pop wrote later in his mission debrief: 'From Lt Aceto I learned that, as far as he knew, no other "bodies" had been dropped that night, but two other aircraft had dropped stores at scattered points.' From this my father deduced that something had happened to Campbell's party and that the other four members of Clarion had either failed to arrive or had elected to turn back. He had no means of checking this with No.1 Special Force, because the Clarion W/T set had been with Telegraphist Bill Banks in the second plane and the partisans were without any form of radio communication. From the returning search party, they also discovered that a further seven stores containers in a second load had landed around 15km away and a third load had been dropped on to the German garrison at Garessio, 25km to the southeast. The two other loads were most likely from the aircraft that Aceto and the San Giacomo group had been primed to expect. At some point during that first morning, the lawyer Verzone offered to take a message to Darewski to let him know that the Clarion drop party had landed some 40km from its intended position, reinforcing the point that word had not reached Lt Aceto's group that Darewski had been killed. Verzone did say that it would be far too dangerous for Bob and Cauvain to attempt to make contact with 'Flap' in the Langhe, as the Germans were still engaged in a major operation against the partisans there. He mentioned instead that he knew of a radio set under the control of an English colonel in the neighbouring valley and that this, perhaps, would be the best way for Pop to get word to Monopoli and Flap. The 'English colonel' was a reference to Colonel Cope, the man who had arrived in the Langhe to gather up Darewski's possessions before flying out in a Lysander. Cope had left his radio operator, Corporal Williamson, at a house near Baracco – the W/T station that had been operating under the codename 'Coelum South'.

As Pop was still unable to move, he sent Cauvain with a message to Baracco, stating their whereabouts and, as he put it later in his mission debrief, 'the general (factual) position'. Baracco was only around 10km to the east of San Giacomo, but in a different valley. To get there, Cauvain, together with his Italian guides, had to scale steep-sided slopes, rocky ridge lines, fast-moving streams and forests pitted with snowdrifts. After the war, my father was fulsome in his praise for the way in which Cauvain performed his duties – 'especially just after we had dropped, when I was unable to walk far'. Cauvain, he said, was 'tireless when walking to outlying groups, no matter how far or what time of the day or night'. There was, sadly, no record of the 'Stanley–Livingstone moment' when Cauvain linked up with Williamson in Baracco, but there is evidence of the ensuing message that Williamson managed to get through to Monopoli. Sitting in the dark of the Signals Office there, the FANY on duty almost fell off her chair when the Coelum South W/T set, which had lain dormant for weeks, suddenly sprang into life. Williamson dutifully relayed the 'general position' that had been put together by my father, before adding that he had a postscript for one of the FANYs – Ensign Marjorie Lewis.

The message was short, to the point and completely counter to regulations. It ran: *Bob sends love to Marjorie.*

Pop had done what he said he would. He'd let my mother know that he was safe.

Chapter 14

'Multi-coloured 'chutes'

Mondovi, Northern Italy, November 1944

Pop arrived in Baracco three days later, after a slow, painful hike across the mountains with Cauvain and his guides, a group that included Sergio Curetti.

On the way, he had his first opportunity to take in the spectacular setting he now found himself in. From San Giacomo, as I discovered when I visited it myself, you could see the ridge lines of the four finger-like valleys that stretched away to the south of Mondovi – peaks that pushed above the pine and deciduous forests, the pastures and streams that occupied the valleys and the lower slopes. Beyond the ridges, to the north and west, lay the Alps, rising sharply from the plain between Mondovi and Turin, 100km away.

As he took in the view, Pop may have had cause to wonder how he was still alive. His Halifax pilot had been able to manoeuvre the aircraft to drop them at less than 1,000 feet. At that altitude, many of the mountain peaks would have towered above the aircraft and been barely visible at night.

Not visible from where he had landed, but known to him from briefings, was the area known as the Langhe. To the north and east of Mondovi, the Langhe was a region of rolling hills and forests, famous in happier times for its wines, cheeses and truffles, where the bulk of the partisans under Mauri operated. It was in the Langhe that the German assault on the partisans had started. And while there were some isolated attacks by the Germans on partisan units in the valleys south of Mondovi during the middle of November, in the main, an uneasy period of relative peace existed there for the rest of the month. In retrospect it was the calm before the storm.

At Baracco, Pop was promptly introduced to Captain Piero Cosa, the commander of the 3rd Alpine Division. Cosa was tall, with a prominent forehead and dark receding hair. Contemporary accounts

185

described him as 'intense'. The 3rd Alpine was headquartered in Rastello, a few kilometres from Baracco, and had been formed in the aftermath of a particularly vicious battle in the spring, known as the 'Battle of Easter', when, during the first round of *rastrellamenti* that year, the Germans had launched an offensive against partisan operations in the Val Pesio, one of the four 'finger-valleys' south of Mondovi. The Val Pesio had been a nerve centre of partisan resistance in the months following the armistice and Capt Cosa one of its original and most charismatic leaders.

The Battle of Easter commenced on 8 April when around 1,000 German troops stormed up the Val Pesio against a far inferior force under Cosa's command. After an 11-hour pitched battle, the partisans were forced to retreat up the valley, eventually crossing into the more remote and secure Val Ellero. It was here that they reformed into the 3rd Alpine, with its hub at Rastello and sub-units in the surrounding villages. When my father met Cosa, he was told that he had around 1,500 partisans under his command. The number of partisans, however, available to the Val Ellero Brigade, which would be in the thickest part of the fighting, was far smaller: around 300 men. The combined force of Germans and Italian fascists that they faced totalled in excess of 7,000 heavily armed troops.

In his post-mission report, Pop described Capt Cosa as 'very highly organised, having a firm system of rationing and distribution of stores'. However, he also found major problems within the regional resistance network, based largely on the fact that Cosa had an 'intense scorn and hatred' of Major Mauri, the leader of the 1st Group Alpine Division, to which the 3rd and 4th Alpine Divisions were subordinate. Supply drops, Pop quickly found out, were a key source of the disagreement, as they did not always get to the units that needed them most. The only bright spot in an otherwise dire picture of non-cooperation was the fact that Capt Cosa and Lt Aceto got along reasonably well. The first thing Pop did was to hand Cosa two of the money packages that he had brought with him – a sum totalling five hundred and fifty thousand lira, or around a thousand pounds sterling – having heard that funds previously supplied by Darewski and Cope, which had been used to lubricate the local economy – mainly through the supply of food – were all but used up. The second thing he did was to make direct contact via Williamson's radio with No.1 Special Force, whereupon he was informed by Colonel John Stevens to stay where he was – i.e. with the radio – and to 'await further orders from Monopoli'. Stevens had been flown in to Darewski's landing ground in the Langhe, which had now been given the codename 'Abraham', two days earlier in a twin-engine B25 bomber.

Air operations into Piedmont, I learned, had been started by Charles Macintosh, who, having helped in the taking of Florence in August, had moved there permanently in October in order to establish a forward tactical headquarters on behalf of No.1 Special Force. This was principally for liaison with the US Fifth Army as it probed the Gothic Line. But it also became useful as a channel for the short-notice delivery of vital supplies and for extraction operations. In addition to the B25, this unofficial 'air force' of No.1 Special Force also included a captured German Fieseler Storch, an aircraft that had even better short take-off and landing capabilities than the British Lysander.

On the ground, Stevens, a solicitor in peacetime, had quickly become exasperated by what he had found. Following the German attack that had led to Darewski's death, Mauri's partisans had been split into three separate groups, with each more or less at each other's throats, and all of them so demoralised that many of them had elected to go into hiding rather than fight or engage in the intelligence-gathering function that was so vital to SOE. 'Under such circumstances, it is not possible for me to establish a command in the field, but only to inspect and clutter up an area that is not very healthy at present,' Stevens communicated to Monopoli despondently. It was unsurprising, therefore, that he gave orders to Pop to stay put at 3rd Alpine headquarters.

For his part, Pop would have had time, too, to reflect on the situation that he found himself in; the reality on the ground being very different from anything he would have been briefed on in Monopoli. The partisans of the 3rd Alpine were Communist and so dedicated to the Communist cause that he spent much of his time, he said later, 'enthusing them to fight the Germans, rather than the other enemy, the Christian Democrat partisans'. The limited availability of weapons and ammunition was another major problem, as were communications. Because they had no radio equipment, the partisans relied on dispatch riders. As the partisan network grew, these communication lines became ever more stretched, making cohesive action a near-impossibility. Poor communications also contributed to a partisan tendency to be very rigid in defence of their territory, rather than fight the way they should have – as small bands conducting hit-and-run raids against the Germans, then melting into the mountains, valleys and forests when they were counter-attacked.

It was fortunate, therefore, as Pop reported after the war, that for the next two weeks the Germans were only active along the Cuneo–Mondovi–Ceva–Acqui road, which ran from the west in an east-northeasterly direction 10km or so north of the 3rd Alpine's headquarters. This permitted Pop to engage only in limited activities while he was at Capt Cosa's headquarters: primarily making preparations for receiving and distributing stores on the Abraham dropping ground and looking for a suitable dropping ground in the San Giacomo area for the 4th Alpine Division. 'This was necessary for two reasons,' he explained in his post-mission report after the war. 'Firstly, because Cosa thought that everything arriving on the Abraham dropground was intended for *his* group; secondly on account of the difficulty transporting stores by mules.' Monopoli asked if there was a suitable Lysander ground in the area, 'but as we were hemmed into the foothills, and the valleys were very narrow, no convenient place could be found'. Cosa, meanwhile, spent the same period 'occupying himself in regrouping and preparing for the winter'.

Prior to making the trip, I knew the 'bookends' of Pop's time during this period, but not much more – the fact that he had parachuted on the night of 16 November and had been captured on the night of 12 December. Thanks to Marco Ruzzi, the lead archivist at the 'Resistance Archive' in the provincial capital, Cuneo, which I visited (with my friend Pier Riches acting as translator) in a second research trip to the area, I was given some telling insights into how Pop spent his time with Cosa, while the latter 'prepared for the winter'. It is evident from some of the radio traffic that survives in the archive that

Cosa was desperate for supplies and saw Pop's unexpected appearance from the skies as manna from Heaven – his own direct channel to SOE. On 18 November, he drafted a W/T message to Monopoli to say that the 3rd Alpine hadn't received any supplies from No.1 Special Force 'for three months' (this despite the stores that were recovered from Pop's Halifax) and that the group was 'not in a position to defend itself' from attack. Pop, it seems, spent much of the next two to three weeks with Cosa drafting proper, considered inventories of supplies that were needed – a more effective means of getting SOE's attention than the blanket, scatter-gun demands Cosa had dispatched up until then. Many of these lists survive in the Cuneo archive, an 18 November 'shopping list' for 54 88mm mortar rounds, 224 50mm mortar rounds, two 80mm mortars, as well as various other weapons and items of clothing. In another typed message, I found evidence that Pop had also acted as a mediator between the various partisan groups in the region – one request coming from the wife of a senior partisan from a rival group, who was begging Pop to help her find out what had happened to her husband, who was missing with no word of his whereabouts. It was clear from the archive that Pop had dropped into an atmosphere of organised chaos where trying to keep on top of the paperwork and fencing amongst rival factions had become the norm.

At the beginning of December, Pop asked Monopoli whether, in view of the Allies' air superiority, daylight missions might be flown over the area. He was promptly told that stores could and would be delivered by day, but that personnel could not be, and that the rest of the Clarion party would be coming in, as planned, by night. This was puzzling, as it was quite the opposite of what was being discussed with Duncan Campbell in Monopoli. Not surprisingly, Campbell was growing increasingly frustrated with his lot; the weather, which remained appalling, having consistently prevented them from making the trip.

Thanks to Campbell's unpublished memoir, which had been provided to me in an act of great generosity by his son, whom I had managed to track down several weeks earlier, I had a ringside seat on what was happening in Monopoli as well.

After landing back at Brindisi on the morning of 17 November, Campbell, Irving-Bell, Telegraphist Banks and Corporal Stephens had returned to Monopoli, where Campbell spent the next few days trying to persuade the powers-that-be to get them back to Piedmont on the first available aircraft.

It must have seemed like déjà vu, with the party hanging around waiting in vain for good weather or the availability of a plane that could fly them north. Campbell, impatient by his own admission at the best of times, began to press No.1 Special Force for an aircraft that would fly them in to *land* them behind the lines, rather than dropping them in by parachute. 'It seemed to me ludicrous that we could not be flown in,' he wrote in his memoir. 'Why on earth couldn't they pop us over from a forward landing strip just behind the front line, [where] they would easily know the weather conditions in my [assigned] area?' Following a series of increasingly vociferous pleas from Campbell for this course of action, Monopoli eventually agreed: instead of jumping, they would be landed by aircraft, presumably at the Abraham site.

No.1 Special Force sent a message to Pop ordering him to prepare to receive the rest of the Clarion party at noon on 9 December – this in direct contravention to the advice Pop had received at the end of November that daylight drops of personnel, as opposed to stores, would not be taking place. Campbell and his Clarion party, in the meantime, had flown up to a base just outside Pisa, from where they would make the relatively short hop across the lines to Piedmont. Campbell had argued for a night-time flight, but, for reasons that remained unclear, headquarters maintained that this was not possible – citing, spuriously, a smaller transport aircraft's (as opposed to a Halifax's) inability to perform such an operation. When told that they would be running a gauntlet of enemy fighter sweeps, Campbell requested – and was granted – an escort of eight US P47 Thunderbolts to protect them in enemy airspace.

However, somewhere between this request and the actual flight, the plan changed. At the last minute, instead of a landing, it was decided that they would jump instead. On the morning of the 9th, on a beautifully sunny day with unlimited visibility, Campbell and his three comrades took off from the airfield in a pair of RAF DC3 transport aircraft. Their route to the Abraham dropping ground took them across the Gulf of Genoa on a northwesterly heading towards the Ligurian Alps. It was while he was in the air that Campbell started to be nagged by feelings of unease over the course of action he had pressed so hard for. 'Looking about me,' he wrote in his memoir, 'it was some sort of comfort to see the fighter escorts manoeuvring about the sky in our vicinity, but I began to have doubts about the wisdom of the decision which I myself had prompted, of doing this sort of clandestine work in broad daylight.' He settled himself with thoughts of the fiancée he had left behind and found the courage he needed to go on by glancing from time to time at her photograph.

After less than an hour in the air, the dispatcher told them to prepare to jump. As Campbell stood hooked up by his static line next to the door, he caught a glimpse of the drop-zone (DZ) and was alarmed by the small size of it. The DZ sat on a mountain ridge with a precipitous drop hundreds of feet into the valley below if you didn't hit it bang-on. It was too late for doubts, however, and, with a shout from the dispatcher, he leaped into the slipstream. On the way down, he became concerned he wasn't going to hit the DZ, but he needn't have worried. The landing – on rocks covered by a thin layer of snow – was hard, but all four of them landed intact. Their relief turned to joy when they realised that their reception committee included Pop and Cauvain.

As soon as he landed, Campbell swapped his jump-helmet for his glengarry, the boat-shaped red and white checked hat of his regiment, the Argyll and Sutherland Highlanders. I reflected that it could not have been easy for Pop suddenly finding himself under the authority of another BLO after three weeks of more or less independent action during his stay with the 3rd Alpine Division. But it was clear, too, that, in the short time he had got to know them, Pop had established a strong rapport with Campbell and Irving-Bell and, as a result, would have deferred without question to their authority. There was no hint either that he expressed surprise or dismay at the sight of Campbell's party – or the stores that they had brought with them – floating to the ground under multi-coloured parachutes during daylight. There was, however, a hurried discussion about what to do with the stores, with Campbell concluding that 'caching' everything they didn't need in a nearby cave was the best option. When he had got to know the lie of the land, he told the rest of the party they could retrieve the stores and see to their distribution to the *partigiani*. His orders, he now shared with Pop and Cauvain, were to get the Clarion party into the seaboard area centred on the port city of Imperia between Genoa and the French border. From there, they would take steps to safeguard Italian infrastructure against 'scorch' operations in the wake of what was seen as the Germans' impending withdrawal from Italy. It is unclear whether Pop had been given these same instructions prior to his departure or whether the 'Imperia brief' was an update to the original mission – liaising with the partisans, coordinating their supply requests and training them to fight.

'To be able to do this,' Campbell reported later, 'we had to get ourselves from the north slopes of the western end of the Ligurian Alps to the southern slopes and then filter down towards the coast.' The simplicity of this plan belied the true nature of the picture, as Campbell began to appreciate soon after the party set off towards Rastello to meet with Captain Cosa.

'As we sped down the mountain paths and I was admiring the beautiful views of the valley laid out in the bright evening light, it began to dawn on me that our multi-coloured parachutes must have been seen for miles around and that the news would be disseminated along "the grapevine".' He was right to be anxious. After meeting up with Corporal Williamson in Baracco and dumping his equipment there, he made the short journey along the valley to Rastello to meet Captain Cosa. As soon as he arrived at the 3rd Alpine HQ – led there almost certainly by Pop – he found Cosa apoplectic with rage. The Germans, Cosa told Campbell, were already engaged in a sustained anti-partisan campaign in the area and he had sought to explain to SOE that supply operations should be undertaken as clandestinely as possible. 'And then I came fluttering down with parachutes every colour of the rainbow into the middle of it all,' Campbell wrote. He felt wretched, he said, about the impetuousness that had led to the decision to drop the party in by day.

Cosa had objected to the drop in the strongest possible terms as soon as he'd heard it was being planned, he wrote later, because of the German mopping-up operation that was then underway. In a piece of testimony at The National Archives in Kew, the Italian said that he had 'warned Lt Clark about this and had energetically suggested that the drop should not take place'.

The following day, Cosa, still fuming, told Campbell that he had no choice but to order his men to scatter into the surrounding countryside in anticipation of the *rastrellamento* that the Germans and Italian fascists would inevitably now launch up the valley. According to the account in The National Archives, he suggested that they should head for the Langhe, away from the valleys, but that Campbell insisted on withdrawing higher into the mountains 'to avoid the uncertain fate of being mopped up'. This gelled with Campbell's own account. With some trepidation, he asked if Cosa could lend him some guides to help them get through the mountains and down to Imperia. Cosa reluctantly agreed and somewhere in this exchange it was confirmed, too, that Campbell would assume responsibility for an escaped British POW and a couple of American airmen who had been hiding out with the 3rd Alpine for a few weeks. A post-mission report stated that one of the guides assigned to the group had been attached to the 'Flap' mission as Darewski's interpreter.

Amidst mounting, frenetic activity to evacuate the area, Campbell realised that it was every man for himself and that the Clarion team needed to disappear into the forests as quickly as possible. First, though, he had to take action over the equipment that had been left near the landing ground. He dispatched Irving-Bell and Cauvain to the cave with authority to distribute the equipment or blow it up depending on the situation they found when they arrived. On no account, he told them, was any of it to fall into enemy hands.

They said their goodbyes and arranged to meet further up the valley the next day.

At midnight, according to the account left at The National Archives by William Banks, Clarion's telegraphist, the remaining members of the Clarion party – Campbell, Pop, Stephens and Banks – left Rastello, along with the two guides, Williamson, the POW and the two American airmen. They walked in the darkness up the eastern slope along a narrow, circuitous path until they crossed into the next-door valley. Along the way, Banks buried his radio set and Campbell hid much of the remaining money. After descending the slope on the other side of the ridge line, they arrived at around two o'clock in the morning, Banks wrote, on the outskirts of the alpine village of Frabosa Soprana. On the far side of the valley lay San Giacomo, where Pop and Cauvain had parachuted to earth three-and-a-half weeks earlier.

At Frabosa, the party decided to split, Banks related, for security reasons: the two Americans and the British POW in one party; Campbell, Pop, Banks, Stephens, Williamson and the two guides in the other.

In his memoir, Campbell described how they were then 'led by the nose' by their two guides along an unpaved road that wound along the bottom of the valley beside a river, with little clue where they were heading, except that it was in the general direction of Imperia, some 50km to the south. In the darkness, they came across a pony-trap and loaded their equipment on to it, then took it in turns to pull the trap along the road. A little further on, their guides called a halt. There was a narrow bridge ahead, they explained – the only crossing point on the river for miles. The Italians told Campbell that they wanted to reconnoitre the bridge in case the Germans or fascists had posted guards. Half an hour later, they returned with the news everyone had feared – that the bridge was now in the hands of the enemy. Pop had encountered a couple of light *rastrellamenti* in the previous weeks and had been relatively unbothered by them – you lay low and waited for them to pass you by, he told me many years later. But this was evidently very different. For the fascists to be this far up the valley was a confirmation of Capt Cosa's worst fears – that a major *rastrellamento* – something unprecedented in scope and size – had penetrated deep into the area.

The enemy's forces, in fact, had managed to advance almost to the head of the valley and were already in charge of the main crossing points on the river. After their *rastrellamento* in the Langhe, which had been successful enough to split Mauri's partisans into three groups and drive them into the surrounding hills, the German and Italian Republican forces had launched an offensive against the partisans in the valleys south of Mondovì. It remained unclear whether the assault had been triggered by the parachute drop, but German troops and Italian Black Brigades had stormed up the Ellero and Pesio valleys, clashing with partisans along the way and posting soldiers at key points to secure the ground they had captured. The bridge on the road to Frabosa was one such spot and Campbell therefore took the only decision he felt was open to him – he issued orders to abandon the road and head into the hills. Their two guides took this as their cue to leave. Abandoning the pony-trap, Campbell, Pop, Banks, Stephens and Williamson headed up the slopes on a southerly heading, guided by the first light of dawn.

Laden down by their gear, progress was slow, but after a couple of hours they spotted houses ahead. As their eyes became accustomed to the light, they picked out other details: a church with a bell tower on one side of a small piazza, with houses on the other two sides and a steep drop on the fourth into a valley. From the map, they knew the settlement was Fontane, a hamlet tucked under a rocky ridge line at the head of the valley. Staying in the trees, they put the village under observation and soon spotted some women walking between a cluster of houses on the edge of the village. This, as Campbell noted in his memoir, came as a relief. 'We were told that the Italian women were reliable and on the whole anti-fascist,' he said. How accurate this was is debatable, but it emboldened him to make a decision to go down into the village and 'parlay' with them. Without Irving-Bell, who did speak fluent Italian, the only decent linguist amongst them was Pop. But, at best, Pop had only a smattering of Italian. Campbell didn't record how many of the group went into the village to speak with the women, but what emerged from the discussion that ensued with them was that there were no men in the village – that they had either been press-ganged into fascist military units or deported to Germany. The women they spoke to told them that fascist forces, working in small groups, had been combing the area since the previous day, but had not yet entered Fontane. They were still talking to the women when a villager rushed out to warn them that soldiers were coming up the valley. Everyone fled back into the woods, with Campbell so alarmed by what he'd heard that he buried what remained of their lira in the roots of a tree, covering it with leaves.

From their hiding position they watched as lines of troops – they identified them as RSI fascists – combed the valley below. As it grew darker, they could see that the dragnet had moved past them and that the enemy was on the ridge line above the village. But with nightfall, the temperature dropped and, with no choice but to spend the night in the open, Campbell ordered them all to lie on a groundsheet 'like spoons in a drawer', with each man taking it in turns to occupy the outside positions. Campbell himself 'took the first stint on the sharp end', as he put it, and recalled in his memoir his feeling of joy whenever it was his turn to be the 'lucky Alfonse' in the middle. When the light came up, they spotted a small building – it appeared to be a woodman's hut – some distance from the edge of the village and further up the mountainside, around 65m above the road that led into the valley. Everyone was so cold that they considered it worth the risk to head for the hut so they could light a fire and warm themselves inside. As dawn broke, the sentries posted to watch for signs of enemy troop movements reported zero activity anywhere.

At around 9.30am, they discussed what to do and decided that their best course of action was to try once again to solicit help from the women of the village – and that Pop, as the nominal linguist, should be the man to communicate with them. They watched through binoculars as he picked his way through the trees to the village perimeter. He then rounded a corner and disappeared from view. The minutes ticked by. Campbell scanned the slopes above and below them for a sign of the enemy, but still saw no movement. Then somebody said that they could see Pop making his way back. Campbell watched his approach through the binoculars and allowed himself to breathe again. 'Though he was taking care, his movement suggested that there was no threat from the direction of the village,' he wrote. But somebody else noticed that Pop wasn't alone. Two men had suddenly appeared and were strolling up the road from the direction of the bridge they had skirted around the night before. Watching them through his binoculars, Campbell saw that they were in civilian clothes. As they passed by the hut, very close to his viewpoint, he could see them watching Pop as he picked his way back up through the trees. From my father's relaxed gait, it was apparent to Campbell that Pop had not seen these men.

They disappeared into the village just as Pop made it back to the hut. From Campbell's account, the most detailed that exists of events that unfolded at Fontane, Pop had met and spoken with someone in the village, who had told him that it was 'clear' and that the enemy had 'moved on'. If this was the case, however, it was a lie, because suddenly they all heard, as Campbell's account had it, the 'tramp-tramp-tramp' of feet below them. Peering over the edge of the hut's porch, Campbell spotted around 30 soldiers in marching formation on the road. As the soldiers drew level with the hut, they turned and ran up the slope towards them. With barely time to think, Campbell had to make a snap decision: whether to fight it out or throw in the towel. As the enemy outgunned them at least five to one, he made the decision to surrender. Moments before they came out with their hands up, Banks had the presence of mind to hide all of his codebooks. Somebody else tossed a burning log into the hayloft. By the time they were all out in the open, the inside of the hut was an inferno. With their winter parkas, German weapons and black forage caps, troops of the Black Brigades could, from a distance, look like Germans. The moment he realised that they were Italians, Campbell thought they were doomed. 'They hated the partisans and anyone to do with them,' he wrote in his memoir. He thought then about making a run for it, 'on the grounds it was more sporting to shoot (or be shot as) a running target than just to wait for it'. But in the end, he elected to stay put. One of the Italians barked an order for them to strip naked. They were standing in the cold, shivering half to death, when there was a shout from below and a German officer appeared. He yelled at his Italian counterpart, who, embarrassed at being ordered by his ally, told the prisoners to get dressed again. As Campbell was placing his glengarry back on his head, however, the Italian snatched it from his hand, spat on it and rubbed it in his face. 'Perhaps I deserved it for my part in the failure of my mission,' he wrote.

Campbell was still full of remorse for having pushed for their flight to originate in Tuscany, although, as he made it plain subsequently, he'd had no idea before leaving the heel of Italy that this would entail them dropping in broad daylight. They were piled into trucks and driven under heavy escort back down the valley towards Mondovi. Along the way, they had time to ruminate on the events that had led to their capture. 'Did the women in the village spill the beans, or was it the two strolling Italian men who had spotted Bob... and were there for the purpose?' Campbell wondered in his memoir. He strongly suspected the latter. My father, however, was in no doubt at all. When the Italians stormed up the hill, Pop, Williamson, Stephens and Banks had managed to scoot out of the back of the hut and hide in a pile of leaves. It hadn't done them any good. Thanks to the 'traitor' who had tipped off the enemy, Pop recounted after the war, the RSI troops had known exactly where to look. Who this 'traitor' was was never made clear, or even confirmed as fact, although Pop did hear from Sergio Curetti years later that, a few days after their capture, a man from Fontane had been identified as the person who had betrayed them. According to Sergio, he was lynched by a combined group of locals and partisans, taken into the woods and summarily executed.

Chapter 15

'Twenty-first'

Mondovi, Northern Italy, December 1944

As soon as they arrived in Mondovi, Campbell, Pop, Banks, Stephens and Williamson were bundled into the guardhouse of a Republican Army unit and the business of interrogation began. The questioning, from Campbell's point of view, 'was rather abortive', because, as he wrote, 'he [Campbell] had not been around long enough to know anything'. This, however, was altogether different for Pop, who would need to disguise this fact at all costs from his interrogators.

As Cauvain was on the run, Pop, the only other member of Clarion to have been with the partisans for any length of time, would have without doubt claimed that he, too, had jumped with the main group on 9 December. Be that as it may, he was now a prisoner and this was something he had never contemplated happening to him. 'Suddenly, there was no present, only a possible future – and release,' he said, when he recalled this moment long after the war. Release at that point, however, would not have entered his mind. For now, all any of the Clarion party were thinking about was survival and the protection of information at all costs. This adjustment, from what until then had been a military mission, must have been considerable.

After two nights in a police jail in Mondovi, they were transferred to the civilian prison in the nearby town of Cuneo. The cell in which they were held, according to Campbell's memoir, was on the first floor of the building; the same floor was also given over to the administrative offices of their captors.

It was here, according to Campbell, that they were told – not by their RSI interrogators, but by the partisans in the other cells – that, irrespective of their British military uniforms, they would be shot. This moved Campbell to point out, whenever he got the opportunity, that they were regular military personnel and had been 'merely carrying out their orders'. When this appeared to cut no ice, Campbell noted that, as the war wasn't going so well for the Germans and their allies, it might be to their advantage to show them some mercy – or, as Campbell put it, 'to leave behind a good smell'. If this argument registered with their jailers, however, there was little sign of it; quite the reverse, in fact. The immediacy of the threat of execution was conveyed by the regular evening visits of priests to the cells of those partisans who were due to be shot the next morning. In a further bid to make it quite clear that they were all regular combatants, the Clarion team shooed away the priests with protestations that they were 'not of their faith' and therefore did not need confession or absolution. In truth, they were making a point: that they didn't consider themselves in the same boat as the partisans, who requested, and were granted, absolution before being shot. For the next two weeks, they whiled away the time as best they could, although, as Campbell pointed out, a cell of around 10 by 10 feet didn't yield much scope for entertainment.

It was Pop, according to Campbell, who suggested that they play chess. 'A chess set was, of course, not part of the fixtures of a felons' prison, so we made a set by chewing up a mixture of paper and bread,' Campbell wrote – red wine being used to dye the darker pieces. Pop and Campbell also set each other crossword puzzles and recited verse to one another. Campbell also told how one day he was taken from the cell and put through another round of interrogation – this time by two Gestapo officers. To his considerable alarm, they both held stick grenades in their laps as they questioned him across a table. Despite this, Campbell said, their interrogation technique was 'abysmal' – while he stuck to the 'name, rank and number' convention, they were more interested in conditions on the home front. Campbell told them, pointedly, that morale was high owing to the British conviction that Germany would very soon be defeated. He put this point across so forcefully, he said in his memoir, that he was 'amazed they didn't start waving their stick grenades about'. He came away from this session with the very strong impression that he had just been put through a 'comic opera' and that the two Germans, with their grenades and leather coats, had come straight from Central Casting. Later he learned from his jailers that the grenades were a precaution against attack by the partisans, who 'were getting bolder as the Germans got weaker'.

This, in fact, was hardly true. As a result of the *rastrellamento*, the resistance was in disarray. Two days after the capture of the group, most of the partisans of the 3rd and 4th Alpine Divisions had been driven from their positions in the valleys into the Langhe. Those who had stayed behind found themselves in a desperate fight for survival in the valleys' upper reaches.

Lt Aceto's band of partisans, which included Sergio Curetti, briefly occupied Frabosa Soprana, but, finding themselves under attack, retreated to Fontane, following the route the Clarion party had taken days earlier. It was while they were in Fontane that they were able to root out the man who had betrayed the Clarion party to the Republicans and mete out their summary justice. Eventually driven out of the village by renewed German and RSI attacks, a small band of partisans, including Curetti and Aceto, tried to reach the outskirts of Mondovi, where safety of a sort awaited them, the population there being more loyal to the partisan cause than the people living in the valleys. They were unable to reach the town, however, because of a heavier than expected German presence in the lower part of the valley, so they turned around and headed back into the mountains. There, on a mission from Lt Aceto to pick up some information from a partisan hiding out in a farm on the edge of the isolated village of Corsagliola, Curetti had a very narrow escape.

Reaching the farmhouse, he found it deserted, except for a woman sobbing uncontrollably in a room on the upper floor. He tried to find out what was wrong, but without success. Suddenly, from below, a guttural male voice shouted for him to come down with his hands up. Curetti, with documents in one hand and a gun in the other, assessed what he needed to do. He had unloaded the gun – it may well have been the shotgun that Pop had given him – because it had a tendency to discharge at the slightest knock, even with the safety catch on. Yelling to his would-be captor that he was on his way down, he reached the courtyard and, without turning around, made a dash for it. Bullets whizzed past his head, but, despite falling flat on his face while failing to clear a barbed-wire fence, he picked himself up and managed to make it to the woods without being hit.

Terrified by the experience, he asked local farmers if they would hide him until the immediate danger subsided, but they refused; some of them even driving him from their land, frightened at the thought of what the RSI and the Germans would do to them if he were found to be on their property.

Curetti eventually made it back to the part of Mondovi where he lived – a suburb that was mercifully free of German troops. There he crept back into his house and lay low until the worst of the fighting was over. Captain Cosa, meanwhile, managed to escape the Val Ellero, ending up at the Shrine of Santa Lucia, an imposing convent just outside the town, where the Catholic sisters hid him in the roof. He, too, would remain there until the fighting subsided. Mauri, meanwhile, who had been joined by an SOE BLO – Captain Hugh Ballard, a South African who had flown in with Colonel Stevens's party to help coordinate the parachute drops – ordered his partisans to split up again and to regroup when the German assault was over. It would, in fact, be another two months before they would be able to reform. Only by lying low did the partisans manage to avoid total annihilation during the two weeks of the *rastrellamento*. From 11 December to Christmas Day, the attacks and reprisals continued unabated, with the Germans and Republicans vying with each other to carry out the most brutal acts of oppression and suppression.

On 20 December, German troops rounded up 2,000 people from Mondovi and its environs – old men, women and children mainly – and forced them to march 30km through the snow to Cuneo. Along the way, they were filmed by Republican propaganda units and portrayed in newsreels as 'a column of rebels' captured during military operations in the valleys south of Mondovi. Only after the intervention of the Bishop of Mondovi were the Germans persuaded to release those who had survived the journey and allow them to return to their homes. Meanwhile, the commander of a detachment of Cacciatori degli Appennini, one of the RSI's most brutal instruments of suppression, had established himself in Mondovi's town hall, where he set about interrogating anyone suspected of dealing with the resistance.

According to Carluccio, two former boxers were brought in to Mondovi specifically to beat up suspects under interrogation. Their boss, Lieutenant Alberto Farina, used to interrogate suspects while hanging them from a beam by their wrists. Another favourite technique was to beat them while they kneeled on a board of nails. It was said that a German sergeant was so disgusted by what he found when he stumbled across Farina's torture chamber, while Farina himself was in the midst of a particularly violent bout of questioning, that he spat in Farina's face. 'The fascists were extremely tough and tortured partisans without pity,' Carluccio told me. 'The Germans were easier to deal with – they either took you prisoner or killed you.' Carluccio also managed to lie low until the *rastrellamento* ran out of steam in February 1945.

Four days after Christmas, the Clarion team received a welcome, and yet unwelcome, addition to the cell: Eddie Cauvain. Cauvain, who had been on the run for two-and-a-half weeks since separating from the rest of the group to destroy the equipment in the cave, told them how he and Colin Irving-Bell had managed to hide out in the woods close to Frabosa and Fontane during the worst period of the *rastrellamento*. But how also, in a severe lapse of judgement, as he told them, they'd decided to go to Fontane to escape the cold and look for food – in the hope, also, that the villagers would know what had happened to the rest of the Clarion group. They'd had no idea, of course, that Fontane had been the village where the main party had been betrayed.

Irving-Bell had insisted on walking through the woods. Cauvain, however, thinking the Germans and Republicans had left the valleys, elected to stay on the road. A German armoured car had swept without warning around a bend and, with nowhere to run to, Cauvain was captured. After a night in Mondovi, he, too, was brought to Cuneo. He had survived on next to nothing while they had been on the run and was just about all-in when he was reunited with the rest of the group. Only Irving-Bell, whom Cauvain revealed had been with the US airmen when they split up on the road to Fontane, was now still at large. He would eventually reach safety by linking up with Colonel Stevens's BLO mission in the Langhe. In the meantime, amidst the chaos of the *rastrellamento*, no one at No.1 SF HQ had the least idea whether the six members of the Clarion mission were alive or dead.

They would remain in the dark over the mission's fate for several more months.

In the depths of a particularly cold night in Cuneo at the end of December, Pop, Campbell, Cauvain, Banks, Stephens and Williamson were shaken awake, dragged out of their cell and ordered into the prison courtyard. As Campbell described it in his memoir, he was sure they were to be shot. The six German soldiers prodded them at rifle-point into the back of an open truck, gave them a single blanket and told them that they were being driven to Le Nuove prison in Turin, a journey of around 60km.

As part of my wish to understand the lie of the land in which Pop found himself while he'd been with the partisans, I'd made a number of trips to follow the journey he had taken from Fontane to Turin as a prisoner. On the last of these, I had travelled out to Italy with Mop, who had insisted that she too wanted to visit the places where Pop had been held in the aftermath of his capture. We had driven from Mondovi along the Val Ellero, tracing the contours of the river that Pop, Campbell, Stephens, Williamson and Banks had followed as they'd made their way to Fontane from Cosa's mountain HQ. We'd stood in Fontane on a wet, grey day, looking up at mountains around us, knowing that 70 years earlier Pop had stood in this very place as he'd parlayed with the people of the village; knowing, too, what he had *not* known – that (as I allowed my mind to drift a little deeper) within minutes he and the rest of the Clarion group would be betrayed to the Republican forces that had been out there, combing the woods for *partigiani*. I had tried – and failed – to find the woodman's hut where they had taken refuge the night their luck had run out, maybe, I reflected, because it had burned down after that log had been hurled into the hayloft. I had managed to inspect the courtyard of what had once been the police jail in Mondovi where they had spent their first two nights of captivity – and all these places had resonated with the narrative as I now understood it.

In the cold and the dark of these places, I had been able to experience a hint of the isolation and fear that Pop, as a 20-year-old, must have experienced – as, all around him, the Germans and the Italian fascists had embarked on their wholesale annihilation of the local resistance movement.

In the depths of winter, as it had also been for him, these places had managed to imprint some remnant of the past on me, but nothing had remotely prepared me for Le Nuove, the state prison in the middle of Turin, where Pop, Campbell, Cauvain, Banks, Williamson and Stephens were shuttered into a cell on the first floor of the SS-run wing in the small hours of 30 December.

According to Campbell's memoir, and to Banks, whose report is in The National Archives at Kew, prisoners were free to wander the corridor by day, but were locked in their cells at night. Most were partisans, Campbell wrote, the odd felon and 'one quite unacceptable Australian', who, the Germans had told him, had been transferred from a nearby POW camp because his captors there wanted nothing more to do with him. Campbell – the epitome of the upstanding British officer – hated the man, describing him as 'wild, noisy, swearing' and 'unfit' for human companionship. Pop had referenced the fact that at one point at Le Nuove he had shared a cell with a hairdresser who had been charged with murder, 'a very nice fellow', as he'd described him. He'd also painted a vivid portrait of the warder, a man straight out of Gilbert and Sullivan, 'all beard and bristle', with a huge belt jangling with keys.

An underground corridor in the southwest wing had been given over to the *condannati a morte*. Seventy years on, this part of the prison, despite Le Nuove now being a museum, had lost none of its starkness. Black and white photographs pinned to the walls attested to the almost industrial manner in which the Republicans put the *condannati* to death: tied to a chair in a courtyard and executed by firing squad, the shots audible from all points of the prison.

Pop stated in his oral deposition at the Imperial War Museum that he was 'interviewed' several times by the Gestapo during his time at Le Nuove. They were, he said, particularly interested to know why his identity card stated that he was attached to a ship, HMS *President*. This, in fact, was part of Pop's cover story – HMS *President* being nothing more than an old steamer tied up on London's Embankment close to the War Office.

It was difficult to second-guess from published testimony whether the 'interviews' to which the members of Clarion were subjected were more brutal affairs than any of them admitted to. In the interview in which he talked about his City career, Pop admitted that the Italians were much 'better interrogators' than the Germans – and infinitely more brutal in the way they set about trying to obtain information. In the post-war report at The National Archives of the team's capture and subsequent incarceration – its author isn't named, but everything points strongly to it having been Colonel Stevens, the former solicitor who had flown in by B25 to the Abraham landing site after Darewski's death to take charge of all BLOs in the area – it stated specifically that they were *not* interrogated; Campbell, on the other hand, stated that they were. Whatever the truth, the conditions – brought alive in Campbell's extraordinarily personal account (I reminded myself, too, that Campbell had been in Le Nuove, Stevens hadn't) – made it clear that he considered their lives forfeit from the moment they arrived there. Although the Germans were nominally in charge of their wing, their day-to-day treatment was meted out by Italians – brutal ones at that.

Campbell stated that their 'animal instincts' kicked in as soon as they arrived at Le Nuove – 'we were cold, we were hungry and we were lousy,' he wrote. The lice were everywhere and impossible to kill in the usual manner with forefinger and thumb. 'The best way was to fry them up on our stove by opening up the seams [of our clothes] and dragging [them] across the hot metal before the cloth caught fire.' In order to fuel the stoves, they had to resort to burning their bed-boards; and when all the wood was gone, they raided the beds in the other cells. 'The Australian's cell, which he had to himself because neither friend nor foe would share with him, was an obvious target,' Campbell wrote.

As for food, Campbell could only remember that it was 'scant and meagre'. They were fortunate, however, in that they, at least, had water. The political prisoners were not allowed, as they were, to roam their corridor, being kept instead in a state of permanent isolation. In his memoir, Campbell wrote that years later he could still hear the cries of '*acqua, acqua*' coming from their cells. Their only access to food and water was provided by some nuns. The sole advantage of the cold in which they lived, Campbell added, was that the freezing temperatures froze the slop water in the wing's communal toilet.

One day, he wrote, a *Wehrmacht* general paid a visit to the prison and, hearing of it, he and Pop demanded an audience with him to discuss their conditions – Campbell 'as the Senior British Officer and Bob with his fair command of German'. Campbell described the general as a 'very nice man' who listened patiently and sympathetically to their complaints and especially about the lice and lack of ablution and washing facilities. Campbell stressed – again to make the point – that they were regular military officers and that their German counterparts did not get treated this way as POWs. The general promised that he would do something about it, but nothing ever happened.

Instead, Campbell stated in his memoir, 'Bob and I were taken for yet another interrogation round somewhere in Turin.' On arrival, and waiting to be summoned, they were told that on no account were they to talk to each other – and this, in itself, conveyed the very real sense that this was a different kind of 'interview' from the one with the grenade-wielding Gestapo officers in Cuneo.

Campbell was worried because when he had been captured and searched he had had on him a piece of paper with the name and address of a woman in Imperia who had been a friend of his aunt before the war. Campbell freely acknowledged in his memoir that this was very foolish of him, but by the time he reached the interrogation centre he was determined to undo any damage he had done. Now, though, he had to enlist Pop into helping him – and he had not had a chance to discuss his strategy before their arrival.

As they'd waited to be questioned, Campbell started to hum a tune that he had picked up in Italy called '*Torna a Surriento*', which he'd chosen deliberately to allay any suspicion on the part of his Italian fascist guard. As he'd hummed, he started to introduce English words and phrases that would gradually communicate the message that he wanted to get across to Pop: that the address he had had on him had been nothing to do with the mission, except in so far as he thought that it might be a useful place to stay after the Germans had departed – all of which was true. Although the strategy was hardly original, it worked. Pop got the gist of the message. They were then hauled in individually for questioning. Again, there was little indication from either my father or Campbell about the form these interrogation sessions took, but I assumed them to have been intense, extremely physical and underscored by the threat of death at any moment.

On their way back to the prison, Campbell described how they were escorted for a short way through the streets where they passed posters emblazoned with imaginative depictions of London in flames. It was the time of the V1 and V2 attacks and this had provided a boost to fascist morale.

As they were marched at rifle-point back to their waiting truck, they were jeered and jostled by groups of Germans who shouted, 'London *kaputt*' at them. Campbell, with commendable courage, took it upon himself to correct this impression at every turn, informing their tormentors that London was very far from *kaputt* – this on the basis that he had been dining there only a few weeks before. 'They did not like it,' he wrote, 'and I was glad that our guard pushed us into our awaiting "carriage" – the truck that took us back to jail.'

On 6 January, a week after they arrived at Le Nuove, my father turned 21. He chose to share this seminal moment sotto voce with his companions, telling them that he never expected to come of age in a prison.

Campbell decided that he couldn't let this milestone go uncelebrated and that they would do everything they could 'to do him the honour of seeing in his majority'. Being SOE, Campbell wrote, 'we, of course, had ways and means of concealing valuable things about our person – minute compasses sewn into our clothing and money, in the form of lira notes, hidden in our boot insteps'. Between the various members of the Clarion group, they were thus able to put together a 'fair sum'. This, however, did not get them very far, because the alcohol they wanted to exchange it for was, needless to say, outside the prison walls. Campbell approached an Italian guard – one better disposed to them than most – with a hypothetical proposition. *If* some money could be found and *if* the guard were able to buy some alcohol, *might* it be possible to celebrate the coming of age of their young officer with a harmless drink or two? After some protracted negotiations, in the course of which a large backhander was introduced into the hypothetical discussions, to their enormous surprise, three bottles of vermouth suddenly turned up in their cell, allowing them, as Campbell put it, to 'give Bob a very commendable beano'. As they hadn't had a drink for weeks and were in a state of near-starvation, the alcohol went straight to their heads. Pop had even gone so far as to include the hated Australian in these celebrations, although this had some unfortunate consequences. As Campbell told it, the Australian was so 'alight' after several sips that he announced his intention to rush the guards and initiate a mass breakout. 'Had we not locked him back in his own cell, he would have led the assault there and then,' he said. Pop made no mention of this impromptu celebration in his verbal deposition at the IWM. The only reference he made to anyone about his 21st birthday – myself included – had been to point out the generosity of a nun, who had given him a hard-boiled egg, which – under the circumstances, Pop had told us – couldn't have been a better or more meaningful gift. But, as the testimony of someone in whom Pop confided just a few years before he died bore witness, this was not the whole story, because something else happened on his 21st birthday – something that provided me, shortly after my visit to Le Nuove, with reason to re-evaluate my father's whole experience of SOE and the war.

Back in London shortly after my trip, Gerry Pattinson, my ex-MI6 friend who had been at the 70th anniversary dinner for SOE with Pop at the Imperial War Museum, recalled some further crucial details about the conversation that night. He had spoken to Pop about a former colleague who had also been held prisoner in 1944 by the Italians. The colleague said they had been particularly brutal – far worse than the Germans – and that they had tortured him. It was after this, Gerry said, that the conversation took an altogether different turn. 'It was as if your father', he added, 'suddenly wanted to talk.' Gerry, I could see, was hesitant to tell me any more, but I urged him to go on.

'He was talking to Susan,' he said. Susan was Gerry's wife and, like him, had also been in MI6. She, too, was a good listener. Pop, know-ing of their ties to the security services, would no doubt have felt a bond of trust with them both. I sat up and listened closely. Gerry told me that Pop had revealed that the Italians had, as he put it, 'biffed him about a bit too'. I asked him when this had happened and he told me: on Pop's 21st birthday. 'He wasn't physically tortured. This was psychological torture,' Gerry said. He paused, then added: 'But of the very worst kind.' He told me they had put Pop in front of a firing squad and fired twice – he then stopped, remembering something. I could see he was trying to recall what Pop had said word for word. 'No, he said that they fired once and then – and then he said that he'd lost control of himself.' The Italians, seeing Pop had wet his trousers, began to laugh. He mentioned this specifically, Gerry told me, that they had been Italians. He then said they fired a second time. Both times just above his head.

Gerry added that he had been intensely moved by what Pop had told him – especially as he made it clear that he'd never spoken about it before. 'He was clearly quite emotional, but in a very understated way. Looking back, I think he found it therapeutic to talk. It had been in an atmosphere conducive to his wanting to speak. I felt privileged he'd done so to Susan and me.'

As remarkable still, I thought later, was Pop's determination not to let this prejudice him against Italians as a whole. Perhaps his reluc-tance to speak had been a nod to the suffering of the many partisans and civilians tortured by the Nazis and Italian fascists – in a nuanced variation on the standard line: *that whatever I suffered, your suffering – the suffering of the partisans and the Italian people – had been worse. And so, what do I have to complain about?*

Pop's final word on the subject of death and reprisal was contained in a few succinct lines in his oral deposition in the archives of the Imperial War Museum. After almost a month of captivity, he relayed to his IWM interviewer, he and his SOE colleagues were informed by their German captors that they would not be put on trial. With their 'impeccable logic', Pop said, they informed the Clarion group that, as German citizens were now fighting the Allies *in* Germany, this placed the Italian partisans – and those who assisted them – on the same footing. Resistance fighters thus had the same status as POWs and would be treated as such. This may not have been policy, or enshrined in a 'Führer order', but it said something about the relationship between the Germans and their allies that even the SS had considered the RSI's methods of oppression to have been beyond the pale.

In one further postscript, Pop had once told me that during a business trip to Turin in the 1960s he had wandered off, in a moment when he had had 'nothing better to do', to take a look at Le Nuove. Quite by chance, he ran into his former jailer outside the main gate, the 'bearded and bristled' figure who'd doubled as a character from Gilbert and Sullivan. After shaking his hand warmly, the jailer offered to show him his old cell. Pop accepted. To his surprise, the murderous hairdresser was exactly where he had left him and welcomed him back with open arms. Now that I knew what had *really* happened here, I was amazed that my father could have been persuaded to revisit the place he had been put through a double mock-execution – but this, in a sense, was very typically him. Pop had never wanted his life to be in any way constrained by the ghosts of his past – and this visit, perhaps, was one way of exorcising them. Another had been simply to clam up about the detail of his experiences. Beard and Bristle then showed him his entry in the prisoner log for December 1944 and the two men departed – Pop, as far as I could tell, without any trace of bitterness. For both of them, he said, it had simply been 'the war'.

Chapter 16

'Trains and transit camps'

Turin, January 1945

Before dawn on 14 January, Pop, Campbell, Stephens and Williamson were woken by a German officer and told to gather their scant possessions. They were being driven to a transit camp, he told them, for onward transportation to Germany. Cauvain and Banks, for reasons unclear, were to follow on later.

Outside, under the glare of lights, they were bundled into the back of a truck, which, to Campbell's amusement, was powered by a wood-burning stove bolted on to the rear of the cab. One of their guards, 'a rather pleasant Rhinelander', told them that the camp they were headed to was located just outside Mantua – Mantova in Italian – a drive of around 200km.

Given the privations of the time, the journey was too long to accomplish in a single day and they broke the trip in a small town with a civilian jail where they were locked up for the night. The numerous short stops they'd made along the way for 'relief and sustenance' had allowed them to contemplate escape, although not here: 'the streets,' Campbell wrote, 'were solid sheet-ice and it would be difficult enough to keep one's feet, even [when] walking'.

Before leaving them, the Rhinelander told their jailer, who was almost certainly RSI, to treat them properly and to give them adequate blankets – with the added instruction that the group was to let him know in the morning if they had any cause for complaint. As soon as the Rhinelander departed, however, they were locked in adjoining cells without a blanket between them; and so, as the temperature plummeted, they began to shout the place down. When the jailer came running, they told him in no uncertain terms what the Germans would do to him if he didn't play ball and this yielded unexpected results – he put them in the guardroom where there was a stove, and they ended up enjoying their warmest night in weeks. 'We were able to give the Rhinelander a good report in the morning,' Campbell's memoir said drily.

They reached the transit camp in Mantua the next afternoon. Campbell didn't give the camp a name, but from my own research I knew it must have been 'Dulag 339' – 'Dulag' for *Durchgangslager* or transit camp. In the wake of the armistice, when the Germans had taken over the administration of camps run by their former Italian allies, the policy had been to collect POWs and hold them at Dulag 339 before onward transport to Germany. Dulag 339 had been designed to hold POWs for just a few days, but as 1944 wore on, and as Allied air attacks caused more disruption to transportation and communications links, days often became weeks. Kitchen facilities, a shower and an air-raid shelter had to be added to the limited facilities of the camp, which was described in other accounts as having next to no heat and lighting. According to Campbell, they were told they would be detained for no more than 24 hours and that the next day they would be put on a train that would take them through the Brenner Pass, the mountainous route between Italy and Austria, and from there to Germany. 'This was bad news,' Campbell observed. Once into Austria, there would be little to no chance of escape.

The next morning, they were marched the short distance from the camp to the station where a train to the Greater German Reich awaited them. Under the Geneva Convention, trains transporting prisoners of war were supposed to be marked with 'POW' in highly visible lettering as protection from air attack – but theirs, Campbell noted, had no markings. Further, he wrote, 'I was horrified to see that our train [included] fuel trucks.' Bundled on to the rear, behind the fuel and a guard's van, were the cattle trucks that would take them into Germany. As senior officer, Campbell demanded to see his German opposite number – 'the OC Train' – a warrant officer, who told Campbell rather smugly that the letters 'POW' *had* been painted on the roofs of the cattle trucks – as well as on the guard's van. 'That's a fat lot of good,' Campbell barked back at him, 'as there's four inches of snow on them.'

The *Feldwebel* remained unmoved and ordered him, Pop,

Williamson and Stephens – along with several hundred other POWs – on to the train.

The two cattle trucks were so crowded that there was standing room only. As a result, all officers were ordered into the guard's van. Straw was scattered across the floor for them to sleep on. Wall-to-wall and floor-to-ceiling barbed wire deterred any thoughts of escape. 'There was no way out except with a claw-hammer,' Campbell said, 'and we didn't have one handy.'

After an interminable wait, the train suddenly lurched forward and soon began to make progress, judging from the clickety-clack of the wheels on the track as they headed north. Campbell could see the mountains rolling by through a 4-inch head-height ventilation slit in the side of the wagon. It was at this point in his account that I was struck by the feeling that Campbell, Pop – the whole Clarion group – must have felt: that surviving the war – something that must have seemed inconceivable (to a captured SOE agent under threat of execution prior to the rescinding of the Führer order) a few weeks earlier – was now a distinct possibility.

Several hours later, as the train rolled to a halt, Campbell, straining for a view through the slit, informed them that they had reached Bolzano and that he could see that they were in a large marshalling yard. Bolzano was 30km from the Austrian border and the train had partially emerged from a long tunnel. Suddenly, they heard aero-engines. As the sound grew louder, Campbell saw the engine driver sprint past them towards the front of the train. A second or two later, there was a lurch and the train began to shunt backwards into the tunnel. Glancing up, Campbell could now see planes high overhead and then he heard the whistle of bombs. There was a giant explosion that felt like one enormous bomb, Campbell wrote – the first of a wave of continuous explosions to hit the marshalling yard. The pressure wave from the first giant explosion tore through the tunnel, rocking the train. A paraffin lamp that had been hanging from the ceiling fell to the floor and set the straw alight – which they only just managed to put out. The train pulled back into the tunnel. As bomb after bomb rained down, they counted the explosions, feeling them as dull vibrations, knowing that the yard and the town were being flattened.

They could see nothing, however. Everything was pitch-black. And there they remained. A day passed, then another. 'They were not pleasant,' Campbell recorded in another dry piece of understatement, 'especially for the other ranks in their disgustingly cramped conditions in the cattle trucks.'

To begin with, everyone bore their lot stoically. But as time wore on, with the train still in the tunnel and their food and water running out, Campbell, as the senior officer in charge, once again demanded to see the OC Train. The *Feldwebel* showed up and Campbell did his best to take charge, suggesting that the guards mount machine guns at each entrance to the tunnel so that the men could be released from their airless carriages.

The *Feldwebel* prevaricated. The train, he said, would be allowed to continue on its way soon. All prisoners would remain in the cattle trucks.

The train, however, did not move and day succeeded day and 'night succeeded night, as it was all the same to us,' Campbell wrote of their appalling conditions. Their only comfort was the warmth of the stove – something that brought forth new problems. 'The lice, with which we were all infected thrived on the conditions of dark and warmth and had a feast,' as Campbell described it. They heard other trains moving through the tunnel, but these, they were told, had priority as they were packed with troops heading back into Austria and Germany. Hope turned to frustration and frustration to despair as their train stayed in the tunnel. From snatched conversations with their guards, they learned that growing numbers of soldiers were being pulled out of Italy to defend the homeland against the Red Army, which had just taken Warsaw. They received scraps of food from one guard, even though he was terrified of his NCO, an ardent Nazi. It wasn't until 25 January, after about a week, that the train finally emerged and they started on their way again. By then, however, as Campbell observed, 'two of the other ranks had died, the rest were in a very bad way and we ourselves were much debilitated by lack of food and the attentions of the lice'. They were, though, miraculously, alive.

Looking down from the cable car that I rode up the mountain, I was able to see the entirety of the Bolzano marshalling yards stretched out below. They were huge – a choke-point for trains moving to and from the Greater German Reich and an obvious strategic target. Records showed that numerous points along the 'Brenner Line' had been hit between 15 and 18 January by Mitchells and Havocs of the US 9th and 12th Army Air Forces – aircraft that had been tasked with disrupting German transport links during a break in the bad weather that had prevailed since the autumn. From the top of the mountain, it looked as if nothing much had changed. The station and the marshalling yard were still there – the whole area, indeed, remained a hub for the movement of goods across the nearby border with Austria. The town, confined between the mountains, had been rebuilt, and the railway line that had brought Pop, Campbell and their companions up to Bolzano from Mantua was clearly visible beside the river. To try to understand the horror of such a long period of confinement underground, I spent several hours attempting to locate the tunnel, but nobody professed to know anything about it and so I pressed on, following the railway as it threaded north through the tunnels and cuttings of the Brenner Pass. Today, it is a two-and-a-half hour drive from Italy across Austria into Germany – and quicker, even, by rail. During January 1945, the journey would have taken days, not hours, as the Brenner Line had been almost permanently in the crosshairs of the 9th and 12th Air Forces.

What would Pop have felt as he'd left Italy? On the one hand, I knew that there would have been relief: relief that he had no longer been under the threat of immediate execution; and relief that he was no longer in the clutches of the Italian fascists. But as Pop had always maintained he'd not been able to imagine himself a POW, I knew, too, that he would have hated this period of confinement. It would have been an altogether better day, therefore, when he reached the next waypoint on his journey: Stalag VIIA at Moosburg. In early February 1945, Stalag VIIA had been an installation under a great deal of pressure. Built as a camp for US Air Force NCOs, it eventually took on the role of a transit camp via which Allied POWs captured in North Africa and Italy were 'processed' before being transferred to permanent camps in Germany. But it retained a role as a permanent camp as well. Situated on a flat plain in the lee of hills that rose sharply towards the Bavarian Alps, Stalag VIIA, not far from Munich, was ringed by a double barbed-wire fence interspersed by seven guard towers. It was roughly square shaped and was divided into three main compounds, which, in turn, were subdivided into three small 'stockades'. These were still evident when I arrived in the town of Neustadt after my journey through Austria from Italy.

Extraordinarily, there was still quite a lot of the camp left to see. Neustadt, or Newtown, had grown up around the Moosburg camp soon after the end of the war. Following some maps I had found online, I was able to find several former barracks blocks, looking much as they had in 1945, on Sudetenlandstraße, a long residential street. These were not the wooden huts burned into my memory from films like *The Great Escape*, but brick-built buildings – solid enough to have survived the ravages of seven decades and serving still as both residential accommodation and as offices. A memorial close by gave me some inkling of what Pop would have found when he'd arrived in early February. The *Nordlager*, or North Camp, held newly arrived POWs – usually for a period of a few days – while they were searched, medically examined and deloused. One of two other *Lager*s held Soviet POWs, while the third held French, Polish, Yugoslav, British and Americans. The memorial told me that, of the 80,000 POWs at Stalag VIIA at the end of the war, approximately half came from France, with the next biggest country contingent being that of the Soviet Union – there were more than 14,000 Red Army POWs, all in their own segregated barracks and all appallingly treated.

On 2 February, the camp's numbers were swelled by an additional 2,000 prisoners – Allied officers transferred from the south compound of Stalag Luft III at Sagan, the Luftwaffe-run POW camp made famous by *The Great Escape*. The Germans had taken the decision to move the prisoners to Moosburg due to the rapid advance of the Red Army. Five days later, 2,000 additional prisoners arrived, this time from Stalag Luft III's middle compound. All were held in Moosburg's *Nordlager*, where groups were searched and deloused before being sent to Moosburg's main camp. According to reports drawn from the US Military Intelligence Service War Department written after the war, the German administration was unprepared for the influx of new personnel and seemed completely disorganised. 'German rations were unbelievably poor,' the reports stated, 'no inside sanitary facilities existed and there was no hot water.' This tallied with Campbell's account of the 'deteriorating conditions' inside the camp when he, Pop, Williamson and Stephens arrived there in the middle of the prisoner influx from Stalag Luft III. The delousing they received in the *Nordlager*, however, was very welcome. 'I have never felt so clean as I did when I ceased to play host to those pests,' Campbell wrote. 'In our new, pure state, we joined other British POWs in the British compound. They had been tenants for varying lengths of time and were mostly from the Italian front,' he reported, although there were some newly arrived from the Ardennes, the scene of Hitler's last-ditch effort to drive the British and Americans back to the coast in the offensive that became known as 'The Battle of the Bulge'. Campbell wrote how amused he'd been at Moosburg by multiple Americans coming into the camp complaining, after long journeys, of aching backs and 'busted asses' – and, all told, this let me know that he and Pop considered themselves to be in a better, lighter environment than any of the other confinements they'd found themselves in since their capture six weeks earlier. From Pop's testimony, and evidence I unearthed later, I estimated him to have spent a week at Moosburg. As an RNVR officer, he was about to be transferred to a 'Marlag', a camp for naval officers – part of the Marlag und Milag complex – in the village of Westertimke, near Bremen. After six weeks of operations and incarceration with his SOE colleagues, the time had come for Pop to say goodbye to them.

In early January, soon after the New Year, No.1 Special Force had begun the difficult process of transferring its headquarters from Monopoli to Siena. All the FANY wireless operators and coder/decoders, including my mother, were transported on 12 DC3 flights between 25 January and 6 February. Overseeing the move, and the technical complexity of completing it without any disruption to signals traffic, was Derrick Scott-Job, the man who had accomplished the same task with such dexterity during SOE's exodus from Massingham to Monopoli almost 15 months earlier. Oddjob's challenge, as relayed by FANY Margaret Pawley, who made the move during March 1945, revolved around the availability of equipment and the 'retuning' of No.1 Special Force's communications sets to work over the shorter distances between Siena and SOE's agents in the field. This required changing the crystals in the transmitters to allow them to operate at the new frequencies.

The HQ at Siena was a former school, the Istituto Tolomei, which had been partly converted into a hospital during the German occupation. Unlike in Monopoli, here there was plenty to do. There was an American cinema at which the films changed frequently, a lending library, a dry-cleaner, a hairdresser and a canteen. An Allied Officers' Club had been set up in the grand surroundings of a Sienese palazzo, with chandeliers and a parquet floor for dancing. At headquarters, a van arrived each day selling tea and cakes in the courtyard and there was even a public bathhouse nearby where women could bathe on Mondays, Thursdays and Saturdays. The pressure of work on the FANYs, however, already intense, was even greater in Siena than it had been down south. With more than 100 BLOs and almost as many Italian agents in the field, wireless operators and coders were at full stretch dealing with the traffic. Everyone was waiting for Field Marshal Alexander's long-awaited final offensive against the Gothic Line; the assumption being that it would come in the spring. But in late February, spring was still more than a month away – and, for Mop, still with no news of Pop, a month seemed like a lifetime.

Since receiving Williamson's illicit message via the Coelum South radio set at Baracco – the message that Pop, laid up with his broken ribs in San Giacomo, had asked Cauvain to transmit to her – Mop had heard nothing from Pop or anyone who had anything to do with Clarion. As the *rastrellamenti* continued and, with Colin Irving-Bell still on the run (he would remain at large until March, when he reached Stevens's field headquarters in Piedmont, only to be captured shortly thereafter at Savona), and with the 3rd and 4th Alpine partisan divisions' communications in tatters, the fate of the Clarion group had become lost in the fog of war. It was as if the Clarion team had dropped off the map, which in a sense it had. It was against this gloomy assessment that my godfather, Robin, wrote to Mop, on 30 December, to say that he was now with '20 Det' in Nice. After several abortive attempts to deliver Capt Robert Bentley's 'Saki' BLO mission to Liguria by sea, he was waiting for the weather to clear before launching one final attempt in the first week of January – one that would turn out to be successful. He had also written to tell Mop that he felt deeply for her over the lack of news from my father. *Bob is the best friend I have had in this part of the world,* he told her, *and I can sincerely believe how he could evaporate in this untimely fashion. I can only say that the circumstances point to them all being well...* Here he reiterated his fervent belief that Pop, Campbell and Irving-Bell were very much alive. *If I know those three, they won't be very long standing idle if there's the faintest chance of getting away – which there always is: look at Gallegos!* (Adrian Gallegos, a remarkable SOE agent, had been captured by the Germans after his MAS boat had been blown up by a mine near Rome in 1943, but, masquerading as an Italian, he'd managed to escape a year later.)

Shortly after Pop had jumped, Mop had taken it upon herself to write to his parents – the first time she had contacted them, and finding it difficult because there was so little she was able to tell them. But from the tone of the letters she received back – letters I was now able to read, and which had always come from Gladys, my grandmother, never from my grandfather – it was clear that Granny Clark knew that Pop was behind the lines. Much later, Pop revealed that he had had to tell his parents shortly before the mission that he might be 'travelling' and out of touch for a while. On 30 November, she thanked Mop for letting her know Pop 'had gone' and had 'arrived safely'. 'I wonder if there is any hope,' she added, 'of him being back for his 21st?' She wrote again on 7 December to thank Mop for telling her she had received a 'personal message' from him – this after Pop had 'sent his love' from the Coelum South W/T set. Granny Clark said she hoped it wouldn't be too long before he returned. And then, on 12 January, she wrote to say she had received news that Pop was missing. *The news broken to us by you, Marjorie Dear, is so much softer than the official notification which we shall get and we are very thankful to you for writing.*

On 9 February, Granny Clark wrote again, this time in a happier frame of mind, as it seemed that there was some hope, at least, that Pop had been captured, not killed. This had been provided, I learned, from Colonel Stevens, who used to write regularly to the families of BLOs in his charge in the Turin area, to offer encouragement if they were posted missing. *We are hardly breathing*, Gladys wrote, *until something more definite comes through, but in the meantime life seems to be brighter.* Two weeks later, Granny Clark wrote a letter to Robin – a letter that had come to be in Mop's possession – in which she congratulated him upon the award of his DSC, which she had spotted in *The Times* on 20 December. *I could not believe my eyes*, she told him, *when I read R.A.C. Clark, but when I saw your name with his, I knew it to be true.* And I could only imagine the reserves of courage she'd managed to summon when she added: *My husband and I send you our heartiest congratulations too and feel very proud of your wonderful job of work. It seems such a pity that Bob didn't get out this time…* I reread this last part several times. *Such a pity Bob didn't get out this time* – the epitome of British sangfroid in the face of the most terrible anxiety. Granny Clark concluded her letters to Mop by saying how interested she and Grandpa Clark were to hear that Mop was in a 'better place' (Gladys's quotation marks) – a reference to the Siena move. It had come just in time for Mop, who, while maintaining a cheerful front for my grandparents, was worried sick about 'her Bob'. Mop had adapted well to the new location and was grateful for the distraction of her coding/decoding assignments, which helped to keep her mind on other things. The work was particularly interesting, she told me, because it was enabling her to gain a sense of the unfolding strategic picture in Italy and the wider war. The messages that she transcribed in the Signals Office allowed her to see that Germany was in retreat on multiple fronts and that the end was in sight.

Chapter 17

'Phone Tudor 1686'

Moosburg, Bavaria, February 1945

After leaving Campbell, Williamson and Stephens at Moosburg, Pop was put in the charge of a lone guard and led on a journey across Germany, 'stopping off at the odd prison', as he described it later. The journey would take him around two and a half weeks to complete. Munich to Bremen, his ultimate destination, was around 700km as the crow flies. With US and British forces approaching Germany's borders from the west, Soviet troops advancing from the east and the infrastructure of Germany pummelled by American and British bombers day and night, there was no way of reaching Bremen directly. Pop's details of this journey had always been sketchy, to say the least, but in his deposition to the Imperial War Museum he provided its essential waypoints: from Munich to Berlin, where he got caught up in an RAF bomber raid, from Berlin to Hamburg and from Hamburg to Bremen. Remarkably, he once told me, given the punishment that the Allies were meting out from the air, he wasn't in any way ill treated by his escort or by the civilians he met along the way. From Bremen it was roughly 20km to the village of Westertimke and the nearby Marlag und Milag POW camp. Changing trains in Berlin and Hamburg to reach his final destination, and, no doubt, with multiple stops en route to avoid being attacked from the air, Pop would have witnessed the utter destruction of two of Europe's finest cities. From Berlin, as he travelled westwards, he would have joined streams of refugees heading in the same direction. He would have witnessed a German Army all but crushed by the impossible task of defending the Fatherland from the east and the west. In March, the Red Army was massing to the east of the German capital preparing for its final assault – the race to the Reich Chancery and Hitler's bunker. The Americans had crossed the Rhine on 22 March and were heading for the heartlands of Thuringia and Bavaria. The British were pushing towards the

German cities of the northwest, including Hamburg and Bremen; and it was to Bremen that I now drove, with spring breaking, more than three years after Pop died, in an attempt to track his movements in the final weeks of the war.

Map 3

Marlag und Milag Nord was a large German camp complex for Royal Navy and British Merchant Navy POWs. Marlag, the RN camp, was divided into an 'O Compound' for officers and an 'M Compound' for NCOs and ratings. At the beginning of 1945, conditions in 'Mar–

224

lag O', where the officers were almost entirely British, were reasonably good. There was a football pitch, a theatre (converted from one of the huts used as living quarters), a mess room, a galley and even a refrigerator plant. In early February, however, around 2,000 RAF officers arrived at Marlag und Milag from Stalag Luft III at Sagan – part of the same POW migration, triggered by rapid Soviet advances, that had led to the sudden influx of prisoners at Moosburg. This placed considerable pressure on the camp, as it more than doubled in size, and virtually overnight. The prisoners' treatment at the hands of the *Kriegsmarine*, at least, was better than the treatment meted out at Army-run POW camps. Pop, I knew, had arrived at the camp in late February. On a recent visit home, Mop had told me she'd dug up a postcard that he had sent to her home address in Wales – clearly he had no option but to do anything else for security reasons. Mop, of course, being in Siena, never knew about the card until after she was demobbed. The card, written by Pop in pencil, was dated 26 March 1945. *I have now been just a month in my new camp and it is a great improvement on the previous two months, so morale is, within limits, high,* he wrote. The front of the card had been date-stamped by the German *Kriegsgefangenenpost* (prisoner-of-war mail) '17.4.45' and most probably would not have been delivered to the Allies for several more weeks (it seemed incredible that in the chaos of the Nazi collapse the service was still functioning) – it is doubtful, therefore, if the card would have even reached Wales by the end of the war. The rest of the news, as I expected, was perfunctory, but told me a little more about his mood.

> *The glorious sunshine of the past days [has] brought back the happiness of last August and September, my darling The biggest drawback here is no news of you. I hope you got to hear I was safe quickly and now I must just wait patiently for the end. Until then, all my love, Bob.*

As I would discover later, SOE *had* received reports at the end of December that the Clarion team had been captured, but had elected not to pass this information on. Mop would remain in the dark about Pop's fate right until the end of the war. As for Pop, he said little about his time at Marlag O, except that he had had the privilege of sleep-ing beneath a bunk occupied by Godfrey Place VC. Place had won the Victoria Cross for a daring attack on the German battleship *Tir-pitz* in Kaa Fjord, northern Norway, in September 1943. The damage inflicted on the *Tirpitz* from the charges laid by two midget sub-marines, one of them commanded by Place, ensured that this pow-erful German battleship was unable to be put to sea again until April 1944. Awarded his VC for an act of outstanding courage, Place was nonetheless extremely modest about the award – as Pop would doubt-less have discovered when he arrived at the camp. That he made an impression on Pop was never in any doubt, as Pop had mentioned the fact that Place had occupied the bunk above his several times to me. Perhaps, I reflected, this might have had something to do with the appreciation he had held for submariners after his own experiences in the *Marea*. Pop did not have time to strike up anything more than a cursory acquaintance, however, because, on 9 April, orders were issued by the camp commandant, *Fregattenkapitän* Schmidt, that, with the British Army advancing from the southwest, all prisoners would march to a new camp to the north of Hamburg. *Kapt* Schmidt did not say it, but the British Second Army, which had crossed the Rhine on 23 March, had reached the banks of the River Weser a few days earlier and was now poised to cross it. The Weser was less than 50km to the west of the camp. The POWs were able to keep up with these devel-opments thanks to news reports on an illicit radio.

When I arrived at Westertimke in glorious spring sunshine, much like the weather Pop had described in his card to Mop, I was, for the first time, lacking any direct testimony from my father or any of his close colleagues about the daily routine of his war. There was, however, in The National Archives in Kew, a detailed report of the march that he was about to undertake, compiled by Captain E.H.B. Baker RN, who had been the Senior British Officer at Marlag O. Armed with a copy of this report, I had already determined that I would drive the route that Pop had taken on foot. Locating its start-point, however, proved more problematic than I'd thought, as, in contrast to Stalag VIIA at Moosburg, there were no visible traces of the camp at Westertimke and the people I spoke to there were unaware there had even been a POW camp in their midst during the war. Just outside the village, however, I came across a business park that might, I felt, have been built on the site of a camp. Sure enough, some people I spoke to there said that it had been a military camp just after the war – and that prior to this it had served some 'quasi-military purpose'.

In front of the office buildings was a large square expanse of land with the trace remains of a grid structure on it like the one I'd seen at Moosburg, where the huts had been laid out in a chequerboard pattern. Here, now, surrounded on two sides by tall pines, I could picture the moment that *Kapt* Schmidt had mustered the camp at 3pm on 9 April, according to Baker's testimony, with Schmidt relaying orders for all prisoners to be ready to march within three hours. No transport was provided for prisoners, but German guards were able to make use of horse-drawn carts for their own equipment. Most POWs used handmade rucksacks and containers to transport the few possessions they had – which, extraordinarily for the time and the conditions, amounted mostly to food, mainly thanks to the Red Cross. Each man carried an average of two-and-a-half parcels of food, in addition to their German hard rations. 'From the moment that the order for the march was given there was complete chaos in and outside the camp,' Baker wrote. 'Most of the guards had disappeared and some of those remaining opened the gates of the compound and also lifted the barbed wire around it to help officers and men to escape and to hide in the nearby woods.' Relatively few escaped in this wave as some semblance of order was shortly restored. To shorten the distance between them and the advancing British Second Army, Baker instituted a foot-dragging policy to slow down their departure. It was interesting to me that the decision had been taken to march the men at night – but there were reasons for this, too; reasons that would become clear as I read on. The column – comprising 1,832 RAF officers and NCOs, 223 naval ratings and marines, and 244 naval and marine officers – eventually set off on 10 April. Approximately 550 POWs who were deemed unfit to travel were allowed to remain behind at the camp. Some POWs were allowed to load water and provisions on to some of the hand-drawn carts.

In his report, Baker did not conceal his contempt for Schmidt and his officers as they struggled to maintain order and discipline on what was expected to amount to a 10-day march to their final destination: Oflag XC at Bad Schwartau on the northern outskirts of Lübeck. 'Schmidt... was entirely ineffective, was rarely to be seen or got hold of, and it was evident that the whole undertaking was far beyond his power to control,' Baker wrote. Even Schmidt's officers, he added, complained of his refusal to accept responsibility and of his being 'un-getable'. Baker lifted his order banning further escape attempts, although numbers would be limited to 15 that day to avoid detection. The following day, however, it was reinstated – this after 12 officers and nine ratings had managed to slip away from the Marlag O column.

Campbell, Williamson and Stephens remained at Moosburg for the remainder of the war. Three weeks after Pop's departure, they were joined by Cauvain and Banks. It would be a further three weeks before Moosburg would be liberated – by troops of the US 14th Armored Division.

Mop, meanwhile, left Siena towards the end of March and, together with two other FANYs – Nancy, who had been with her from the start, and Mary de Fonblanque, who had become a good friend during the period Pop had been missing – made her way to Naples, where she boarded a ship for Liverpool. This date, when I asked her, she did remember – it had been Easter Day, 1 April 1945. Her friend Mary had been engaged to a marine officer and had recently received news that he had been killed in action. They had been the 'most attractive couple', my mother told me, adding, sadly, that wherever Mary went she had carried his beret with her. She and Mop were amongst the first FANYs to head home – Mary had been allowed home on compassionate grounds and Mop had been deputed to accompany her.

By now, she had received a glimmer of hope that Pop might be alive.

A file in The National Archives revealed that on 7 March No.1 SF had been aware for two days that some members of the Clarion mission, at least, had survived. *Information received from the field (vide*

Maryland telegram 5258 of 5 March) indicate that the above British officers who were captured in a skirmish with the enemy towards the end of 1944 are POWs in Turin. The two officers were Pop and Duncan Campbell. Aside from the inaccurate intelligence that in early March they were still being held in Turin, the message also revealed that Maryland had been aware of reports since 22 December that a party of 'seven British prisoners' had been captured in the Val Ellero (it cited the point of capture as Frabosa, the village next to Fontane where the capture actually took place) and that further information had been received on 31 December that the prisoners included Pop and Campbell. Why this information had not been passed on to Mop is not known, but can likely be put down to the authorities not wanting to raise hopes on the basis of unconfirmed reports. A Naval Intelligence Division report in The National Archives seemed to back this up. On 25 February, *request not to contact next of kin as circumstances not yet definite,* it noted. On 13 March, NID said: *Clark, Cauvain and Banks should not be publicly listed as missing, but their relatives had been informed that they were missing presumed POWs.* This was when Mop had written to my grandmother to offer hope. But there wasn't as yet – and wouldn't be until the end – any confirmation that he was alive.

After a sea voyage of around a week, Mop arrived back in Liverpool where she and Nancy were met off the ship by Grandpa Lewis, Mop's father. They travelled back to London and that night went to see a musical in the West End – a strange decision, Mop reflected years later, although she felt that my grandfather had been doing his best to 'cheer them up'. After almost a year and a half away from home, the sights and sounds of London felt unreal – as if, she told me, she was seeing everything in a dream. To describe to her father how this felt, however, as close as she was to him, was impossible.

The following day, she went back to Wales, where she received a call from FANY HQ telling her to report to Poundon, near Oxford, immediately. Nobody, she was informed, had given her permission to leave. Poundon – formally known as Station 53B – was one of two large SOE hubs on the UK mainland for handling communications traffic to and from Europe. One of the first things she had to do on walking through the door was to pay for personal items of clothing and equipment – including mess tins and a greatcoat – that she had left behind in Italy. At Poundon, a large requisitioned country house, she waited for news – any news – of Pop. Even though the war in Europe would drag on for another four weeks, she had already received word that she would be amongst the first wave of FANY WTOs and coders/decoders to be demobbed. After 15 months of service – and the indignity of being forced to pay for kit she'd been ordered to leave in Italy – she was ready to go home.

At 3.30pm on 11 April, a day after leaving Marlag und Milag Nord, Pop and his fellow POWs halted in the village of Seedorf. The rear party, according to Baker's very detailed account of what happened next, consisted of three horse-drawn wagons – one of which had been donated by the German guards for transporting the sick and their baggage – and a handcart containing some general equipment as well as medical supplies. The cart was marked with a red cross, although in retrospect, Baker admitted, it was not very prominent – but 'the best that could be done in the time and with the materials available'.

The rear of the column had halted just outside the village and was lined up on the road that led into it – highly visible in the flat, open countryside that characterised this area of northwest Germany. Allied fighters had been seen the previous day, as well as during the morning, and 'the general impression,' Baker reported, 'was that we had both been seen and identified as POWs'. As a result of this, he added, the general policy was to stay on the road and wave, rather than duck for cover whenever an Allied plane was spotted.

As a result, with the column now at rest, no one gave too much thought to two silver-winged USAAF P-47 Thunderbolts (from a unit that to this day remains unidentified) as they flew over the village – in fact, it is more than likely that many of the men, recognising them as Allied aircraft, came out from behind buildings to wave and cheer them on. The pilots, spotting the column as they roared over it, hauled the aircraft back round for another pass. As they did so, the POWs saw that they were readying to attack. They ran for cover, but the rear of the column, which was clear of the buildings, stayed exposed. The P-47s opened fire as the POWs found what cover they could – two very shallow ditches on either side of the road. Fifty-calibre bullets ripped into the wagons killing one man instantly and severely injuring four others. The P-47s came around again, but this time flew over without shooting. The wounded were taken into farm buildings situated close by. Despite the best efforts of medical staff, led by a Captain Maclean, two more men died of their wounds.

Much of this was clear to see as I drove into Seedorf. Helped by the fact that there was only one road in and out of the village, the long, straight avenue of trees where the men had dived for cover was obvious the moment I spotted it. And being a pilot, I could imagine it from the air, too. Here were men who must have thought that they were in with a chance of surviving the war – only to end up being killed by their own side. Pop, I reckoned, must have known – or known of – the men who'd died. 'As bad luck would have it,' he relayed many years later, 'they had been prisoners since 1940.'

Baker described how he had been halfway up the column at the time of the strafing. As soon as the Thunderbolts had gone, he ran to the front to tell the officer in charge of the Marlag O section of the column, a particularly ineffectual *Oberleutnant* called Schoof, that the rear had been attacked and that Schoof had to call the column to a halt. But Schoof was all for carrying on. Yet despite repeated attempts by Schoof to move the column forward, Baker and the senior cadre of officers with him refused, citing an urgent need to get the wounded to hospital. 'After some blustering and trying to force us to move, [Schoof] finally agreed to stay in the village and camp was made in the small wood at [its] east end,' Baker wrote. An ambulance eventually arrived from the nearby town of Bremervörde, but for two of the wounded it was too late.

That night, according to Baker, who had moved most of the men into a small wood just outside Seedorf, was 'a disturbed night for all' due to aircraft dropping flares in the countryside around them and shooting up roads close to where they lay. He called the whole company together and told them that there would be no further escape attempts. 'I considered it my first duty to get the column through to its destination and finally home to England without further casualties,' he explained later, 'and I could only do this by giving my personal assurances to the Germans that no one would escape when taking cover in the woods when our aircraft were road-strafing in the vicinity.' He said, too, that he did not believe that anyone attempting to escape from then on had much chance of doing so successfully, since he had been told that the Germans were combing the woods for deserters as well. The next day, the column moved on and three days later, wracked by fatigue and sickness, at last reached the River Elbe. They spent a very cold night in the open at a village called Cranz on the river's southern bank, the skyline illuminated by fires burning in the middle of Hamburg, a few kilometres to the east of them.

When I arrived in Sülldorf, a leafy suburb across the river from Cranz, I knew that at this point in the war, the German 1st Parachute Army had been preparing to meet an attack on the city by British VIII Corps and that the battle itself would rage for more than two weeks and turn out to be one of the last major engagements of the war. It struck me as all the more remarkable, then, that Schmidt, Schoof and the other Germans in charge of the column had so doggedly stuck to their brief. Somehow, amidst all the preparations then underway to defend the city, the German officers had managed to find barges to transport the POWs across the river, around 500m wide at that point.

From my viewpoint on the cliffs, which overlooked the giant Airbus factory in Hamburg, I imagined the scene below me as it must have been then – a vision of Hell: smoke columns rising from the opposite bank, the docks next to the Airbus works all but destroyed by bombing designed to soften up the city's defences before the British 7th Armoured Division spearheaded VIII Corps' attack. The POWs spent the night in Sülldorf, according to Baker's story, before marching on to Lübeck, still around 80km away. Baker reported attacks of dysentery in the column, as well as sore feet and blisters, but on the whole said that morale was good, although, after the shoot-up by the P-47s, everyone had become extremely edgy whenever they heard any aircraft – 'although it was evident to a great many of us,' Baker said, 'that our aircraft had recognised us all and knew where we were'. To avoid any further misidentification, he ordered that 'RAF' and 'POW' should be spelled out in large letters with sheets and towels in any field where they set down to rest.

By now, transport of varying types and quantities – still hand drawn – had been supplied for ferrying the sick and their heavy baggage. This, at least, was one aspect of the journey that had improved since their departure. The general conditions, however, were still terrible. Their guards had provided no hot food and no hot water – 'the only rations supplied being bread and tinned meat and fish'. The next night, they camped in a village with a good supply of water and a large unoccupied communal cookhouse that had been set up for refugees. The friendliness of the German people towards them came as quite a surprise. 'They did their best to provide us with hot water at the camp sites. Along the march, through the villages, people put buckets of water at their gates for us to drink and fill our water bottles,' Baker said. 'They were for the most part very sick of the war and were looking forward to the British or Americans arriving. They had a horror at the thought of being taken over by the Russians.' The Marlag O contingent – around 300 naval officers – had by this time separated from the main body of the column, which consisted of almost 2,000 RAF personnel, and was now making its own way to Lübeck.

The British, meanwhile, had assumed complete control, the Germans having lost any authority they ever had after the strafing at Seedorf. No further orders were issued by the Germans, in fact, unless they first came from Baker. This remained the state of affairs when, at midday on 23 April, the Marlag O column arrived at its destination, crossing the Elbe–Lübeck canal on one of the few road bridges in the city left standing. 'German soldiers, German women and POWs were milling around all trying to seize accommodation and anything they could lay their hands on,' Baker wrote. Schoof, unsurprisingly, was nowhere to be seen. In the chaos, Baker added, 'no German had any initiative and orders and counter-orders were being given by all and sundry'.

Bad Schwartau, where Oflag XC had supposedly been located, was the final destination for me, too, as I retraced Pop's march from Bremen.

I spent the morning wandering around the town trying to find out where the camp had been, but, as at Westertimke, nobody seemed to know. The tourist office couldn't help (former POW camps weren't, I supposed, the kind of image you'd necessarily want to project for your town) and the museum, where I had expected them to know, wasn't sure either. The only clue I had from Baker's testimony was that the POWs had been housed in a German Army barracks and, from separate research, I had the address – the corner of Friedhofsallee and Vorwerkstraße. Things became clearer when it was pointed out that this address was in Lübeck, not, as had been portrayed in the Baker account, in its neighbouring town, then a suburb, Bad Schwartau.

Armed with this vital new piece of information, and following the satnav, the only barracks I could find was now the regional headquarters for the German Federal Police, the *Bundespolizei*, and, thinking this to be the place, I headed inside. There, for some reason, I was taken to see the director of training, a man called Peter. After we sat down in his office and I told him my story, Peter smiled and said he could help. The barracks where my father had been, he told me, was now a holding centre for refugees and immigrants. It was situated close by. He gave me directions and I set off again, finding it eventually next to the autobahn that cut through the outskirts of Lübeck.

I drove in, parked the car and took a few moments to absorb where I was. The architecture was almost identical to that which I'd just seen at the police headquarters – five-storey red-brick buildings set within a large compound that was still surrounded by chain-link fencing. It even had an old wartime bunker. Standing next to the bunker, I took out my notes and read the last few lines of Baker's account of the march. By late afternoon on the 23rd, he reported, the Marlag O POWs had settled into one of the blocks and were awaiting the arrival of their RAF comrades, albeit with mixed feelings. As much as they wanted to know that they had made the rest of the journey without incident – they had been separated since the attack at Seedorf – the chaos when they arrived, everyone knew, would be worse than it already was.

When the RAF party did show, just before nightfall, *Kapt* Schmidt was with them – his capacity to reach a decision as ineffectual as ever. Somehow, room was found to accommodate 2,000 additional personnel and an uneasy peace settled on the camp. There, with captor more or less subordinate to captive, both sides awaited the arrival of Allied troops.

Oflag XC was liberated on 2 May by the British Second Army, the same day that Berlin fell to the Soviet Army and German forces in Italy announced their surrender. On 3 May, Hamburg capitulated and the day after, on the 4th, Field Marshal Bernard Montgomery took the unconditional surrender of all German forces in the Netherlands, Denmark and northwest Germany. The document was signed in a tent in a forest clearing on Lüneburg Heath, around 150km south of Pop's location. According to his own later description of these events, he was taken from the camp by his liberators on 2 May and flown to an 'advanced RAF base where they were celebrating the German surrender'. The reason for this was revealed by Pop many years after the war: the British authorities had been keen to debrief Pop as soon as possible – giving him special early release status – to find out who had betrayed Clarion, not knowing that the *partigiani* had already taken justice into their own hands.

Pop's 2 May memory of his release is most likely a conflation of the date of the camp's liberation and the surrender of German forces at Lüneburg – the actual date of Pop's departure in all probability being the day after Lüneburg, not the liberation of Oflag XC. In any event, I knew that the 'advanced RAF base' was Celle, a Luftwaffe airfield that had been taken over by the RAF soon after its capture by British forces on 16 April. Celle was 50km northeast of Hamburg and 100km southeast of Lübeck, and it was there that I decided to head next. This would be no simple undertaking as it was still an active military air base – home to the German Army's School of Army Aviation. Fortunately, however, the airfield is open to civilian air traffic and, as I was a pilot, I contacted the authorities to see if I might gain permission to fly in. A few weeks after making this approach through Chris Harper, a senior RAF officer and fellow member of the Royal Air Squadron, I received an email from *Hauptfeldwebel* Martin Borchert, informing me that the necessary permissions for my flight had been given. All I had to do was hand over thirty-nine euros in landing fees (in cash!) upon arrival. A few weeks after that, with i's dotted and t's crossed, I took off from an airfield just north of London and headed out across the North Sea, excited that I would be flying into the very base that had played host to Pop's flight back to Britain in the final days of the war, but a little anxious, too, as to what I might find. On 5 May 1945, the likely date of Pop's arrival, Celle was a damaged but fully functioning airfield, with a single runway, a control tower and five large hangars. It had been an important airfield since before the war, when it had played a key role in covert efforts by the Luftwaffe to train pilots for the coming conflict. Arriving at the base, instead of Messerschmitts, Pop would have found Spitfire XIV and Tempest V fighters of the RAF's 125 Wing, commanded by the legendary Battle of Britain veteran and fighter ace Group Captain Johnny Johnson. That night, at what must have been a stupendous celebration, Pop was given his first drink in six months (apart from the glass or two of vermouth he'd received on his 21st birthday in Le Nuove) – a shot of whisky – by Johnson himself.

Pop, by now dangerously underweight – in the time he had been in Italy, both at No.1 Special Force and as a POW, he had dropped to just 6 stone – took a couple of sips and promptly keeled over; and it was with this image in my mind – the very last fact Pop ever provided of his time on the continent during the war – that I touched down on Celle's runway and taxied my aircraft to the dispersal area in front of one of the hangars.

In the building next door, where I'd been taken to fill in the requisite paperwork, I met Sergeant Borchert and we started talking. Soon a friendly reception committee of Borchert's colleagues had gathered around us, each eager to know what had brought me here – it turned out that Celle received very little civilian traffic and news of my arrival on a quiet Wednesday morning had created something of a stir. When I told them about the journey, how far I had come, and how much I had learned about my father's war, I wasn't altogether sure how the news would be received. But the next thing I knew, photographs and albums were produced of Celle as it had looked during the war, with row upon row of aircraft with swastikas on their tails lined up in front of the hangars, and I was taken on an impromptu tour of the base, being shown the clover-leaf dispersal areas where Me109s had deployed in the war. In the modern era, Celle had become a training base for helicopters, not fixed-wing aircraft, but other than this it had altered very little. All the main wartime buildings – and four out of the five hangars – were still standing. My plane, in fact, my hosts told me, was parked in the very spot where Pop's aircraft would have been parked – the aircraft he'd boarded two days after Monty had taken the surrender of Hitler's forces in north Germany – this less than a week after Hitler himself had committed suicide in his Berlin bunker. Nursing what would have undoubtedly been a king-sized hangover, Pop had been flown back to Biggin Hill, the RAF fighter base in Kent. From Biggin's railway station at Bromley South, he caught a train to London. The date of his arrival home is provided in a naval telegram dispatched to the Admiralty in London and to SOE in Italy. *Sub/Lt R.A. Clark repeat Clark of Clarion mission returned UK Sunday fit and in good form following release from* Marlag und Milag *POW camp at Bremen.* Overlooking the fact that he was released from Oflag XC at Lübeck, the telegram confirmed my father's own recollections of the day that he arrived back – 6 May.

With just a few shillings in his pocket, he took a Tube and a tram to the stop at the bottom of my grandparents' street, Creighton Avenue, in East Finchley. On the BBC, it had just been announced that Admiral Dönitz, Hitler's successor, had signed Germany's final and unconditional surrender at Eisenhower's HQ in Reims, France. In Britain, 8 May had been designated a day of celebration, but, by the time Pop reached East Finchley, the festivities were already underway, with the first flags and bunting appearing in and outside the shops, as well as in people's houses and gardens. The weather in London that first week in May had been unseasonably wet and cold, but the 6th heralded a period of finer weather, the spring warmth swelling the crowds that had begun to take to the streets. As he hopped off the tram and started up Creighton Avenue, Pop would have felt the excitement in the air.

There is confusion at this point as to how much my grandparents knew when Pop arrived at the door of Number 227. The Navy telegram in my possession, dated 13 March, had stated only that relatives of the Clarion team had been informed they were 'missing and presumed to be POWs'; whether *confirmation* of their status as POWs ever reached them is unclear.

Whatever the truth, the story as it related to Pop was as follows. My grandfather was sitting in the bay window in the front of the house when he suddenly caught sight of a tall young man – very thin, bearded, dressed in shabby fatigues and with a rucksack over his shoulder – walking up the street.

Until this point, the story had it, nobody had the least idea Pop was alive, let alone that he was in England. Seeing the unkempt soldier coming up the path, my grandfather went to the door, opened it and realised only then that it was his son. They stood for a second or two looking at each other and then they shook hands. In all the times I have been told about this moment, I have tried to imagine it, but always failed to do it justice. We live in an age of vulnerability. We show our emotions, often to all and sundry. My father had always had this tremendous reserve, but through his letters to Mop I had seen a different side to him – a man who'd had highs and lows: that 'varied graph' as he'd once described it to her in a letter. But in that handshake I recognised the Pop I'd known and loved: warm, unflappable, dependable… *there*. And, after the journey I'd been on, this, perhaps, is what I had come to value most: that Pop's way of keeping order in his life, the order he had promised my mother and had given to us, his children, was to maintain that even keel, not to rock it even for a second. Talking about his war would most likely have done just that. And so, until the very end, he had chosen not to – to us at any rate.

Did I regret going on the journey? Did I regret learning the details of his war – the details I'd craved from that early age? Not a bit. Pop, were he alive, might have discouraged me from immersing myself in the detail of his time with SOE, but I would have happily argued the point; and, in the end, I think he would have agreed. We talk about the sacrifice of those who gave their lives during the Second World War – and of those who gave the *best part* of their lives to it – but it had been in the detail of Pop's journey – from schoolboy to SOE agent to POW – that I had come to understand what that actually meant. On his 21st birthday, he had endured the most terrifying experience imaginable. On mine, I'd opened presents, knocked back a glass or two of bubbly and blown out some candles. The journey had given me a window, too, on the extraordinary circumstances that had brought my parents together, as well as a whole new appreciation of what Mop had sacrificed. In her quest for 'adventure', she had given up a place at Oxford and seen friends die. Her health had suffered too. Always the extrovert, she had chosen not to speak of these things either. But as Pop now told my grandparents in those first few joyous moments of reunion back at home in East Finchley, my mother was *the one*.

Later that day, he sent a telegram to her that read: *Arrived home from Germany. Please phone Tudor 1686 if possible tonight. Love Bob.* It had been sent to Poundon, where Pop had learned from my grandparents that Mop was waiting to be demobbed.

My mother had to wait eight days before she was allowed to take the train from Oxford to London. She was so nervous, she told me, that she spent most of the journey in the loo. Pop had borrowed my grandfather's Rover and had driven it from home to Paddington to meet her off the train. When they saw each other, instead of embracing, they, too, shook hands. Hanging over them both was a very big question mark – the matter of his deployment to the Far East: with the end of the war in Europe, Pop and my godfather Robin had received orders that they were being re-deployed to fight the Japanese.

During their meeting in London, Mop had tried to persuade him not to go, that he had more than done his bit already. But this wasn't Pop's way. As he wrote to her two days later: *It is no case of mad patriotism or wish for glory – I must go. I could never live with myself if I stayed here. I have only been in the 'service' for three years and have had a very lucky and easy time really.*

Two days later, he wrote to her again about how he saw the future: *While in prison, I thought so much about what I was going to do with myself and now after six months, I still cannot say I have much of a clue; all I know is that first comes the Far East show and then after being demobbed, what?*

And then, suddenly, all his doubts and fears seem to melt away: *But, at the moment, I think it is quite hopeless to do any worrying; just live for the immediate future.* The sentiments behind these words, some would say, formed the backdrop to the rest of his life. He signed off as he always did.

All my love. Bob

The power of Pop's love for my mother brought forth a memory – an image from the journey I had not thought about much until now. During our three-day trip to Monopoli, I had suggested that we drive up the coast and visit Termoli, the forward operating base used by Laming, Robin, Pop, Tom Long and Roy Taylor for mounting missions northwards in the Italian MAS/MS boats.

When we arrived in Termoli after a two-and-a-half hour drive from Monopoli, we found a somewhat charmless harbour town off the usual tourist path, its approaches marked by industrial estates. But making our way down to the port, through half-closed eyes, I could easily imagine how it had looked 70 years earlier – its breakwaters and the old castle on the promontory appearing exactly as they would have when the Germans had left in 1943.

I drove as far as I could along one of the breakwaters and parked. A sharp autumnal wind was blowing in off the sea and I asked Mop if she wanted to walk with me to the end of the breakwater where I would take a few pictures and stop there a while. I wanted to see if, in my mind's eye, I could summon an image of the MAS/MS boats as they slipped out of the harbour at night at the start of another journey up the coast. Mop, feeling the cold more than me, I thought, said she preferred to stay close to the car. So, I wandered off…

When I came back, I found her standing at the breakwater's edge, looking out to sea. She was unaware that I had returned – or that I was standing close enough to hear her singing to herself. It was a song I recognised: 'The Way You Look Tonight', one of Pop's favourites.

Some day, when I'm awfully low, And the world is cold, I will feel a glow just thinking of you, And the way you look tonight…

When she turned, I saw that she was smiling.

Epilogue

'Mop and Pop'

London, England, June 1945

In June, a little over a month after the war in Europe had drawn to its end, Pop embarked for the Japanese theatre of war on a Sunderland flying boat, flying from the UK via Iceland and Newfoundland to Boston, where he picked up another aircraft to the US West Coast. From California, he made his way on a Liberator bomber across the Pacific to Australia via Fiji and Auckland.

With him was Robin – the two of them having been dispatched by SOE to serve with an Australian special forces unit called the SRD, the Services Reconnaissance Department. The SRD was tasked with intelligence-gathering, reconnaissance and raiding operations in Japanese-held territories and islands and was loosely based on experience gained by SOE, with which it had close ties. Robin had been told that he would be running missions to agents in Japanese-held territory in 'Welfreighters', mini-submarines that had been dreamed up by SOE's technical department, the Inter Services Research Bureau (ISRB), to deliver men and matériel behind enemy lines. Robin, the engineer, considered the Welfreighter to be a death-trap, 'designed by automobile engineers in a backyard in Welwyn Garden City', and was mightily relieved that the war in the Pacific ended with the dropping of the atomic bombs over Hiroshima and Nagasaki in August 1945 before he could be deployed in them. This, in effect, freed him up to join Pop on his designated mission: as skipper of their old boat the *Eduardo*, which had been shipped out to the Australians under loan by the Royal Navy during March. The *Eduardo* had a crew of 10 and carried out what Pop described as 'odd jobs' in the Pacific for much of the following year. Pop and Robin sailed the vessel from Darwin via Borneo, the Celebes (now Sulawesi) and the Philippines to Hong Kong. Along the way, they accepted the surrender of Japanese soldiers who had been cut off from the main Pacific battlegrounds,

241

some of them not all that willing to accept the news that the war was over. Pop finally made it back to the UK in mid-1946.

Before he left for the Far East, he had told my mother that his ambition had been to join the Colonial or Diplomatic Service, because, out of the RNVR, and short of money, he would be badly in need of a job. It was not something that particularly appealed to him, but he felt it was the sensible thing to do – and the first on a series of steps that would allow him and my mother to marry. Following his service with SOE, Pop always believed that he had been blessed with remarkable good fortune and, soon after he returned to the UK, he experienced what he would later describe as one of the best strokes of good luck he could possibly have had. Strolling along the Strand, on his way to an interview with the Colonial Office, he bumped into Hilary Scott. His old boss, as stunned as Pop was by the impromptu meeting, asked him what he was doing and Pop told him. The chap he had been in prison with in Turin, he told Hilary – the 'chap' being Duncan Campbell – had filled Pop with an enthusiasm for Sudan, having spent some time there before the war in the Sudan Defence Force. Hilary promptly invited his young protégé at Monopoli to meet his partners at Slaughter and May over lunch and my father accepted. The rest, as they say, is history. As soon as he qualified as a lawyer, Pop found himself working mainly with banks. Discovering he had an aptitude for the large and sometimes bitter takeover battles that would characterise some of Slaughter and May's most important business transactions, his aptitude translated into rapid promotion and he became a partner at the age of 32. Banking was an association that would change his life. He joined a fast-expanding merchant bank – Philip Hill, Higginson, Erlangers – in 1961, which merged shortly thereafter with Samuel and Co. to form Hill Samuel, one of the City's biggest banking firms. He rose to become its chief executive. In addition to banking, a string of advisory positions and chairmanships followed with some of Britain's best-known companies. He also joined the Special Forces Club so that he did not cut himself off completely from his wartime experience.

He was knighted in 1976 and became a director of the Bank of England the same year. When the Mirror Group Newspapers scandal broke following the death of Robert Maxwell, and the appearance

of a vast black hole in its pension pot, Pop, a director of the group –
and as horrified as everyone else by the scale of Maxwell's fraudulent
activities – grabbed the tiller and steered MGN through the storm.
Somehow during this period, he managed to maintain his sangfroid –
a steeliness beneath his good nature – that was admired by friends and
foes alike. It was, perhaps, only right to imagine that after the horrors
and deprivations of Le Nuove – a period that he never discussed for
reasons that were now all too clear to me – he managed to see the
stress of business as something that, in the big scheme of things, could
and should be risen above.

Without doubt, however, it was his marriage and his family that
Pop considered to be his greatest achievement.

Three years after returning from the Far East, he fulfilled his
promise and married my mother.

He remained devoted to her, as well as to Will, Catherine and me
and our children, his grandchildren, throughout his long and remarkable life.

The war exploits of a very brave bear (not to mention his master)

Valentine Low meets a flying Scotsman and other heroes from Churchill's dirty tricks team

Sir Robert Clark with Lady Clark, his wartime radio link, and Falla the bear

BOB Clark has never told his story in public before. How his disability led to selection for the most secret force of the Second World War, how he parachuted into Italy with a highly unusual companion, what happened to that nice girl who was his wireless operator: all this was known only to those closest to him.

But this week, one of the more extraordinary gatherings hosted by the Imperial War Museum was as good a moment as any to recount his tale.

Assembled beneath the Spitfire that takes pride of place in the museum's main hall were 29 of the last surviving members of Winston Churchill's dirty tricks department, the Special Operations Executive.

Or 30 if one counts Falla, and perhaps one should: after all, he landed in Italy with Clark — now Sir Robert — was taken prisoner with him and still managed to make it to the Special Forces Club dinner to be addressed by its patron, the Princess Royal. More on Falla in a moment...

Created to carry out sabotage and subversion in Nazi-occupied Europe and beyond, the job of the Special Operations Executive (SOE) was, in Churchill's words, "to set Europe ablaze". Secrecy was its byword and for years after the war its activities remained a closed book.

Sir Robert's war was going nowhere before he joined the SOE. Consigned to a desk job with the Navy because of his colour blindness, he secured an interview at SOE's Baker Street headquarters and by 1943 found himself being parachuted into northern Italy to train partisans and to carry out sabotage.

Tucked inside his battledress was his childhood teddy bear, Falla. "I had had him since I was four years old and I rather liked him," Sir Robert, 86, said. "Since then he has been everywhere with me."

Dropped miles from his target, he landed in a tree and had to be rescued by a young partisan called Sergio Curetti. Fifty years later, in 1993, Sir Robert would receive a letter from an old man wondering whether he was the same Robert Clark whom he had once pulled out of a tree. "He was a retired accountant by then, instead of an 18-year-old with a Sten gun. He was a lovely map. As a young man, he had been very dashing."

As well as training partisans to use British weapons, Sir Robert's speciality was sabotaging rail lines. "Blowing up railway engines was really great fun," he said.

Sabotaging rail links was a priority of the Special Operations Executive

Meanwhile he had met an SOE wireless operator called Marjorie, who used to send his messages back to Baker Street. "It was nice to have female company," he said, understatedly; perhaps his true feelings were revealed after he went missing for several months. Marjorie had no idea whether he was alive or dead. Then,

in complete breach of the rules, a message came over the radio to her in plain English instead of code: "Bob sends love to Marjorie."

Eventually his luck ran out. "We were hiding from the Germans, about five of us. We were in a haystack. But we were given away, and I rather ignominiously gave myself up." Falla was captured with him. Bob was able to keep him throughout his time as a prisoner of war. "He used to sit inside my battledress."

Once more Marjorie had no idea whether Sir Robert was alive until she got a telegram at the end of the war: "Arriving London from Germany. Meet me London."

Telling the story now, she marvels at how differently young couples in love behaved then. "I went to meet him. My knickles! Can you imagine? And we shook hands! We shook hands ..." Sir Robert and Lady Clark are still married today.

Notes on Sources

As stated at the beginning of *Monopoli Blues*, Nick and I started out with just a few pages of handwritten notes on Mop and Pop's story, culled from my various (truncated) conversations with them (Pop, particularly) over the years. I have been helped enormously, however, by numerous published and unpublished sources since then, the most important and useful of which I list below. Where I talk in the text about Pop having 'discussed' events in the book after the war, I am referring primarily to two talks that he gave: one in 2005 to the Imperial War Museum for its Oral History series; the other in 2000 to the pupils of Westminster School. The Internet being vast and, in places, untrawled, I was astonished to discover, just a few months before publication, a third source: a long interview, published in partnership with the British Library, in which Pop talked about his career in the City. This includes details of his early life as well as observations on his wartime service. It is typical of him that he never mentioned this to us – but exemplifies, too, the challenge that Nick and I faced in researching the details of his war. Some information comes from Pop's personal correspondence, discovered after his death, to and from various organisations and individuals associated with SOE, including the Special Forces Club and Christopher Woods, who wrote a history of SOE in Italy (where he served as a BLO). I am also indebted to the Resistance Archive in Cuneo for information held there on partisan activity. Inevitably, the greater part of the facts behind the background to Pop's journey come from files held at The National Archives in Kew. They are far too numerous to detail here, in what is essentially a non-academic work, but principally comprise the HS6, HS7, HS8 and HS9 series for those interested in SOE naval operations, No.1 Special Force and SOE land missions in Italy. Other primary sources are listed below.

Books:

Acton, V. & Carter, D. (1994). *Operation Cornwall 1940–44: Fal, the Helford & D-Day.* Truro: Landfall Publications

Allan, S. (2007). *Commando Country.* Edinburgh: NMS Enterprises Ltd – Publishing

Bailey, R. (2014). *Target Italy: The Secret War against Mussolini 1940–43.* London: Faber & Faber

Battistelli, P.P. & Crociani, P. (2015). *World War II Partisan Warfare in Italy.* Oxford: Osprey Publishing

Cull, N. (1997). *Selling War: The British Propaganda Campaign against American 'Neutrality' in World War II.* Oxford: Oxford University Press

Curetti, S. *Meglio di Niente*

Dodds-Parker, D. (1984). *Setting Europe Ablaze.* Windlesham: Springwood Books

Gianola, A. & Ruzzi, M. (2008). *Italia 1943–45: Resistenze a Confronto.* Cuneo: Associazione 'Resistenza Sempre nel Rinnovamento'

Morris, E. (1993). *Circles of Hell: The War in Italy 1943–45.* New York: Crown Publishers

Ogden, A. (2011). *A Spur Called Courage.* London: Bene Factum Publishing

Pawley, M. (1999). *In Obedience to Instructions.* Barnsley: Leo Cooper

Peniakoff, V. (1950). *Popski's Private Army.* London: Jonathan Cape

Pickering, W. & Hart, A. (1991). *The Bandits of Cisterna.* London: Leo Cooper

Richards, B. (2004). *Secret Flotillas, Volume I: Clandestine Sea Operations to Brittany 1940–44.* Barnsley: Pen & Sword Books

Richards, B. (2004). *Secret Flotillas, Volume II: Clandestine Sea Operations in the Western Mediterranean, North Africa & the Adriatic.* Barnsley: Pen & Sword Books

Rigden, D. (Introduction) (2001). *How to be a Spy: The World War II SOE Training Manual.* Toronto: The Dundurn Group

Stafford, D. (2011). *Mission Accomplished: SOE & Italy.* London: The Bodley Head

Tudor, M. (2011). *SOE in Italy 1940–1945.* Newtown: Emilia Publishing

Woods, C. (2005). *Special Operations Executive: A New Instrument of War.* London: Routledge

Unpublished Manuscripts:

Campbell, D. Untitled (Major Duncan Campbell's wartime memoir, parts of which have been reproduced by kind permission of his son, Angus)

Damini, E. (1998). My Days at War (kindly provided by Annalise Nebbia)

Articles:

Low, Valentine. (6 Nov 2010). SOE Celebration Hails Sir Robert Clark and Sir Tommy Macpherson. *The Times*

Websites/Blogs/Online:

Extract from diary of Leading Seaman Thomas Nevin detailing Mop's convoy to Algiers: http://www.bbc.co.uk/history/ww2peopleswar/stories/12/a2373112.shtml

World War II Escape Lines Memorial Society (ELMS): https://www.iwm.org.uk/collections/item/object/80024812

Interviews/Oral Histories:

Sir Robert Clark, Imperial War Museum: https://www.iwm.org.uk/collections/item/object/80025694

Robin Richards, Imperial War Museum: https://www.iwm.org.uk/collections/item/object/80024812

Sir Robert Clark interviewed by Cathy Courtney for National Life Stories, City Lives (in partnership with the British Library): https://sounds.bl.uk/related-content/TRANSCRIPTS/021T-C0409X0102XX-0000A0.pdf

Manuals:

Special Operations Executive Manual: How to be an Agent in Occupied Europe. (2014). London: William Collins

Acknowledgements

This book could not have been written without the great help of many people who have provided information, given advice and supplied support over the five years which this project has taken.

We must start with the Curetti family – Daniela in particular but also her sister Paola, her husband Diego and her mother, Adriana (Sergio Curetti's wife). The reunion between Pop and Sergio almost 50 years after the war is one of the amazing parts of Pop's story – and it laid the foundations of a strong relationship between the Clark and Curetti families. Daniela has provided information, photographs and the introduction to Carluccio Dalmasso whose wartime experiences with the partisans – and his recollection of them – are extraordinary and who was very generous with his time with us. The Curetti family also introduced us to Sergio's book – *Meglio di Niente* – and to the partisan magazine – *Autonomi* – which included the story of Pop and Sergio's reunions.

We also received great help in Italy from Egidio Gavazzi (two of whose uncles were distinguished partisans) and Pier Riches who greatly aided our understanding of the partisan movement – as well as providing invaluable interpretations in our visits to the Le Nuove prison in Turin and the Partisan Archive in Cuneo.

We are also grateful for the assistance which was provided by the director of Le Nuove prison and Dr Marco Ruzzi, the curator of the Istituto Storico Resistenza Cuneo (the Partisan Archive in Cuneo). The director showed us the particular part of the prison in which the Clarion team was held during an inspirational tour on the eve of Italian Liberation Day for a group of impressively attentive 15-year-old schoolchildren – and us. Dr Ruzzi was very generous with his time and very patient in dealing with our often vague requests for information. Simon Offord, archivist at the Imperial War Museum, London, kindly showed Mop and us around the IWM's SOE exhibition at an important juncture of our research.

Otherwise in Italy we received great help from Clara Muzzarelli, the niece of Max Salvadori who played such an important role in SOE's operations in that country. As mentioned in the introduction, she was completely unfazed by our surprise appearance at her house and gave us not only great help in researching the role of the Salvadori family and their connection to Pop's story, but also introduced us to an extensive body of source materials and to others who could provide assistance. These included Annalisa Nebbia to whom we are very grateful for telling us about the important contribution of Ettore Damini and other invaluable snippets relating to SOE and POW escape lines in Italy.

Not the least of the surprises during the last five years was to discover that Oliver Pawle, whom we had known as a leading investment banker, is a nephew of Max Salvadori. Oliver and his sister, Audrey, have been unfailingly helpful, including putting us in touch with Cristina Odone who has widened awareness of the story and Max's son, Clement, who has recently edited a new edition of his father's book – *The Labour and the Wounds.*

In the context of helpful surprises, it is hard to overestimate the discovery – through his son, Angus – of the unpublished manuscript written by Major Duncan Campbell – the commander of Pop's Clarion mission. The manuscript effectively unlocked the story of the mission and in particular the two months between the capture of most of the team and the first part of their journey in captivity from Mondovi to Munich. To Angus and his family go our very sincere thanks.

We decided relatively early on in the project that it would be important to visit the places which play a significant part in the story. A number of these places were only accessible – we convinced ourselves – by light aircraft. So we flew in a small aircraft to Arisaig, Helford and Celle. Our companion on these flights was Tony Ryan. Tony is a former BA pilot and flying instructor and good friend. He not only guided us through some of the more challenging aspects of these trips, but was also indefatigable in searching for the locations of the story – in particular, the POW camps in Northern Germany, many of which are difficult to find in their current urban environment.

These trips began with visits to Arisaig and Helford. In Arisaig, we met Henrik Chart (an expert on SOE activities in that area) who gave us valuable information on the training of SOE agents as well as an expert guided tour of the various buildings requisitioned by SOE during the war. In Helford, we greatly appreciated the generosity of Dr Thomas Blythe who allowed us to look around Pedn Billy, the house where Pop lived during his training in Cornwall.

Our final trip was – fittingly – to Celle – the airfield from which Pop flew back to England shortly after his release from captivity in May 1945. It was a great privilege to be allowed to fly into this German military base following an introduction very kindly arranged by (Air Marshal Sir) Chris Harper and his deputy at NATO in Brussels, Col. Arnt Kuebart. We were shown great hospitality by the officers at Celle – in particular, *Hauptfeldwebel* Borchert and Warrant Officer Plexnies – which included not only a guided tour of the airfield but also access to their photographic archive of historic pictures of the airfield.

During some of these trips, we were accompanied by Nellie Maclaine who has been an important part of our family for over 10 years. Nellie lovingly helped to look after Pop in the last few years of his life and, since his death, has been the close companion of Mop. Nellie brings a sensitive determination – and humour – to everything which she does – and that was very true of the times we spent together in putting together the story.

A number of people have provided invaluable help in piecing together this story and in understanding the role which SOE played in Italy (in particular, the missions along the Adriatic coast). We are particularly grateful to Roger Stanton and the Escape Lines Memorial Society to whom we were introduced by our friend Reg Francis and the Monte San Martino Trust (Vanni Treves and Nick Young – who has written movingly about his father's experiences as an escaper from Fontanellato POW camp near Parma).

In starting out on this book, when we only had enough information to fill five A4 pages, we were hugely indebted to Catherine Forrester, who did much of the initial research into Mop and Pop's connection to the SOE narrative in Italy. Amongst the many people who assisted Catherine with that initial research, we are particularly grateful to Steven Kippax for his help.

We are also very grateful to two people who helped and encouraged us from the early stages of our research. Dr Roderick Bailey (Departmental Lecturer in the History of Medicine at the Wellcome Unit for the History of Medicine at the University of Oxford), who some years ago had interviewed Pop for the Imperial War Museum, provided many insights into the history of SOE. He also very generously read the manuscript of the book – twice – and gave us valuable suggestions on SOE operations in Italy. We also received great support and encouragement from Caroline Griffith (a member of the Main Committee of the Special Forces Club). Caroline gave us numerous suggestions of people to contact who might shed light on aspects of the story and, very helpfully, provided us with a copy of the papers from the 1987 Anglo-Italian Conference in Bologna which discussed many aspects of SOE and partisan operations.

We would also like to mention Eugene and Jane Curley who were responsible for my parents' attendance at the Special Forces Club dinner in 2010 at the Imperial War Museum and for the discovery of some important parts of Pop's experiences.

We are enormously indebted to Mark Lucas – Nick's agent – for helping to bring *Monopoli Blues* to the wider world – Mark, and his wife Mindy, by coincidence, having holidayed a number of times in Monopoli, thereby connecting them to the story long before we actually wrote it. Also, to Rowland White – author, publisher and friend – for bringing the story to the attention of some very eminent writers and historians. We would like to mention particularly James Holland for his encouragement and help and for the opportunity of introducing Mop and ourselves to our first audience experience – the Chalke Valley History Festival.

Both of us have enjoyed the experience of working with Unbound for the first time. We were impressed by their publishing model and their focus on bringing a wide range of stories to the public and at a speed that is impressive by the standards of the industry. We are particularly grateful to our editor, Richard Collins, who made many helpful suggestions for the narrative and structure of the book while being enormously supportive of the project. His professionalism and engagement were brilliant. We also appreciated the work of Mark Ecob in designing the cover of the book. He was quick to understand the key elements of the narrative and to reflect them in his design. Grateful thanks also go to other 'Unbounders' who helped bring the book to production: Kwaku Osei-Afrifa, Annabel Wright and Xander Cansell.

We were delighted when Paddy Ashdown agreed to write an introduction to the book. Amongst his many talents, Paddy is a leading expert on special forces in the Second World War and his reflections on the story and the reasons why we should remain interested in the experiences of an earlier generation are a tremendous addition to the book. We are hugely grateful to him for both his foreword and also the great encouragement which he has given us during the course of the project.

One piece of advice which we received was to include multiple pictures – and we have sought to achieve this by including photographs which illustrate the various parts of the story notwithstanding the constraints on photography in wartime, especially in special operations. The work of Tim's wife, Caroline, in this aspect can only be described as indefatigable. An accomplished photographer, she has not only supported us enthusiastically and tirelessly with invaluable advice on the choice and layout of the photographs, but has achieved miracles in enhancing the quality of the pictures so that they can be used in the book. The result has been dramatic – and we owe her an enormous debt.

In the context of pictures, we are hugely indebted to Ben Richards. Ben brought his great talent as a director and cameraman to the making of the short film which was included in the description of the book on the Unbound website. His film illuminated the story – and was, we are sure, one of the main reasons why we were able to reach the target for pre-sales in such a short time.

And finally, there are many other people throughout the five years of the project who have encouraged us to undertake and complete the book and tell this extraordinary story. They are too numerous to mention here but they include many friends of Pop and Mop and of ours – and their support has been invaluable. We would, however, just mention one person – David Hargreaves. David was a housemaster and history teacher at Westminster School and he persuaded Pop to come and speak to the John Locke Society at the school – a speech which provided some of the initial information for the story. Since then David – who is himself an author – has been a source of unfailing encouragement and advice.

For all the others who have helped us in a myriad of ways, we hope that you will not regard the omission of your names as any indication of a lack of appreciation. We are hugely grateful to each and every one of you.

Unbound is the world's first crowdfunding publisher, established in 2011.

We believe that wonderful things can happen when you clear a path for people who share a passion. That's why we've built a platform that brings together readers and authors to crowdfund books they believe in – and give fresh ideas that don't fit the traditional mould the chance they deserve.

This book is in your hands because readers made it possible. Everyone who pledged their support is listed below. Join them by visiting unbound.com and supporting a book today.

Stephanie Bretherton
Martin Broughton
Alan Brown
David Bucks
Lisa Burger
Mark Cardale
Rhiannon Carey-Evans
Bill Carey-Evans
Joanna Carolan
Laura Carstensen
Edward Chaplin
Nick Clark
Vic Cocker
Edward Codrington
Dick Collier
Simon Collins
Hugh Comerford
Kate Cook
Steve Cooke
John Cooper
Elizabeth Copeman
Mark Coreth
Richard Cotton
E R Andrew Davis
Marcus de Ferranti
Anthony Dhanendran
Marnie Dickens
Lloyd Dorfman
Graham Earles
Simon David Eden
Janet Ellis
Leo 'the Lion' Evans
Heide Eyles
Sarah Fane
Tom Fattorini
Sophie & Peter Fernandes

Deborah Finkler
Stephen Foley
Michael Forbes
Sophie Forgan
David and Diane Frank
Charlie Geffen
Linda George
Micci Gorrod
Richard Grant
Eric Grove
Oscar Grut
William Hall
Ian Hamilton
Richard Harvey
Natalie Harvey
Giles Henderson
Basil Hersov
Rachel Hirst
Gregory Hodkinson
Elizabeth Holden
Nick Holt
Penny Horsburgh
Gerry Humphreys
Marie-Josée Hunter
Mark Johnson
Chris Jones
Simon Jones
Janie Joynson
Sandeep Katwala
Tom Keevil
John Kerr
Dan Kieran
Paula Laird
Peter Langley
Hester Larkin
Kate Lascelles

Sarah Lee
Richard Lloyd
Dom Loehnis
Rachel Lomax
Alison & Lorraine
Sian Lucas
John Macaskill
Ian Macfadyen
James MacLachlan
Nellie Maclaine
Michael Marshall
Alec Meadows
Jon Midlane
Marcus Missen
John Mitchinson
Stephen Morant
Anne Morddel
Kate & Greg Mosse
Carlo Navato
Peregrine Nelson Hood
Tim Nicholson
Casey Norman
Emma O'Hea
Robin Ogle
James Olley
Simon Pain
Vinay Patel
Rupert Pennant-Rea
Justin Pollard
David Ponte
Ian Powell
Charles Randell
John Redford
Michael Regan
Tom Reid
Matthew Rhodes

Hannah Richards
Benjamin Richards
George Rolls
Jonathan Rushworth
Matthew Sandham
Julian Sanger
Jonathan Scott
Bill Scott-Kerr
Mary Rose and Jeremy Selman
Christopher Sharples
Adam Signy
Fiona & Nick Spilman
Patrick Sprunt
Georgie Stack
Dennis Stevenson
Richard Thornhill
Vanni Treves
John Trotman
Andrew Trotter
Keith Tutt
William Underhill
Anne Van der Merwe
Nicholas Vetch
Charles Walford
David Walker
Simon Ward
Robert Welsford
Martin Whelton
Graham White
Miranda Whiting
Nicholas & Penny Wilson
Sarah Wilton
Andrew Wimble
Mark Wippell
Patrick Wolrige Gordon
Martin Wood

Stephen Wright
Jon Yarrow
Ado Yoshizaki Cassuto
Sir Nick Young